CULTURAL LEGACIES OF VIETNAM:

Uses of the Past in the Present

COMMUNICATION AND INFORMATION SCIENCE

Edited by
BRENDA DERVIN
The Ohio State University

Recent Titles

Laurien Alexandre • The Voice of America: From Detente to the Reagan Doctrine
Bruce Austin • Current Research in Film Volume 5
Barbara Bate & Anita Taylor • Women Communicating: Studies of Women's Talk
Donal Carbaugh • Talking American: Cultural Discourses on Donahue
Kathryn Carter and Carole Spitzack • Doing Research on Women's Communication: Perspectives on Theory and Method
Fred L. Casmir • Communication in Development
Gladys Ganley & Oswald Ganley • To Inform or to Control Revised Edition
Robert Goldman & Arvind Rajagopal • Mapping Hegemony: Television News Coverage of Industrial Conflict
Enrique Gonzalez-Manet • The Hidden War of Information
Karen Joy Greenberg • Conversations on Communications Ethics
Gary Gumpert & Sandra Fish • Talking to Strangers: Mediated Therapeutic Communication
Robert Jacobson • An "Open" Approach to Information Policymaking
Manfred Kochen • The Small World
John Lawrence and Bernard Timberg • Fair Use and Free Inquiry Second Edition
Sven B. Lundstedt • Telecommunications, Values, and the Public Interest
Thomas Mandeville • Understanding Novelty: Information Technological Changes and the Patent System
Richard Morris & Peter Ehrenhaus • Cultural Legacies of Vietnam: Uses of the Past in the Present
Susan B. Neuman • Literacy in the Television Age
Eli M. Noam & Joel C. Millonzi • The International Market in Film and Television Programs
Eli M. Noam & Gerald Pogorel • Asymmetric Deregulation: The Dynamics of Telecommunication Policy
Gerald M. Phillips • Teaching How to Work in Groups
Carl Erik Rosengren & Sven Windahl • Media Matter: TV Use in Childhood and Adolescence
Michael Rogers Rubin • Private Rights, Public Wrongs: The Computer and Personal Privacy
Ramona R. Rush & Donna Allen • Communications at the Crossroads: The Gender Gap Connection
Majid Tehranian • Technologies of Power: Information Machines and Democratic Processes
Sari Thomas • Studies in Mass Media and Technology, Volumes 1–4
J.M. Wober • Fission and Diffusion: The Possibility of Public Power Over and Through the Machine

CULTURAL LEGACIES OF VIETNAM:

Uses of the Past in the Present

EDITED BY

Richard Morris and Peter Ehrenhaus

with an introduction by Murray Edelman

Printed in the United States of America.

Library of Congress Cataloging-in-Publication Data

Cultural legacies of Vietnam : uses of the past in the present /
edited by Richard Morris and Peter Ehrenhaus : with introduction
by Murray Edelman.
p. cm.—(Communication and information science)
Includes bibliographical references and index.
ISBN 0-89391-713-3 (ppk); 0-89391-635-8 (cloth)
1. Vietnamese Conflict, 1961–1975—United States. 2. Vietnamese
Conflict, 1961–1975—Influence. 3. United States-
-Civilization—1945- I. Morris, Richard Joseph, 1953-
II. Ehrenhaus, Peter Charles. III. Series.
DS558.C85 1990
959.704'3373—dc20 90-971
CIP

Ablex Publishing Corporation
355 Chestnut Street
Norwood, New Jersey 07648

This work is dedicated to
Colin D. MacManus,
who was killed in Vietnam on February 16, 1967.

Contents

Preface

Cultural Legacies of Vietnam: Uses of the Past in the Present is the culmination of a project begun in 1985, when both of us were members of the faculty at Rutgers University. Our plan at the time was to organize and conduct a conference at which scholars and individuals who had contributed in various ways to a "reawakening" of America's Vietnam-related experiences would bring to bear widely divergent interests and perspectives to discuss the implications of "The Cultural Legacy of Vietnam."

Our experiences with and at that conference suggested several important problems that led to and helped shape this book. Some of these problems we deal with in the "Epilogue," but one series of problems seems to us especially germaine to our present discussion of the subject, purpose, scope, and method of this volume. We quickly realized how foolish and naive we had been to imagine that America's Vietnam-related experiences could be circumscribed by a single cultural legacy. Having come to this humbling realization, we concluded that "cultural legacies of Vietnam" more accurately insinuates our subject. Having concluded this much, we also realized that no single conference or scholarly work—however comprehensive—could encompass all or even the majority of the significant issues implied by the term "cultural legacies." This in turn posed the kinds of problems that give editors insomnia and ulcers and paint sympathetic looks on the faces of family, friends, and colleagues.

Rather than continuing with a flawed assumption by attempting to accomplish the impossible, we acknowledged that our volume would be an exploration, an initial effort to stimulate others to think seriously about the issues that the contributors to this volume have raised. Hence, we make no claim to have exhausted the cultural legacies of Vietnam, the subdivisions that constitute the three major divisions of this work, or available methodological or disciplinary perspectives.

In pursuing our exploratory purpose, we have sought to impose as few restrictions as possible on the authors. We did encourage the authors to think carefully about how the specter of Vietnam reveals itself in the present. We also encouraged the authors to write thoughtfully about ways in which America's Vietnam-related experiences have shaped or helped to shape American foreign policy, popular imagination, and cultures. And, like most editors we know, we mercilessly nagged, cajoled, corrected, suggested, and picked at nits. Finally, we encouraged the authors to regard their audience as diverse, as being composed of intelligent and thoughtful individuals, regardless of their relationship to academe. Nevertheless, at every possible turn we have trusted the contributors to do what they do best. The result, we believe, is an engaging collection of essays bound together by subject and purpose, but not limited by disciplinary or methodological concerns.

ACKNOWLEDGMENTS

Working with talented and insightful individuals more than compensates for the myriad of travails necessarily associated with creating a scholarly work. We were particularly fortunate.

Late in the autumn of 1985, while we were attempting to locate funding to support a conference on "The Cultural Legacy of Vietnam," we happened upon Robert A. Glassman, a 1964 graduate of Rutgers University. Several years after his tour of duty in Vietnam, Bob learned that his friend and college roommate, Colin D. MacManus, had been killed in action. Bob then contacted the Rutgers University Foundation to inquire about establishing a scholarship in memory of his friend. The Foundation informed Bob of our plans, we met with him to discuss our plans, and he immediately and enthusiastically provided us with moral and financial support.

With Bob Glassman's assistance we were able to pull together scholars, Vietnam veterans, and others who were seriously interested in discussing how Vietnam-related experiences shape America's present. We wish to thank all those who attended and took part in that initial conversation—especially David Alcaras, Dennis Benson, Edwin Black, Charles Braithwaite, Barry Brummett, Stanley Deetz, George Dionisipoulos, Murray Edelman, Sandie Fauriol, Lydia Fish, William Gamson, Todd Gitlin, Harry Haines, Sal Lopes, Myra MacPherson, Tod Marder, Jan Scruggs, James Skelly, Patricia Walsh, and Philip Wander.

Following the conference, we began to think about more succinctly articulating the major areas of concern that emerged repeatedly at the conference. Believing in the merits of building one project on another, Bob Glassman again provided words of encouragement and urged us to press beyond the successes of the conference, to use what we had gathered and learned as a foundation for creating a more permanent contribution. We gratefully acknowledge our indebtedness to Bob, whose interest, encouragement, support, and vision have been invaluable. We also applaud his views concerning which individuals may shape the past legitimately: "Whatever views that people have—both those who went and those who did not—I would be the first one to say that each of those views is precious. Each of those people is equally deserving and entitled to articulate their view."

Finally, in seeking to create a more permanent contribution, we could not have hoped for a more competent, diligent, sensitive colleague than Brenda Dervin. Her encouragement, enthusiasm, and endless patience as series editor have made this volume possible.

The order of editorship is arbitrary.

Richard Morris
Philadelphia, Pennsylvania

Peter Ehrenhaus
Portland, Oregon

Introduction

Murray Edelman

The Vietnam War polarized America while it was taking place; the essays in this anthology examine many ways in which it has continued to do so in the decades since the War's end. The intensity and endurance of the concerns the War fostered make it clear that much more was involved than the wisdom of sending American troops to fight in Southeast Asia in the 1960s. The Vietnam War epitomized a long-standing clash of values in America respecting a set of related anxieties, including the actuality of a military threat from communist states, the bases of American strength and prestige, the benefits and costs of resort to military action in Third World countries torn by ideological dissension, racism and chauvinism in foreign policy, public control over executive decisions to deploy military force, and the morality of a war in which Southeast Asian peasants and the young, the poor, and the minorities in America were most at risk.

The items in this short list of issues are typically viewed as disparate, but the Vietnam War made it clear that they are linked and reflect contending philosophies. Because the Vietnam War calls up in people's minds a wider set of connected concerns than its name denotes, "Vietnam" has become one of the pivotal condensation symbols of the 20th century; for it is the key property of a condensation symbol that it concentrates the evocations of a set of seemingly distinct observations so that they reinforce each other. In accepting one view of the War and rejecting the other, spectators of the political and historical scene define themselves as well. (I do not mean that individuals who take a position on one of these issues always take on the expected position on the others as well. The point, rather, is that to a large body of political spectators each issue symbolizes or condenses a common set of beliefs.)

While the symbol reinforces both of the conflicting ideological positions, beliefs about the War did not remain static during the years it was being fought. Instead, skepticism about its rationale, the way it was waged, and its consequences increased substantially after 1964, so that by the end of the 1960s, most Americans opposed the War (see e.g., Mueller, 1973). And for a large part of the population, the skepticism intensified in the decades after the formal end of the Vietnam War, presenting a continuing and exasperating challenge to the official view, which was also the position of the political right. The frequent decisions to embark upon military ventures since World War II (Korea, the Bay of Pigs, Vietnam, the Mayaguez incident, the Iran hostage rescue effort, the bombing of Libya, the Grenada invasion, support for the Nicaragua Contras) can be understood in part as an effort to express the symbolism of anticommunism, chauvinism, military power, vulnerability to foreign attack, and national honor and duty, while each of these actions also kept alive and fresh the premises animating the opposition to these policies. Vietnam focused the polarization with uncommon intensity, helping to shape the meanings of the ventures that preceded and followed it.

The resulting division and the effort of each grouping to proselytize have found expression in many aspects of American public life in the post-Vietnam years: literature, popular culture, race relations, gender relations, and the relations among social classes, as well as politics and foreign policy. The forms have varied, as the essays in this volume attest, but these forms have rarely been distinguished for their originality, liveliness, profundity, or value as art or as thought.

There was no great break or opening in new directions in American art, culture, or politics after the Vietnam War, except possibly for some kinds of popular music, but rather a continuation of the trends and issues that had emerged earlier in the century; and, so far as the films, novels, and political discussions dealing explicitly with the Vietnam War were concerned, the level of sophistication started low and, with a few notable exceptions, declined later, as the chapters by Ehrenhaus, Wander and Kane, Dionisopoulos, Jeffords, Mechling and Mechling, and Morris suggest (Chapters 1, 3, 5, 7, 9, and 10).

This continuation calls for reflection because art and culture have often taken strikingly new directions from military defeat, a phenomenon that has been pronounced in other countries after they lost major wars in the 20th century. In the Weimar Republic that emerged from Germany's defeat in World War I, painting, film, architecture, drama, music, and literature exhibited new vitality and new paths; a similar, if less dramatic, resurgence of art and culture appeared in both Germany and Japan after World War II. In the Soviet Union of the 1920s there were striking developments in poetry, music, film, and the novel before the Stalinist repression killed most of them off in the 1930s.

That the post-Vietnam cultural scene in America was not as adventurous was certainly due in part to a key difference in political context. In every other instance just mentioned, defeat in war was the prelude to radical change in political institutions and in class relations: from imperial Germany to a democratic republic in 1918, from Nazism to a parliamentary system in 1945, from imperial Japan to the constitutional government there in 1945, and from Czarist to revolutionary Russia. In each instance a new day seemed to have dawned with a past repudiated, so that emerging art forms and cultural forms were called for to explore and help shape the meanings of the new society.

In the United States, by contrast, defeat in the Vietnam War strengthened the political and social status quo. Higher levels of military spending became the norm, supported by both Republican and Democratic presidents and members of Congress. The influence of the National Security Council and the president in policy making continued to expand. Conservative ideology spread. The groups that had challenged these forms of hegemony in the 1960s lost influence, and organized left wing opposition faded from the political scene.

While a sizeable, lopsidedly female part of the public remained skeptical of military ventures and cold war rhetoric, partly as a result of the Vietnam fiasco, this group wielded little influence in government. It nonetheless posed a threat that kept supporters of the established order anxious. American culture reflected this clash more faithfully than public officials or public policy did. So far as analyses of the Vietnam War in film and writing were concerned, this basic division dominated the depictions and became banal.

Consideration of cultural legacies of Vietnam calls for attention to the subtle and intimate links between art and politics. Artistic and cultural works that deal with social and political issues do not simply mirror public views of those concerns, but help shape them, as American cultural developments during and since the Vietnam War demonstrate. Television coverage of the War focused public attention on disturbing aspects of the conflict that were little noticed in official or public rhetoric or even in the print media: The suffering and deaths of civilians, the impossible tasks and moral dilemmas the American troops faced, and the dubious relevance of foreign military intervention to the infighting among ideological factions of Vietnamese and the economic problems of Southeast Asian peasants. Whether or not these meanings of the War were more realistic than the focus upon communist threat, falling dominoes, and body counts signaling progress toward victory that emanated from the White House and the Pentagon, they increasingly molded American public opinion. And they illustrate the critical sense in which life copies art, because art teaches us to see, to shape meanings, and to focus on some realities and ignore others. Films, novels, stories, essays, memorials, college courses, and other cultural forms have continued to construct the "reality" of Vietnam in the decades since American troops were withdrawn from Southeast Asia. They have continued as well to shape the reality of earlier American wars and later ones, and they have modified the lessons we read into earlier literary and artistic accounts of the range of issues that "Vietnam" evokes. The significance of "Vietnam," " Korea," "Pearl Harbor," or "Appomattox" changes as new political concerns develop, and as cultural and artistic works construct new interpretations of them while masking other meanings.

Still, there is always some tension between artistic and political forms of expression because art strives for originality and insight, while political language is typically banal, appealing to widely held beliefs (see e.g., Orwell, 1957; Edelman, 1988, p. 111). So far as cultural legacies of Vietnam are concerned, political impulses seem to have exerted the stronger influence so far, reducing much of the pertinent art to a kind of political language in itself. In an insightful essay in this anthology, Adi Wimmer (Chapter 4) says some arresting things about the role of literature, public records, and political rhetoric in creating America's purposes and myths before and after Vietnam.

Some of the most banal cultural forms regarding Vietnam were created by the American government itself to manufacture supportive public opinion: the publicizing of the Green Berets as elite troops embodying the noblest manly and patriotic virtues, for example (a development discussed in Chapter 5), the institution of "body counts," and public relations efforts to portray the successive troop commanders in Vietnam as military innovators rather than bureaucrats. The *Rambo* films and their imitations carried on this tradition of constructing personal heroes and fraudulent tests of their success, though those films were critical of a government that had allegedly failed to give the troops the resources to win. The latter claim amounted to a paradoxical use of the very premise that had misled the Johnson and Nixon administrations: That the paramount challenge in Southeast Asia was military in character. Jeffords (Chapter 7) analyzes the sense in which *Rambo* and similar films infantilize audiences, a tactic that the White House and the Pentagon had tried to pursue during the War itself, with deteriorating success. Employing diverse perspectives, the chapters by Ehrenhaus, Ivie, Wander and Kane, Haines, and Morris (Chapters 1, 2, 3, 6, and 10) also deal insightfully with these aspects of the cultural legacies of Vietnam.

In some ways the war in Vietnam highlighted cultural disparities within the American population that had been blurred by political rhetoric about a melting pot, national purpose, and pluralism. The cleavages that now seem most salient stemmed from differences in social philosophy, class distinctions, race and racism, and American regionalism, with the South more supportive of militarism than other areas of the country. All the internal differences on which the Vietnam War focused attention were contemporary manifestations of a much longer history. The news reports now told of resentments of military officers by enlisted men and women, with deplorable consequences for morale and some fragging of unpopular officers; and they told as well of military tactics that defined junior officers and enlisted men and women as expendable in order to make politically useful gains. But disaffection from military superiors and the assumption that the lower ranks can be used as cannon fodder have been characteristic of a great many military actions since the dawn of history, though they may have been more pronounced in a losing war for which there was no persuasive rationale.

The War also highlighted the unequal sacrifices entailed in a conflict fought disproportionately by blacks and the poor. And the postwar years brought growing realization of the profound sense in which Vietnam veterans were considered a class apart from the rest of society, both by that society and by the veterans themselves. Dionisopoulos and Haines (Chapters 5 and 6) discuss the portrayal of the Vietnam veteran as tarnished, spoiled, and corrupted, a scapegoat for the country's guilt about the War and the national defeat it symbolized. This phenomenon is also a more general one, though not always so pronounced. Police officers, minorities, the mentally ill, the poor, Native Americans, and women also see themselves, with good reason, as misunderstood, disparaged, often disadvantaged, and frequently reliant upon rituals to maintain self-respect and to survive. The chapters by Ehrenhaus, Ivie, Braithwaite, and Elizabeth and Jay Mechling (Chapters 1, 2, 8, and 9) bring impressive sensitivity to the social divisions the War accented.

The central division during the years the War was being fought, between its supporters and its opponents at home, was intense and grew more so as opposition to the War mounted and the prospect of military defeat became a certainty. Most of the population now recognized that the protesters had been right all along, though many were unwilling to forgive them for having been right too soon. The planners and supporters of the War suffered little from having been wrong, while those who opposed it received a lot of official blame and little credit for having been right.

These political and psychological consequences stemmed from the continuing ideological contention regarding foreign policy that "Vietnam" came to symbolize: a division over military intervention in Third World countries to suppress opposition to authoritarian regimes. In this regard, one conspicuous legacy of the Vietnam War for makers of American foreign policy was a lesson about the need to manufacture public support at home for military actions abroad. But most of the antiwar protesters of the 1960s and the many Americans who were impressed by them continue to question and oppose militarism as a paramount instrument of foreign policy.

The planners of future military adventures into the Third World will no doubt take greater pains to appease the affluent middle class while again targeting for sacrifice those with minimal political influence and resources. But this is not the only political legacy of the Vietnam War to have already shown its contours. Others include: (a) a record of dubious military competence—in the Iran rescue effort, the invasion of Grenada, the support and guidance of the Nicaraguan Contras, the stationing of marines in Lebanon, and the bombing of Libya; and (b) reliance on borrowing rather than taxes to pay for unpopular causes, forcing future generations to bear the financial costs.

The chapters in this volume make it clear that "Vietnam" is not simply an historical experience that yielded a legacy. Vietnam is a condensation symbol epitomizing sets of conflicting values that polarize late 20th-century America. The conflict continues to express itself in virtually every aspect of American culture. Sometimes its articulation assumes blurred or inconsistent forms, reflecting both uncertainty about which set of values is dominant and the ambivalence of many individuals respecting the issues in question; for this conflict rages within individual psyches as well as between political ideologies. The clash Morris (Chapter 10) describes over whether the Vietnam Veterans Memorial in Washington should be "romanticist" or "heroist" offers an atypically neat instance of the contending ideologies, though it has been typical enough in its resolution in a way that offends proponents of both sets of values.

Perhaps the aspect of Vietnam that is most characteristic of the America in which it took place lay in the inadequacy with which America defined the values at stake. Like the War itself, its cultural aftermath is clouded by conflict that is unclear in its configurations and purposes and that fails to mesh with an impulse for political change.

REFERENCES

Edelman, M. (1988). *Constructing the political spectacle.* Chicago: University of Chicago Press.

Mueller, J.E. (1973). *War, presidents, and public opinion.* New York: Wiley.

Orwell, G. (1954). Politics and the English language. In *A collection of essays* (pp. 162–177). Garden City, NY: Doubleday.

Part I
Vietnam as Political Metaphor

1

On Americans Held Prisoner in Southeast Asia: The P.O.W. Issue as "Lesson" of Vietnam

Peter Ehrenhaus
Department of Speech Communication, Portland State University

In 1987, Oklahoma junior high school teacher Bill McCloud prepared to teach his eighth-grade students about the Vietnam War. As part of his research, McCloud conducted a survey of more than 700 Oklahoma junior high school students to discover what they already knew and what questions they had about Vietnam. He also wrote to a variety of American public figures, asking them their view of the lessons which the Vietnam War teaches us. The responses of 51 men and one woman[1] were published in an article entitled "What Should We Tell Our Children About Vietnam?" in *American Heritage* magazine (McCloud, 1988). Among those who answered McCloud's question were presidents, secretaries of defense, members of Congress, generals, admirals, journalists, novelists, and Vietnam combat veterans. Some answers were brief, a sentence or two having the force of truisms; others provided greater elaboration, weaving together historical, economic, and philosophic foundations of America's role in the world community.

Responses touched upon a variety of subjects and beliefs—for example, on "honorable motives," on the views that there are no "Rambos" and that future decisions to go to war must be based on the presence of "broad, popular support," on the need for an "open policy" with "clear goals," on the belief that wars should be fought only when there is a

[1] The sole response by a woman printed in the article belongs to Frances FitzGerald, journalist and Pulitzer Prize-winning author of *Fire in the Lake: The Vietnamese and the Americans in Vietnam*. While we have no way of knowing how many women were invited to respond or how many did respond, the appropriation of the war as a male-dominated issue and, thus, the (re)production of the war's meanings by males, raises issues of gender-empowerment. For a more detailed examination of such issues, see Jeffords, Chapter 7, this volume.

direct threat to "national security" or to "America's vital national interests." Others praised the "noble cause" of freedom in its struggle against communism, while still others laid bare the "myth" of monolithic communism in the face of national interests. Despite the diversity of these reflections, all 52 statements dealt with Vietnam in the past tense. To speak of the "lessons" of Vietnam, we place Vietnam in the past.

By contrast, the results of McCloud's survey of junior high school students indicates that one aspect of Vietnam remains open. Three of the five most frequent responses to what students knew fall within the purview of "textbook" history: many Americans were killed, the war took place in Vietnam, and it occurred in the 1960s and 1970s. Another response, one challenged by several of the adults who defined Vietnam's lessons, was that the U.S. lost the war. But the most provocative response was that Americans are still being held in Southeast Asia as prisoners of war.

We may wonder how junior high school students would come to believe as fact what the governments of Vietnam and the United States label as unsubstantiated speculation—mere fiction. A convenient answer is that they learned this from the spate of "Bring 'em Back Alive" films of the past several years, and well they may have (see Chapters 5 & 6, this volume). But film is not the only place in which such notions originate.

The nagging question of whether Americans remain captive in Southeast Asia persists. A cover story of *Life* magazine ("MIA: Are any still alive?" 1987) examined "25 compelling cases" that illustrate "the web of rumor, suspicion, self-interest, and fear that obscures reality" (p. 111) and that impede, if they do not preclude, the resolution of the question. Sydney Schanberg (1987), a Pulitzer Prize-winning correspondent who reported on Cambodia during the Vietnam War, writes of "the belief in some quarters that our government has not done, and does not do, enough to resolve the missing-in-action puzzle—to track down leads and clues about possible survivors." This lack of "conclusive evidence," Schanberg writes, is "another way of saying that Vietnam clings to us hauntingly as unfinished business." As if enveloped with that same eerie sense of Vietnam—that our grasp of the matter is obscured, that what we observe is not all that there is to observe, that there is much to which we were not and are not privy—Schanberg states his own position: "The mind says the chance of this being true is very remote, but the stomach says it just might be" (p. C5).

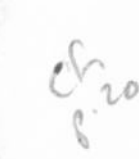

My purpose in this chapter is to explore the uncertainties that characterize the prisoner-of-war (POW) question and to explain how, by its lack of resolution, the issue is denied legitimacy in any discussion of the lessons of Vietnam. By delving into this corner of America's Vietnam experience, we more than just glimpse another facet of American public consciousness; we witness the tensions between national conscience and political expediency, as well as the subordination of one to the other. The following story is instructive in that regard.

On September 17, 1987, a small group of American men and women launched 2,500 copies of a message, each individually sealed in plastic bags, from the Thailand side of the Mekong River. The destination for these notes was the 700 miles of opposing riverbank, the borders of Laos and Vietnam. The message, written in Laotian and Vietnamese, offered 2.4 million dollars for the rescue of American servicemen held prisoner, and it carried a cartoon of a Southeast Asian peasant spiriting an American prisoner to freedom; the peasant's payment was a gold bar. The Foreign Ministry of Thailand had forbidden these Americans to place their messages in balloons; inflated balloons could safely float downstream. But the Ministry did allow the use of plastic bags, believing that they would sink to the river's bottom, never reaching their destination. Of the entire event, the U.S. State Department commented that activities such as this could only hurt official efforts to account for MIAs and POWs, and that direct government-to-government cooperation was the best route to success (Eng, 1987).

This event, like others before it, received little attention in the press. Small wonder: In the absence of direct evidence to support the contention that Americans continue to be held prisoner in Southeast Asia, POW activists, such as those responsible for the sealed messages, are portrayed as a fringe element, obsessed and irrational, unable to admit fully to their losses and let go of a tragic past.

The futility of launching sandwich bags to rescue American prisoners whose very existence remains conjecture is a strangely compelling act for us to consider. While its objective was to stimulate the mercenary impulses of Southeast Asian peasants, it merely produced a mild rebuke from the United States government. And the perfunctory tone of that chiding is suggestive. If direct government-to-government contact was poised to resolve the question of whether Americans are held prisoner in Vietnam, Laos, or Cambodia, we might expect a far more strident reaction; the lack of vigor in that response suggests a lack of commitment to the pursuit, even though President Reagan proclaimed this pursuit to be the "highest national priority" ("Action pledged on lost G.I.'s," 1983, p. A3).

Since 1973, the question of whether live Americans remain in Southeast Asia has been repeatedly subject to scrutiny without achieving resolution. By remaining in the realm of conjecture, the POW issue has been relegated to a political limbo, as much a hostage as any individual held captive in Beirut. Less clear is: Hostage of whom? And to what end? In this chapter I propose answers to both of these questions.

I refer to the *question* of whether the POW issue exists as a hostage, and not to particular persons as hostages. Unlike taking political prisoners in order to direct public attention toward an alleged injustice, holding an issue hostage accomplishes the opposite: It prevents public attention from becoming focused on an issue. When uncertainty persists about the "facts of the matter," argument becomes difficult, if not impossible; we are denied any basis for accepting one assertion or conclusion about POWs over another, or for believing in one source of information more than another (see Fisher, 1987, Chapters 2, 5). The mind may seek to create a firm foundation for belief, but the stomach tells us that the "unfinished business" of Vietnam "clings to us hauntingly" in the victimization of truthfulness and reliability. In the absence of a stable set of elements—of things known—coherent knowledge is undermined. The fragments of the POW issue simply cannot coalesce into a coherent story compelling our belief.

My development of this chapter proceeds in two parts. First, I describe the development of the POW issue as it has been presented by the press from 1973 to 1988. Because of its wide acceptance as a contemporary historical resource, I have relied primarily on the annals of *The New York Times Index*, inclusive of those years. The second section of the chapter explores the significance of those reports. What can we reasonably infer? How is our understanding impeded? The fragments of publicly accessible coverage that define the POW issue enable us to see how the elements essential for a coherent story, and from which clear implications may be drawn, simply have not emerged. What, then, are the implications of the POW issue's failure to achieve narrativity? Since the issue is characterized by what is *not* known, and since it has no closure, how can the POW issue be used in the present? How is it precluded from use? Finally, what positions benefit from its perpetuation as "unfinished business"?

A QUESTION OF FACT

Since the Paris Accords of January 1973, United States policy has been to seek a "full and final accounting" of all Americans held prisoner or listed as missing in Southeast Asia. One provision of the Accords requires the North Vietnamese and the Viet Cong to provide comprehensive lists of Americans held prisoner. However, whether any of these lists was required to include POWs held in Laos or Cambodia was never clearly specified. As the accounting process began, this ambiguity became apparent in the contradictory expectations revealed in statements by the Departments of State and Defense and by the White House ("Communists list 505 P.O.W.s," 1973, p. 15).

The Pentagon, as part of its own effort to account for all POWs, conducted extensive interviews with returned prisoners, and it concluded in early 1974 that there was little hope of finding more Americans alive. However, in a climate of distrust aggravated by the unwillingness of the North Vietnamese to allow U.S. investigating teams into their territory, rumors recurred that some Americans were still being held in the jungles ("Pentagon is not hopeful," 1974).

Fueled by these rumors, the House of Representatives established the Select Committee on Missing Persons in Southeast Asia to investigate the question. After reviewing U.S. intelligence reports of interviews with former prisoners and after following up leads supplied by families of the missing, the panel concluded that "there is no evidence that any of these missing Americans are still alive" ("House panel declares," 1976, p. 1). Further, the committee recommended that the Pentagon should decide whether all those missing should be presumed legally dead. U.S. Representative Benjamin Gilman opposed the recommendation, stating that it would "reduce the significance of the missing-in-action issue" (p. 11). Joining in that denunciation was the National League of Families of American Prisoners and Missing in Southeast Asia (see also "Congress's last word on M.I.A.s," 1976).

The League initiated legal action against the Department of Defense to prohibit the change of status, but in November of 1977 the restraining order against the Government was lifted. The status of 2,400 missing Americans could be changed from missing-in-action (MIA) to killed-in-action (KIA). As reported in *The New York Times* (Seigel, 1977), the judge explained his decision in the following manner: "There is nothing in the record showing the slightest hint that the Government has been less than fully sensitive to the rights and sensibilities of those missing in action and those who seek to represent them" (p. 8).

Changing the legal status of MIAs and POWs accomplished three things. First, it reduced substantially the Government's financial obligation to the families of the missing.[2] It also imposed a symbolic resolution to the issue—since, in the story of a single life, death is closure. Finally,

[2] According to Peterson (1979), "more than 2,000 others whose bodies have never been found have been declared 'presumed dead' and their salaries have been cut off" (p. A3), although the Pentagon continued to carry 120 as MIAs. While the Pentagon took the position that there were no more prisoners in Southeast Asia, the State Department at that time listed somewhat fewer than 100 as "detainees" in that area.

it called into question the credibility of those who clung to the belief that Americans remained prisoners in Southeast Asia. Investigated by the Pentagon and Congress, and ruled on by the courts, no legitimate basis remained for advocating the "live POW" position. Yet, opposition to the Government's conclusion did remain, and it found its voice in accusations of conspiracy. As one member of the League asserted after the court's ruling, "The fact is Americans are being held there. We couldn't prove it because we don't have access to confidential files" (Seigel, 1977, p. 8).

The motif of conspiracy to suppress evidence has continued, as have reports of sightings of POWs. When U.S. Marine Lt. Robert Garwood returned from Vietnam in 1979 to accusations of treason, the press reported that Garwood "hinted broadly" that other Americans may still be in Southeast Asia. Garwood's civilian attorney, Dermit Foley, accused the government of "trying to 'sweep under the rug' the possibility that more Americans were still languishing in Vietnam" (Peterson, 1979, p. A10). A few years later, a former Viet Cong official reported that he had seen 30 to 40 American pilots performing hard labor in the North Vietnam highlands two month after Hanoi declared all POWs had been released. These men, Nguyen Duc Yen believed, were to be used as "bargaining chips" to help Hanoi establish diplomatic relations with the U.S. ("Ex-Vietcong reports seeing POWs alive," 1982, p. A9). Also in 1982, U.S. National Security Advisor William P. Clark publicly stated his belief that some Americans may still be held captive, nine years after the war's end: "The U.S. cannot be certain, even to this day, that the treaty we signed was fully complied with in regard to our prisoners of war and missing in action. . . . Should we find these reports are true, we are prepared to take appropriate action to insure that no American remains a captive" ("U.S. aide cites war missing," 1982, p. A11).

Despite Clark's avowal to "take appropriate action," the impatience of some Americans led to private efforts to discover whether Americans remained captive. In November of 1982, four Americans, who were characterized as "soldiers of fortune," conducted a secret mission into Laos to investigate reports by Laotian refugees that "up to 120 American prisoners of war" were held near the town of Tchepone, and to rescue those captives if the reports proved true. The Americans were led by former Green Beret Lt. Colonel James (Bo) Gritz and accompanied by 15 "Laotian guerrillas." Armed with four machine guns, the rescuers were ambushed by "Laotian paramilitary forces." One American, wounded and captured, was released for $17,000 ransom and medical supplies. The outcome of this raid clearly did not parallel the successes of the cinematic rescues commercially popular at the time (see Chapters 5 & 6, this volume). It should be noted, however, that backing for this undertaking was supplied by Hollywood's own Clint Eastwood and William Shatner ("Private raid on Laos reported," 1983, p. A2).

Fearing that private initiatives such as the Gritz raid might upset "delicate talks" with Laos and Vietnam, the Reagan Administration "resolutely opposed" that raid and all private forays, generally (Ayres, 1983). Thailand then ordered Gritz and his colleagues deported. In addition to staging their raid from Thailand, the Americans had used an illegal radio transmitter to send messages across the Mekong River ("Thais order ouster," 1983). While the press reported on official opposition to private initiatives designed to move the POW issue out of the realm of conjecture, they also published items lending credence to the existence of live Americans in Southeast Asia. The same month that *The New York Times* reported on the ouster of Gritz and his companions from Thailand, it also reported on more than 200 sightings by refugees, many of whom provided polygraph support for their testimony (Taubman, 1983).

The continuing efforts of the United States to locate the remains of American military personnel in Southeast Asia keeps conjecture about POWs alive. In May of 1984, Vietnam was compelled to deny the existence of POWs in Vietnam, Laos, and Cambodia (Tuohy, 1984). In early 1985, other private raids into Laos to locate prison camps were decried by the United States as "illegal, counter-productive," and in "neither the interests of our country nor the families of the missing in action" ("U.S. condemns private raid," 1985, p. 2). The severity of this censure stands in contrast to the government's vehement condemnation and resolute opposition to the 1983 raid; even more circumspect is governmental reaction to the 1987 attempted balloon launch.

A news conference held by POW activists in September of 1985 raised further questions about the government's findings ("Suit claims army blocked POW deal," 1985). One allegation was that recovered remains of Americans were knowingly misidentified. The other was that the government was covering up proof of POWs. The latter claim, made by two former Green Berets, was contained in a federal class-action lawsuit against the government, particularly in the person of National Security Advisor Robert McFarlane, on behalf of any Americans held in captivity. The plaintiffs, Major Mark A. Smith and Sgt. Melvin C. McIntire, alleged that while assigned to the Far East in the early 1980s, they were responsible for identifying and locating POWs, and for assessing the chances of their rescue. According to the lawsuit, Smith and McIntire had located and then arranged for the release of three live American prisoners from Laos. But upon informing their superiors that they were "bringing three live ones out," the rescue was abandoned. As Smith stated, "Someone at the top of the U.S. government needs to explain why on the 11th of May, 1984, there is a distinct possibility that three

Americans stood on one side of a border and there was no one on the other side of that border to receive them" (p. A3).[3]

One month later, Robert McFarlane observed that there must be live Americans in Southeast Asia, that American intelligence sources "haven't yet found the evidence," but that "many of the live sighting reports are coming from sources who have no reason to fabricate them" (Secter, 1985, p. 13). The press also reported that McFarlane believed he was speaking in confidence when making those remarks.

Early in 1986 a U.S. delegation to Vietnam signed an agreement resolving to account for all missing Americans within two years and to investigate continuing reports of POWs. On returning to the U.S., the delegates were told that a half-dozen former military intelligence personnel had filed affidavits alleging that the State Department, the Pentagon, the CIA, and the U.S. Embassy in Bangkok had suppressed reports of live POWs in Vietnam and Laos. Among those filing affidavits was a Southeast Asian businessman, unnamed in the press report, who claimed to have seen 39 heavily guarded men in Laos as recently as three months prior to that date; he was sure that these prisoners were American. The head of the returning U.S. delegation labeled the allegations "specious" and "absurd" (Branigin, 1986, p. A1).

Since 1973, the United States and Vietnam have concurred that no evidence supported the contention that live POWs exist, but that, because of pressures, the U.S. was compelled to consider the possibility and to impel Vietnam to investigate the reports. However, in February of 1986, Vietnam changed its position unilaterally, acknowledging that Americans might be inside Vietnam, held prisoner in remote areas not under full government control ("Hanoi reported to say G.I.s may be there," 1986).

Two months later, *The Wall Street Journal* published an article citing Defense Intelligence Agency (DIA) criteria for "credible proof" and arguing that evidence meeting those criteria did, indeed, exist (Paul, 1986, p. 8). According to the article, two sources independently provided corroboration about POWs—specific in time, location, and circumstance, and "enhanced" by the results of a polygraph test. One source was a Vietnamese refugee who claimed to have seen U.S. prisoners in the courtyard of the Ly Nam De military complex in Hanoi in 1978 and 1982. Based on this refugee's description of the courtyard, the DIA informed President Reagan that the source was lying; as the news story continues, the DIA's own information about the compound was inaccurate. The

---

[3] The distinction between fact and fiction in the POW issue is blurred even further when one considers that Smith places the abandoned retrieval of three live Americans from Laos on May 11, 1984. That same month, "Rambo, First Blood: Part II" was released, and its central premise is that of government betrayal of a rescue mission.

other source was Marine Lt. Robert Garwood who claimed that he was held in the Ly Nam De facility. Upon his return to the U.S. in 1979, Garwood was accused, tried, and convicted of treason. His sightings were dismissed by the DIA without hesitation.

On the other hand, ABC's news magazine, "20/20," broadcast a report that lent legitimacy to the POW activists's position (Corry, 1986). The program labeled as "outrageous" the Army's method of identifying remains of MIAs. It discussed the more than 800 reports of sightings of live American prisoners since 1975. And it examined the DIA's rationale for disbelieving the maps of the Ly Nam De military compound that had been drawn independently by Garwood and the Vietnamese refugee, finding that the DIA's rejection of the evidence rested on a question about the bathing facilities for prisoners.

As a reaction to the lawsuit claiming a cover-up of evidence, the DIA appointed a task force, chaired by Lt. General Eugene Tighe, Jr., the agency's former head, to review all information pertaining to the POW issue (Halloran, 1986). After five months the panel concluded on September 29, 1986 that "a large volume of evidence" pointed to the fact that some Americans are still alive in Southeast Asia. The following day Lt. General Leonard Perroots, the current director of the DIA, cited a "strong possibility" that some Americans remain alive, but added that "no credible evidence, no strong compelling evidence," existed to sustain the possibility. One point was conclusive: There was "no evidence of a cover-up" by anyone in the government.

The debate continues. In October of 1987, two U.S. congressmen released "previously undisclosed government documents" providing details of sightings and other information about 76 missing Americans ("POW papers released," 1987, p. A9). The conservative American Defense Institute is seeking to raise one billion dollars—25 dollars from 40 million Americans—for their "Home Free" rescue and ransom fund ("$1 billion in pledges sought," 1988, p. A18). The Department of Defense continues to examine evidence, asserting that, while it has "been unable thus far to prove that Americans are being held against their will," it proceeds "on the assumption that at least some Americans are held against their will" ("Vietnam to investigate 95 reports on P.O.W.s," 1986, p. A5).

As this brief chronology pieced together from major news stories and brief items reveals, progress on the POW issue has been slow, frustrating, and fraught with contradiction. Fifteen years of direct government-to-government contact has yet to resolve the fundamental question of whether Americans continue to be imprisoned in Southeast Asia. Representatives of the United States and Vietnam intermittently meet, agree to meet again, break off meetings, sign agreements to cooperate, and investigate crash sites for remains.

Caught in a double bind, the U.S. and Vietnam have incompatible agendas. On one hand, the U.S. insists on a full and final accounting of all missing *before* granting formal political recognition to Vietnam. The recognition of normalized relations implies the possibility that Vietnam will receive post-war aid from the U.S., as stipulated in the Paris Accords of 1973. On the other hand, Vietnam insists upon both formal recognition and war reparations *prior* to a full accounting of missing Americans. The U.S. rejects that position, asserting that North Vietnam violated the terms of the Paris Accords, thus nullifying any U.S. commitments made in Paris.

One certain victim of these contradictory injunctions is the POW issue. Less certain, but equally victimized, are any Americans who may be held prisoner. *If* American POWs exist in Southeast Asia, then clearly they are hostages, victims of political terrorism. But this terrorism must operate quite unlike that which we associate with the Middle East. Though power (as in the capacity to take and hold hostages) can be politically legitimating, no nation can take and hold hostages without damaging its political legitimacy. The leverage that American prisoners would afford the Vietnamese stems from public uncertainty regarding the very existence of POWs. Although Vietnam may actually hold hostages, they must deny it. And, to the world community, their efforts to help locate Americans—at a time of their choosing—will invariably be applauded as compassionate. Recall that Vietnam recently indicated that Americans *may* be held inside Vietnam, but in remote areas *not under full government control* ("Hanoi reported to say G.I.s may be there," 1986).

If the United States government had proof that there are American POWs in Southeast Asia, then bringing that information to light would diminish the legitimacy that Vietnam has fostered in the world community. Vietnam's position, demanding diplomatic recognition and post-war aid prior to locating all missing Americans, would cease to be defensible.[4] But, as I have noted, the Departments of State and Defense and the Ford, Carter, and Reagan Administrations have all insisted that they have no credible evidence of American POWs. The search for proof and resolution of the issue continues, unended and seemingly unending.

MAKING SENSE OF THE POW ISSUE

What are we to make of the POW issue? Having poured over newspaper indices and simply happening upon other news reports, I have pieced

[4] This tactic effectively removes one of the contradictory injunctions that create the double bind. See Watzlawick, Beavin, and Jackson (1967), especially Chapter 7.

together what appears to be a coherent story, a narrative. It is not. I have presented only a chronicle, a mere sequence of reported events, beginning in 1973 and proceeding to 1988. Although this chronicle aspires to tell a story, it fails to achieve narrativity. The events do not possess "a structure, an order of meaning" (White, 1980, p. 16). The chronicle has no plot, no "structure of relationships by which the events contained in the account are endowed with a meaning by being identified as parts of an integrated whole" (p. 9). Leading nowhere in particular and building toward no resolution, each news report stands in isolation from all others—this, despite the elements's chronology.

The POW issue will fail the test of narrativity as long as it fails to achieve closure. The chronicle of events provides thematic coherence—the question of Americans living as POWs in Southeast Asia—but there is no conclusion. Unlike narratives, in which the elements of the story take on meaning through their contribution to some outcome that can be judged in terms of moral criteria, chronicles represent "historical reality . . . *as if* real events appeared to human consciousness in the form of *unfinished* stories" (White, 1980, p. 5; italics in original). The chronicle of America's POWs—whether fictive or factual—lacks "that summing up of the 'meaning' of the chain of events with which it deals that we normally expect from the well-made story" (p. 16). Consequently, entries simply terminate in this chronicler's own present. I cannot, in other words, tell you the *meaning* of these events. I can draw no implications from them, no lesson to be learned from the POW issue. All I can relate is that, according to published reports, these things happened. That the POW question continues unresolved, unfinished, with no foreseen conclusion, is simply the way things are.

As with all "unfolding stories," the POW issue presents us with obstacles to interpretation, but far more troubling are its shortcomings of narrative fidelity and narrative probability. The concerns of fidelity are "the individuated components of stories—whether they represent accurate assertions about social reality and thereby constitute good reasons for belief" (Fisher, 1987, p. 105). Through a "logic of good reason," a value-based system of assessment, we judge the truthfulness of each news report. At question here for most is not the press's desire for accuracy, but the veracity of statement that they report. Some might dismiss Robert Garwood's bold hinting at the existence of POWs because he was labeled a traitor. The accusations of governmental conspiracy by families of those still missing may well be understandable in terms of their prolonged anguish. When Robert McFarlane is "overheard" while "speaking in confidence," we may attribute greater credence to his observations.

Particularly when events lack resolution, we strive to make individual elements cohere. In the absence of narrativity we strain "to produce the effect of having filled in all the gaps, to put an image of continuity, coherence, and meaning in place of the fantasies of emptiness, need and frustrated desire" (White, 1980, p. 11). This is the domain of narrative probability, and it is within this domain that Schanberg's stomach tells him that the existence of American POWs might just be so.

Questions of narrative probability concern how convincingly the various elements of the POW issue support each other. This "POW chronicle" fails the test of structural coherence, the internal consistency of the naescent story's elements. The contradictions revealed in this chapter's chronicle test credulity. Because of these contradictions, the coherence of character, of ethos, is also challenged. When officials of the same branch of government contradict each other on subsequent days, and when officials refute their public pronouncements in private, questions of motive abound. Whom can we believe? The problem is fundamental to the search for coherence, for, as Fisher (1987) asserts, "Determining a character's motives is prerequisite to trust, and trust is the foundation of belief" (p. 47).

Governments lie. They dissemble, and perhaps the most dispiriting lesson of Vietnam for Americans was discovering that their trust was so thoroughly violated. Within this context of violation, however, the POW quandary gains clarity. The question of whether American POWs languish in Southeast Asia is but one element in a complex process of structuring the meaning of the Vietnam War in American public consciousness. It is a particularly sensitive element in that process because it concerns closure. War ends not with the cessation of combat and casualties, but through symbolic acts of celebration and remembrance that shape and define the past. As the Vietnam War ended in the spring of 1975, Americans and their institutions turned away from acts of closure at the moment that remembrance was called for (see Ehrenhaus, 1989). But the impulse to bring an ending to the story of war is a strong one. Only when the soldiers who come home are celebrated, when the dead are properly memorialized, and when those held prisoner are returned, is there a sense that closure has been accomplished. The past must be faced and made meaningful before it can be used in the present.

As other chapters in this volume attest, the evolution of the Vietnam experience in film represents one kind of effort to shape the past meaningfully (see Chapters 5, 6, & 7, this volume). The creation of a national Vietnam Veterans Memorial in Washington, D.C. has acted as a powerful release of the suppressed need to remember (see Ehrenhaus, 1988a, and 1988b; see also Chapters 6, 8, & 10, this volume). Moreover, the Memorial has served as a stimulus to the creation of state, regional, and municipal memorials to Vietnam veterans (Franklin, 1986). Parades welcoming home Vietnam veterans, belated as they may be, are another reflection of that impulse. All of these acts of commemoration shape remembrance of the past by "separating the war from the warrior" (Franklin, 1986, p. 26). National unity and reconciliation have been, and continue to be, pursued by divorcing persons from policy (see Scruggs & Swerdlow, 1985; Weinraub, 1980). In opposition to all of these elements of closure, the POW issue confronts us with the inseparablity of the two. Specters from the past, POWs personify the war and hauntingly remind us of failed policies and the assumptions from which they sprang.

As I have argued elsewhere (Ehrenhaus, 1988b, 1989), the end of war carries with it the obligation to *remember*, and remembrance is more than a recounting of discrete but thematically related events. The events we *choose* to remember must be bound together by a purpose or purposes whose legitimacy we collectively endorse (see Chapter 10, this volume). In this fashion the individual elements that we elect to commemorate are imbued with meaning, and the human sacrifices of war are ennobled and justified. Unlike the fragmented chronicle of the POW issue, remembrance of war must have narrative structure precisely because it is fundamentally concerned with events as they may be interpreted within a *moral universe*, informed by both the moral awareness and moral authority of those who shape the past on behalf of the entire community. These remembrances of war not only shape public consciousness, but, insofar as we choose to remember selectively, they reveal national conscience as well.

The POW issue does not lead us to question *whether* Americans and their political institutions should give structured meaning to their past; rather, it raises the question of *how* to remember and *what* merits remembrance (see Chapter 10, this volume). Since the end of American involvement in Vietnam, each presidential administration has taken the position that bringing closure to America's Vietnam War must entail a "full and final accounting," replete with epideictic for those who sacrificed. Never stated but entailed, nonetheless, narratives of closure must also provide a focused and deliberative reaffirmation of the legitimacy of purpose for which those calls for sacrifice were issued; and here is where national conscience and political expediency conflict.

Through narrative acts of closure war is given its meaning; yet, not everyone has the right to shape that meaning. The moral authority for narrative is socially sanctioned; it rests with the collective voices of the community—its political and cultural institutions and those who speak for them. The 52 persons who defined for McCloud's class the "lessons" of Vietnam were invited to offer their views precisely because of their "distinguished" status, precisely because of their institutional standing in politics, the military, the press, and in letters. Invitations to define those lessons not only legitimatize those who tend to our political and cultural institutions by bestowing moral authority upon them; offers such as these further empower them by endorsing their select right of narrative, the right to speak for us and to shape our understanding of the past and its significance in the present. Each of those 52 is concerned with lessons from "the war," but "the war" is not a circumscribed set of events. The boundaries we place on "the war" define "events." Remembrance, therefore, is always partial, always selective, and always positional, reflecting and revealing the interests of those who speak (see Chapter 10, this volume).

Every "lesson" of Vietnam, "however seemingly 'full,' is constructed on the basis of a set of events which *might have been included but were left out*" (White, 1980, p. 10; italics in original). Because narrative operates through "strategies of containment" that repress "the unthinkable which lies beyond its boundaries" (Jameson, 1981, p. 53), remembrance is fundamentally ideological in character. Closing an historical story fulfills a demand "for moral meaning, a demand that sequences of real events be assessed as to their significance as elements of a *moral* drama" (White, 1980, p. 20; italics in original). What we must press is how the resolution of the POW issue and its *inclusion* as an element of that drama changes its moral character.

Suppose for a moment that POWs are alive in Southeast Asia, and it is possible to bring them home. Those empowered to bring the story of Vietnam to closure would be faced with a difficult task. After rejoicing in the POWs' liberation, those who speak for us—and to us—must give meaning to that captivity by reaffirming and justifying the legitimacy of purpose for which those POWs have sacrificed the entirety of their adult lives. Even should the POW issue be resolved, celebration of their return is not a condition that, once fulfilled, relegates the entire affair to some forgotten past. To reiterate: The end of war carries with it the obligation to *remember*.

Simply put, the real events we know collectively as "The Vietnam War," which must be given their meaning within a moral drama, are not necessarily well-suited to the commemorative responsibilities of our political and military leaders (Ehrenhaus, 1989). While they must create a morally justifiable (i.e., ideologically bounded) story that reflects upon their moral authority, remembrance of Vietnam—as war—calls into question that authority. As Hayden White notes, "Narrative becomes a *problem* . . . when we wish to give *real* events the *form* of story" (White, 1980, p. 4; italics in original). The problem of including in a "Vietnam story" elements that call attention to the war, its policies, and its assumptions is that these elements are politically inexpedient; they do not contribute to a morally compelling story. By separating the warrior from the war, however, the problem is obviated. Heroism, bravery, and sacrifice on behalf of community can be commemorated with ease; more troublesome are the exact circumstances of those sacrifices.

Within a context in which matters of conscience are subordinated to the expedient, we find understanding of the interminable and apparently irresolvable POW issue. The foundational premises on which American foreign policy in Southeast Asia was pursued were moral certitude and an unswerving faith in military might and technological prowess. To draw attention to the limitations, if not the failure, of these premises, through the return of men who conceivably have been held prisoner since the 1960s, rattles the very foundation upon which those same assertions are now made in shaping United States' foreign policy. This, as Philip Wander (1984) argues, is "the 'ground' on which foreign policy is debated in this country," a ground "so pervasive, so obvious, so free of challenge that, once articulated, one can but say that such is the nature of foreign policy rhetoric" (p. 353).

Claims of American moral superiority supported by military prowess would seem to be more compelling when unfettered by reminders of a past that calls into question those premises. It is easier—far easier—to dismiss all of those unaccounted for, particularly when the overwhelming majority of them are presumably dead, than it is to cast doubt upon one's moral authority and political legitimacy. I am not implying conspiracy. I merely suggest convenience.

CONCLUSION

Among those who answered teacher Bill McCloud's question regarding the lessons of Vietnam was John Negroponte, a U.S. delegate to the Paris Peace Talks. Negroponte wrote that "For countries, just like individuals . . . You can't win them all." This hackneyed platitude views war as a contest, a challenge of skill, planning, and luck with consequences no greater than "you win some, you lose some." There's always another game tomorrow, and, even if we lose players today, our ability to field another team remains intact. Espousing his lesson on the tactical level, Negroponte believes that Vietnam "will help ensure that we pick our fights more carefully in the future" (McCloud, 1988, p. 72). Negroponte's "ground" is richly fertilized with assumptions of American pre-eminence and its right to seek conflict, albeit justly.

In 1977, the following lesson of Vietnam was offered: "The lesson of Vietnam is one of indecision. The U.S. was not wrong in the purpose for which we fought. While South Vietnam was not totally a free government, they still enjoyed more liberty than any communist regime in

Eastern Europe allows. Our mistake was in not moving decisively when we first militarily intervened to discourage further communist aggression in that country" (Cragan & Shields, 1977, p. 288). Not the insight of any one individual, this assertion is computer-generated, based on a study conducted by John Cragan and Donald Shields with 60 residents of Peoria, Illinois, to discover their reactions to various foreign policy dramas. Notably, this lesson, like so many offered to McCloud's junior high school students, is cast in terms of geopolitics and ideologies—governments, regimes, aggression, liberty, communism (see Chapter 2 & 3, this volume). It ignores the human realities of warfare. Like America's POWs, nowhere is to be found a corporeal being.

War has never been tidy. More than 8,000 Americans remain missing from the Korean War. Vietnam adds a mere 2,400. Even ignoring the dead, these sacrifices can only make sense by clinging to the moral certitude that created them in the first place.

REFERENCES

Action pledged on lost G.I.'s. (1983, January 29). *The New York Times*, p. A3.

Ayres, B.D. (1983, February 7). U.S. fears forays into Indochina may harm talks. *The New York Times*, p. A7.

Branigin, W. (1986, January 8). U.S., Hanoi to intensify MIA search. *The Washington Post*, pp. A1, A24.

Communists list 555 P.O.W.s but give no data on Laos. (1973, January 29). *The New York Times*, p. 15.

Congress's last word on M.I.A.s. (1976, December 16). *The New York Times, IV*, p. 6.

Corry, J. (1986, May 29). "20/20" report on M.I.A.s. *The New York Times*, p. C22.

Cragan, J.F., & Shields, D.C. (1977). Foreign policy communication dramas: How mediated rhetoric played in Peoria in campaign '76. *Quarterly Journal of Speech, 63*, 274–289.

Ehrenhaus, P. (1988a). Silence and symbolic expression. *Communication Monographs, 55*, 41–57.

Ehrenhaus, P. (1988b). The Vietnam Veterans Memorial: An invitation to argument. *Argumentation and Advocacy, 25*, 54–64.

Ehrenhaus, P. (1989). Commemorating the unwon war: On *not* remembering Vietnam. *Journal of Communication, 39*(1), 96–107.

Eng, P. (1987, September 18). Thais bar launching of MIA balloons. *The Oregonian*, p. A7.

Ex-Vietcong reports seeing P.O.W.s alive. (1982, July 8). *The New York Times*, p. A9.

Fisher, W.R. (1987). *Human communication as narration: Towards a philosophy of reason, value, and action*. Columbia: University of South Carolina Press.

Franklin, B. (1986, November 9). 143 Vietnam memorials, vast and small, rising around nation. *The New York Times*, p. 26.

Halloran, R. (1986, October 1). Report says Americans may be in Indochina. *The New York Times*, p. A13.

Hanoi reported to say G.I.s may be there. (1986, February 16). *The New York Times*, p. 8.

House panel declares no American is still Indochina War prisoner. (1976, December 16). *The New York Times*, pp. 1, 11.

Jameson, F. (1981). *The political unconscious*. Ithaca: Cornell University Press.

McCloud, B. (1988, May/June). What should we tell our children about Vietnam? *American Heritage*, pp. 55–77.

MIA: Are any still alive? (1987, November). *Life*, pp. 110–124.

$1 billion in pledges sought for a war prisoners reward. (1988, January 28). *The New York Times*, p. A18.

Paul, B. (1986, April 21). POWs: The evidence is there; now let's act. *The Wall Street Journal*, p. 22.

Pentagon is not hopeful of finding M.I.A.s alive. (1974, February 10). *The New York Times*, p. 36.

Peterson, I. (1979, May 25). Return of Marine buoying hopes on the missing in Southeast Asia. *The New York Times*, pp. A3, A10.

POW papers released. (1987, October 7). *The Oregonian*, p. A9.

Private raid on Laos reported. (1983, February 1). *The New York Times*, p. A2.

Schanberg, S.H. (1987, November 11). Soldiers still missing in action enduring scar of Vietnam War. *The Oregonian*, p. C5.

Scruggs, J., & Swerdlow, J. (1985). *To heal a nation*. New York: Harper & Row.

Secter, B. (1985, October 16). Some MIAs alive in Indochina, McFarlane is quoted as saying. *The Los Angeles Times*, I, p. 13.

Seigel, M.H. (1977, November 24). Missing in action could be declared dead, court rules. *The New York Times*, p. 8.

Suit claims Army blocked POW deal. (1985, September 17). *The Buffalo News*, pp. 1, A3.

Taubman, P. (1983, June 29). P.O.W.s in Vietnam aren't ruled out. *The New York Times*, p. A3.

Thais order ouster of group of Americans. (1983, June 2). *The New York Times*, p. A5.

Tuohy, W. (1984, May 6). No American POWs, top Vietnam editor insists. *The Los Angeles Times, I*, p. 5.

U.S. aid cites war missing. (1982, August 17). *The New York Times*, p. A11.

U.S. condemns private raids into Laos for missing G.I.s. (1985, January 25). *The New York Times*, p. 2.

Vietnam to investigate 95 reports on P.O.W.s. (1986, January 14). *The New York Times*, p. A5.

Wander, P. (1984). The rhetoric of American foreign policy. *Quarterly Journal of Speech, 70*, 339–361.

Watzlawick, P., Beavin, J., & Jackson, D. (1967). *Pragmatics of human communication*. New York: W.W. Norton.

Weinraub, B. (1980, July 2). Carter hails veterans of Vietnam in signing bill for a war memorial. *The New York Times*, p. A14.

White, H. (1980). The value of narrativity in the representation of reality. In W.J.T. Mitchell (Ed.), *On narrative* (pp. 1–23). Chicago: University of Chicago Press.

2

AIM's Vietnam and the Rhetoric of Cold War Orthodoxy

Robert L. Ivie

Department of Speech Communication & Theatre Arts, Texas A&M University

Kenneth Thompson (1981), in his study of the Cold War theories advanced by orthodox and revisionist historians, pointed to a great ideological divide separating mainstream American policy makers from their critics. In one camp, "official" histories blame the Soviets for the Cold War, pointing to communism as the ideological engine that drives Russian ambitions and threatens freedom internationally. This is the view taken by presidents and their advisers since Harry Truman. In the other camp, revisionist histories "shift the blame to American imperialism and the insatiable demands of capitalists for worldwide economic markets" (p. 11). Both theories, Thompson concluded, underestimate the complexities of international politics and the limits of national power. Nevertheless, anticommunism has remained the dominant, ideological motive for resisting Soviet initiatives globally, even after the United States suffered in Vietnam the painful consequences of a containment doctrine grounded in demonological thinking.

Demonological thinking about the Soviet threat has been advanced most recently in what has been called, somewhat ironically, "the continuing campaign of the revisionist hawks to restyle the past" (Willenson, 1987, p. 3). Members of the Committee on the Present Danger, the Reagan administration, and Reed Irvine's Accuracy in Media (AIM) organization renewed in the 1980s the themes of the early Cold War years articulated originally in the Truman Doctrine address, National Security Council Document 68, and John Foster Dulles's rhetoric of liberation. Because the unhappy experience of the Vietnam War taught many Americans, in the words of historian George C. Herring (1979), "the inherent unworkability of a policy of global containment" (p. 270), foreign policy conservatives have made a concerted effort to reawaken the nation to the communist peril, insisting that a red wave still threatens to engulf the free world unless strong barriers are erected and maintained everywhere.

Richard Nixon, in a spree of post-presidential books about real war and real peace with the communist foe, made a particular effort in *No More Vietnams* (1985) to reconstruct the lessons of a war that "has grotesquely distorted the debate over American foreign policy" (p. 13). In his view, the "Vietnam syndrome" has contributed to a "renaissance of isolationism" and an unwillingness to use power globally in defense of national interests. Thus, it is crucial, he argued, for the nation to understand that "Vietnam was lost on the political front in the United States, not on the battlefront in Southeast Asia" (p. 15). Properly steeled by renewed confidence in its righteous cause and military might, the United States must meet the challenge of "totalitarian thugs" who "lick their chops" and "gobble up" Third World nations, who commit "ruthless murders," circle the world "like a vulture searching for fresh carcasses," infect vulnerable victims with "an incurable revolutionary virus," and who enslave the survivors (pp. 210, 220, 221, 224, 227). Thus, for Nixon, Vietnam should be considered merely a temporary setback in a continuing war to contain Soviet-led communism; whereas "No more Vietnams can mean that we will not *try* again, it *should* mean that we will not *fail* again" (1985, p. 237).

Herring's (1979) history of the Vietnam War represents precisely the view to which Nixon and others of his persuasion have taken strong exception. America's defeat, according to Herring, demonstrates a need to reassess the basic premises of the containment policy. In his words:

> The United States intervened in Vietnam to block the apparent march of a Soviet-directed Communism across Asia, enlarged its commitment to halt a presumably expansionist Communist China, and eventually made Vietnam a test of its determination to uphold world order. By wrongly attributing the Vietnamese conflict to external sources, the United States drastically misjudged its internal dynamics. By intervening in what was essentially a local struggle, it placed itself at the mercy of local forces, a weak client, and a determined adversary. It elevated into a major international conflict what might have remained a localized struggle. By raising the stakes into a test of its own credibility it perilously narrowed its options. A policy so flawed in its premises cannot help but fail, and in this case the results were disastrous. (p. 270)

Essentially the same interpretation of America's failure in Vietnam received wide exposure and high acclaim in the Fall of 1983 when PBS aired its 13-part series entitled "Vietnam: A Television History."

However, a little less than two years later, the reconstructionist rhetoric of the "revisionist hawks" was also broadcast over PBS. On June 26,

1985, AIM's counterdocumentary on the Vietnam War, produced with financial assistance from the National Endowment for the Humanities, was aired as an hour-long rebuttal of "Vietnam: A Television History" (see Chapter 3, this volume). In the words of narrator Charlton Heston, "Television's 'Vietnam: The Real Story' " was "dedicated to setting the historical record straight by correcting some of the more serious errors of the PBS series on Vietnam," especially its "underlying myth" that "communists aren't really communists at all" (*Inside story*, 1985, pp. 6, 7). At issue were the basic premises of the containment doctrine and whether America's defeat constituted the failure of a misguided policy or, as AIM contended, a tragedy of lost will.

AIM's counterdocumentary illustrates the continuing ideological allure of anticommunism, which has survived the Vietnam experience as the basis for a confrontational policy toward the Soviet Union. The program perpetuates an image of the communist enemy so primitive that the fear of death is channeled into a potentially suicidal concept of self-defense, the "logic" of which is a rhetorical construction to which Americans have become accustomed through decades of Cold War conditioning.

The source of AIM's rhetorical invention is a system of conventional metaphors from which the premises of Soviet-American confrontation are themselves derived. Specifically, the urgency of America's rivalry with the Soviet Union reduces to a dramatic conflict between underlying images of life and death, tragedy and melodrama, clarity and distortion. These images constitute concepts with sufficient ideological force to impede progress toward a more constructive relationship between the superpowers. Thus, an understanding of the conceptual images at work in AIM's counterdocumentary on Vietnam clarifies the rhetorical task facing those who warn against the dangers of demonological thinking in the nuclear age.

AIM's VIETNAM: A "TRAGEDY" OF LOST WILL

AIM's program was designed to present the Vietnam War as a struggle between the forces of life and death, suggesting that the 13-part PBS series distorted reality by transforming a tragedy of lost will into a melodrama of misguided policy. These basic images constituted a shrewd rhetorical strategy for interjecting a framework of interpretation that, in turn, validated AIM's arguments.

The image of life versus death was projected through words such as "healing," "antidote," "wounds," "trauma," "extermination," and "murder." This verbal imagery was supported by visual images of young spring trees and fresh green grass surrounding the Vietnam Veterans Memorial, shots of a Vietnamese child's limp, emaciated body, panoramas of human skeletons unearthed from Cambodian graves, and so forth. Through vehicles such as these, Charlton Heston and a host of other program participants advanced the premise that communism equals death.

The program's insistence upon characterizing communists as agents of death was apparent in Stephen Morris's testimony (*Inside story*, 1985):

> *Violence* was central to the success of the communists in Vietnam. Back in 1945, in the scenes which we see in the PBS series, there is no mention of the fact that the communists carried out a massive campaign of *assassination* of all non-communist nationalist leaders they could get their hands on. . . . They were simply *murdered*, one after the other, over a period of six months to a year. . . . Not only the *assassinations* of 1945–46 are not mentioned, [but also] the *assassinations*, the *murders*, which took place in the late 40s of other non-communist nationalists, the Hoa Hao and the Cao Dai. . . . Once again, Ho Chi Minh could not accept anybody being independent of him and his organization, so *murders* took place on a large scale there. (p. 10, my emphasis)

Reed Irvine's reference to "the murderous Pol Pot" served a similar function as Stephen Morris's narrative, but with the explicit intent of establishing the program's basic premise. "Unfortunately," Irvine complained (*Inside story*, 1985), the PBS series did not "show the connection between these horrendous events [in Pol Pot's Cambodia] and their cause, namely the imposition of communist rule over all of Indochina" (p. 7). Communism, in short, accounted for all the suffering in Southeast Asia.

AIM also took the PBS documentary to task for associating the American soldier with images of death. It gave a "grim portrait of the postwar life of our Vietnam veterans," Heston complained. He noted especially the PBS segment that suggested many soldiers were "still haunted by the experience," language which William Jayne disliked because it projected "the stereotyped image of the veteran as a loser, a victim" rather than as "well-adjusted," "productive" members of society assuming leadership roles "because of their experience of having served their country." America's soldiers should have been associated with life-saving, productive activities, not with pain, agony, and festering wounds (*Inside story*, 1985, pp. 12, 13, 16).

Thus, PBS was guilty of "reigniting" the questions that "inflamed" debate over the Vietnam War in the 1960s and 1970s. The series should have contributed instead to "the healing of national esteem in the post war era" and to helping to end "the trauma of the Vietnam experience." Whereas AIM's goal of resisting communism was identified with healing and life, PBS was condemned for leaving "the impression that the Indochinese holocaust could be viewed from two equally valid perspectives," thereby abandoning communism's victims to "the howling wind" (*Inside story*, 1985, pp. 6, 14).

The two remaining images in the AIM counterdocumentary associated PBS's perspective on the war with the language of distortion and melodrama, drawing prolifically on terms such as "distorted," "episodic," "kaleidoscopic," "glossed over," "jumbled together," "tar brush," "melodrama," "white hats vs. black hats," "puppet," "myth," "villian," and "bad guys." Just as systematically, the program presented AIM's version of the Vietnam tragedy within a verbal context of clarity, telling the "tragic story" of the war "straight," with "20-20 hindsight," as "bedrock history." Thus, the premise that communism equals death was reinforced by a second premise that defeat stems from disinformation.

Reed Irvine's comments revealed the interaction of images of clarity and tragedy by advancing the assumption that distortion (i.e., any alternative perspective) exposes America to communist encroachments. In his words (*Inside story*, 1985), "Now one of the great advantages of history is that you can take advantage of *20-20 hindsight*. [PBS] didn't do that. . . . And, as a result, they failed to put across one of the most important lessons that should be learned from the Vietnam experience. And that is, the imposition of communist rule inevitably results in great human tragedy" (p. 7, my emphasis).

Instead of "history telling," the PBS documentary presented "a kind of kaleidoscope of images" that "glossed over" the negative side of Ho Chi Minh and "jumbled together" information about the struggle between nationalists and communists (*Inside story*, 1985, pp. 7, 6, 8, 11). This kind of distortion leads directly to melodrama, as Charlton Heston explained (*Inside story*, 1985): "Having portrayed the communists as principled nationalists fighting for the independence of Vietnam, the PBS series shows the South Vietnamese as the bad guys. The story becomes a melodrama—white hats versus black hats. Our friends are the ones in the black hats" (p. 9). A segment featuring Bruce Loebs's critique of the PBS series (*Inside story*, 1985) underscored the interaction between these two conceptual images:

> Now, every myth has to have a hero, and the hero in the PBS series is clearly Ho Chi Minh. But he needs to be constructed as a hero. Every myth has to have a villain. The villain in the PBS piece, of course, is South Vietnam and the United States. Now, to make Ho Chi Minh the hero, it

is necessary to make him the legitimate ruler of all Vietnam. And they do this by distorting the so-called elections that were supposed to be held in 1956 according to the Geneva accords. (pp. 10–11)

Constructing myths about heroes and villains on the basis of distortions suggested that the producers of the PBS series, and the media in general, were acting with malice against the best interests of the United States. Charlton Heston (*Inside story,* 1985), in fact, reported that "scholar Douglas Pike felt that the distortion went beyond error, beyond unfairness." Heston said further that "disinformation" and "deception" were "the deciding factors in the Vietnam War" (pp. 12, 16). He concluded that "this kind of distorted coverage had a cumulative effect on Congress. The results on the battlefield were disastrous." Ultimately, "our people, and our leaders, became confused and suffered a loss of will, with disastrous consequences" (pp. 14, 16).

In sum, the distortions of the PBS melodrama constituted disinformation that led to defeat and death at the hands of the communists and their agents. This was the underlying assumption, or first principle, introduced metaphorically in the AIM counterdocumentary. It established a framework of argumentation within which evidence was interpreted and from which necessary conclusions about the past and the future were derived.

As Ernesto Grassi (1980) has observed, metaphor is the basis of rational thought; it is the mechanism of what Vico called *ingenium,* which is the faculty of "grasping" ultimate principles that themselves cannot be deduced. Metaphor "determines" premises since "they cannot be proven" within the system of logic itself. The image "comes 'before' and provides that which deduction can never discover." Thus, "the concepts through which we come to understand and 'grasp' each situation come from our ingenious, metaphorical, fantastic capacities that convey meanings in the concrete situations with which we are confronted" (pp. 20, 45, 97, 100).

Such was the case explicitly for Reed Irvine, as revealed in his comments during the half-hour discussion aired immediately after AIM's counterdocumentary. In his view, there could be no balanced picture of communism, for "that's like saying let's have a balanced picture of Auschwitz. Let's get the pros and cons of incinerating or gassing all of those Jews, and Poles, and others. . . . To me that's obscene" (p. 22). There was but one true picture of the threat posed by the red fascists, according to Irvine:

I have a point of view. I am in favor of freedom and of democracy. I want to see it *preserved.* I wanted to see it *preserved* in Vietnam, Cambodia, and

> Laos. I want to see it *preserved* anywhere in the world where it exists. . . . Communism *brutalizes* people. (*Inside story* 1985, pp. 22–23, my emphasis)

Fighting communism everywhere was necessary because it was equivalent to preserving life itself.

With this concept grasped metaphorically, the function of evidence provided by Douglas Pike, Stephen Morris, Bruce Loebs, and others on the program was to envelop AIM's image of communism in the aura of rationality, thereby maintaining the guise of flawless reason while criticizing those who argued from different first principles. Both sides in the PBS versus AIM debate were quite adept at rebutting one another from their separate vantage points, as the post-program exchange of written replies demonstrated (see *Inside story,* 1985, pp. 27–53, for PBS's assessment of the AIM counterdocumentary; see Rollins & Banerian, 1985, for AIM's reply to PBS's rebuttal). Thrusting and parrying, each scored occasional points against the other, but neither penetrated the other's shield of rationality enough to expose basic premises. Thus, AIM's rhetoric of anticommunism was sustained "rationally" even as it advanced concepts metaphorically, concepts that associated warfare with survival and diplomacy with death.

AIM's imagery reflects a dimension of Cold War rhetorical orthodoxy that persists despite America's apparent post-Vietnam hesitancy to project power globally. As James Schlesinger has observed, "The public instinct is that we'd better not get into that kind of situation again. But the public also wants a restoration of faith in the country's invulnerability. And these two forces are playing one against the other in our society today" (Willenson, 1987, p. 399). A reversal of life and death imagery pervades even gatekeeping institutions, such as the press—symbolically neutralizing, for instance, opposition to the nuclear arms race. As Robert L. King (1982) has observed, journalists routinely draw upon metaphors that characterize nuclear weapons "as creative, living beings, not as instruments of death on a massive scale." The irony is that positive imagery has become associated with "instruments of death" so extensively that "those who object to the spread of nuclear weapons are metaphorically against life: they advocate 'nonproliferation' or a 'freeze' " (pp. 709, 712).

As AIM's reconstructive rhetoric on Vietnam reveals, a plausible replacement of anticommunism as America's principal operational motive in international affairs must be grasped metaphorically as "for life," symbolically assuring the preservation of freedom without insisting (as does AIM's rhetoric) upon the demise of the Soviet Union. A plausible image of living with the Soviets necessarily would draw upon and redirect conceptual metaphors that presently legitimize a commitment to eradicating the "red virus" (Talbott, 1984, p. 185). Thus, progress toward what Bennett (1984, p. 164) has called a "codification of coexistence" between the superpowers requires renewed attention to the inventional properties of tropes currently in the ideological service of an indiscriminate Cold War containment doctrine (Johnson, 1983, p. 970).

TOWARD A POST-VIETNAM IMAGE OF LIVING WITH THE SOVIETS?

The struggle to articulate a serviceable image of the Soviets—that is, one that reverts neither to anticapitalist revisionism nor to anticommunist ideology—has been implicit in many discussions of America's foreign policy options during the decade of the 1980s. I.M. Destler (1984), for instance, rejects anticommunism as "the political engine for American internationalism," recommending instead a "picture of the Russians as powerful, ambitious, unattractive, opportunistic rivals whose presence on the world scene, however disadvantageous and threatening to us, is beyond our power to alter in any fundamental way. But we have the strength and capacity both to compete with them and to live with them" (pp. 41, 57). Destler's view has been reinforced by Gordon Adams (1984), who argues that "the United States and the Soviet Union will have to live with each other; the alternative is mutual suicide" (p. 171), and by Roy Bennett (1984), who suggests a "fundamental reorientation is required" that involves "(a) United States policy coming to terms with the imperative of living with the Soviet Union on the basis of political equality; and, following from that (b) establishing a system that might be called 'codification of coexistence' " (p. 164).

The effort to envision a new kind of realism in global affairs includes Ralph K. White's (1983) call for "realistic empathy," an attitude toward the Soviets which recognizes their hostility toward the United States without overlooking what he called their "essential humanity;" such an attitude, White argues, would enable the United States to "be tough in ways we should be tough" and "reasonable and cooperative in the ways we must be in order to survive" (p. 122). Realistic empathy would help Americans maintain a more balanced perspective toward their adversaries, such as the view advanced by Bialer and Afferica (1982/1983) that "Soviet leaders do not want war with the West; they fear war as much as we, and are inclined to engage in relatively low-risk adventures to further their expansionist ambitions" (p. 262).

This vision of a kind of competitive coexistence between the superpowers encompasses the twin assumptions of equality and common interests. Unlike the orthodox doctrine of containment, it does not prescribe a radical change in the Soviet system or seek to keep the Soviets in "the position of a junior relationship" to the Americans, with American interests and power paramount everywhere (Bennett, 1984, pp. 157–158). Instead, it acknowledges the global reach of Soviet power and advocates Russia's participation in settlements wherever its interests are engaged. Rather than assuming that every Soviet gain amounts to an American loss, these "new realists" emphasize that the interests of both sides coincide where, for instance, there is a need to stabilize the arms race, reduce nuclear stockpiles, avoid a further spread of nuclear arms, and use finite economic resources to insure healthy economies (Bialer & Afferica, 1982/1983, p. 266; Bay, 1983, p. 502).

These new realists also adopt the potentially reassuring notion that the military balance in Europe is essentially "stable," with NATO and Warsaw Pact forces in a "stalemate," and that neither side controls the "long-term flow of events" in the Southern Tier (Adams, 1984, pp. 171, 180). They reject the notion of Soviet superiority and American insecurity, of "periods of peril" and "windows of vulnerability" (Johnson, 1983), arguing that such language serves only to perpetuate a verbal map drawn by the old realists and substantiated by the consequences of their own, self-validating practices (Rapopport, 1979, p. 311).

Thus, the rhetoric of the new realists attempts to deflect attention from the threatening ideological motives of the Soviets and to avoid magnifying the fragility of American security. It emphasizes the situational constraints limiting the actions of both the U.S. and the U.S.S.R. and criticizes the fixation on evil intentions that blackened President Reagan's view of Soviet leaders (Glad, 1983). Yet, this new vision of realistic empathy, of living securely in a world of competitive coexistence with the Soviet Union, has fallen short of achieving the status of rhetorical orthodoxy. The rhetoric of anticommunism, as reflected in AIM's counterdocumentary, still plays well to the nation's historic sense of mission and tugs with authority at the public's fear of an ideology so alien to democratic, capitalistic, and religious ideals.

Distrust of Soviet motives remained high in the 1980s (Lovell, 1983), with "peace and strength" (pp. 39–40) being identified by pollsters as the "two issues of surpassing concern" to Americans (Schneider, 1984, p. 18). Thus, the Reagan administration's call for peace through strength continues to prevail over the warnings of those who fear for "the fate of the earth" (Schell, 1982). While antinuclear advocates have featured negative images of American madness, pathology, sickness, and death over positive visions of national security (Ivie, 1987a), the resurgent voices of Cold War orthodoxy capitalize on a rhetoric of survival, reconstructing the Vietnam experience to legitimize the continuation of an essentially confrontational policy toward the Soviet Union. The "new realism," which has only just appeared on the horizon of public debate, advances a vision of peace without insisting upon containment at any cost, but also without attending sufficiently to the limits of rhetorical invention imposed by its guiding conceptual metaphor.

On the positive side, the conceptual image of reluctant partnership characterizes the Soviets as an established power with a vested interest in maintaining world order. It integrates themes such as political equality, common interests, and competition. Futhermore, it avoids the historic ideological divide that either accuses American leaders of power lusts, paranoid fears, and delusions of grandeur, or promotes visions of Soviet savagery. An image of the Soviets as members of the established world order symbolically invests them, along with the United States, with protecting civilization from terrorism, revolution, and nuclear destruction. In short, the Soviets are presented as competitors with a deep-seated interest in preserving the system of competition itself.

On several counts, such an image might have proved rhetorically effective. By highlighting the stability of Soviet power and Soviet interests "in the settling of major problems around the world" (Bennett, 1984, p. 165), the metaphor of reluctant partnership invites an image of one world instead of two—an image that draws upon the familiar notions of bargaining, negotiating, and doing business with a strong competitor, of accommodating the conflicting interests of legitimate parties in a dispute, and so forth. Moreover, the metaphor of the U.S.S.R. as an establishment power could be substantiated with evidence showing, for instance, that Soviet foreign policy is conservative by nature and that the Soviets might be counted upon to abide by carefully negotiated agreements (Ground Zero, 1983).

Ultimately, though, the idea of living with the Soviets—of exercising a degree of realistic empathy in order to maintain a state of competitive coexistence—requires a sense of security that is not easily or immediately grasped through the conceptual image of reluctant partnership. The *ingenium* of the metaphor finesses, but does not emcompass or supplant, rhetorical conventions that underscore freedom's fragility and thus America's insecurity. Just as Americans are accustomed to a plethora of decivilizing vehicles that portrays the savagery of the communist adversary (Ivie, 1984), they routinely speak of freedom in terms that converge on a conception of its vulnerability (Ivie, 1987b). Freedom is an experiment that risks failure, a lady in distress, a solitary flickering flame amidst the dark and stormy seas of totalitarianism, a precarious infant, a heroic struggle, and the hunter's prey. Empathy with a powerful partner is discouraged by Lady Liberty's rhetorical insecurity. Thus, the conceptual image of competitive coexistence presumes a sense of national self-confidence that is contrary to the linguistic facts of contemporary American political discourse.

Despite the "lessons" of Vietnam, Cold War orthodoxy prevails rhetorically—boldly advanced by those who would "restore an image of American omnipotence" while rewriting the war's history (Willenson, 1987, p. 2) and essentially unchallenged by those who have attempted to articulate an image of living with the Soviets in competitive partnership. Liberals and conservatives alike generally agree that one of the legacies of Vietnam is greater public caution over committing American troops to combat unless vital national interests are at stake (Willenson, 1987, pp. 381–413). But hawks and doves both overlook the rhetorically grounded image of freedom's fragility that remains unchanged by the Vietnam experience and continues to provide a readily available and reliable resource for constructing "real" threats to the national security, wherever they may appear. For the moment, at least, America has not lost its rhetorical will to fight communism to the death.

REFERENCES

Adams, G. (1984). Restructuring national defense policy. In A. Gartner, C. Greer, & F. Riessman (Eds.), *Beyond Reagan: Alternatives for the '80s* (pp. 167–192). New York: Harper & Row.

Bay, C. (1983). Hazards of Goliath in the nuclear age: Need for rational priorities in American peace and defense policies. *Alternatives: Journal of World Policy, 8*, 501–542.

Bennett, R. (1984). Beyond the new cold war. In A. Gartner, C. Greer, & G. Riessman (Eds.), *Beyond Reagan: Alternatives for the '80s* (pp. 152–166). New York: Harper & Row.

Bialer, S., & Afferica, J. (1982/1983). Reagan and Russia. *Foreign Affairs, 61*, 249–271.

Destler, I.M. (1984). Congress. In J.S. Nye, Jr. (Ed.), *The making of America's Soviet policy* (pp. 37–61). New Haven, CT: Yale University Press.

Glad, G. (1983). Black-and-white thinking: Ronald Reagan's approach to foreign policy. *Political Psychology, 4*, 33–75.

Grassi, E. (1980). *Rhetoric as philosophy: The humanist tradition*. University Park: The Pennsylvania State University Press.

Ground Zero. (1983). *What about the Russians—and nuclear war*? New York: Pocket Books.

Herring, G.D. (1979). *America's longest war: The United States and Vietnam, 1950–1975*. New York: John Wiley & Sons.

Inside story special edition: Vietnam op/ed [transcript]. (1985). Kent, OH: PTV Publications.

Ivie, R.L. (1984). Speaking "common sense" about the Soviet threat: Reagan's rhetorical stance. *Western Journal of Speech Communication, 48*, 39–50.

Ivie, R.L. (1987a). Metaphor and the rhetorical invention of cold war "idealists." *Communication Monographs, 54*, 156–182.

Ivie, R.L. (1987b). The ideology of freedom's "fragility" in American foreign policy argument. *Journal of American Forensic Association, 24*, 27–36.

Johnson, R.H. (1983). Periods of peril: The window of vulnerabilty and other myths. *Foreign Affairs, 61*, 950–970.

King, R.L. (1982). Fatal metaphors. *Massachusetts Review, 23*, 709–713.

Lovell, J.P. (1983). The idiom of national security. *Journal of Political and Military Sociology, 11*, 35–51.

Nixon, R. (1985). *No more Vietnams*. New York: Avon Books.

Rapopport, A. (1979). Verbal maps and global politics. *Et cetera, 36*, 297–313.

Rollins, P.C., & Banerian, J. (1985). *Accuracy in media's reply to the WGBH rebuttal*. (Available from Accuracy in Media, 1275 K Street N.W., Suite 1150, Washington, D.C. 20005).

Schell, J. (1982). *The fate of the earth*. New York: Alfred A. Knopf.

Schneider, W. (1984). Public opinion. In J.S. Nye, Jr. (Ed.), *The making of America's Soviet policy* (pp. 11–35). New Haven, CT: Yale University Press.

Talbott, S. (1984). Social issues. In J.S. Nye, Jr. (Ed.), *The making of America's Soviet policy* (pp. 183–205). New Haven, CT: Yale University Press.

Thompson, K.W. (1981). *Cold war theories*. Baton Rouge: Louisiana State University Press.

White, R.K. (1983). Empathizing with the rulers of the USSR. *Political Psychology, 4*, 121–137.

Willenson, K. (1987). *The bad war: An oral history of the Vietnam war*. New York: New American Library.

3

"Vietnam" and the Politics of History

Philip Wander
Melissa Kane
Department of Communication Studies, San Jose State University

> What the world needs to know at this juncture is that our Nation remains steadfast to its historic ideals and follows its traditional course . . . in the spirit of our Declaration of Independence. And may we never forget that, as Lincoln said, that declaration was not something exclusive to us, but there was "something in that declaration giving liberty, not alone to the people of this country, but hope for the world for all future time."
>
> (John Foster Dulles, 1955)

President Reagan (1984), at the Georgetown Center for Strategic and International Studies, on April 6, 1984, thought it unfortunate that many Congressional representatives believed they were still in the troubled Vietnam era. Congress, he concluded, is not wholly comfortable with both the need for a military element in foreign policy and its own responsibility to deal with that element (p. 5). Reagan was not engaging in some academic dispute. Nor was he merely calling for a new orientation, for shedding the past in order to live more fully in the present. He was making the case for military intervention in Lebanon. He was also implicitly acknowledging that the debate over Vietnam is embedded in the issue of military intervention, that Vietnam, the historical event, has given way to "Vietnam," a place in political discourse over which we debate American foreign policy.

Controversy still hovers over Vietnam. It is not surprising, therefore, to discover that after the Public Broadcast System (PBS) aired its award-winning documentary, "Vietnam: A History," in 1983, it encountered a bitter response from a small, conservative group calling itself "Accuracy in Media" (AIM). The clash between these two perspectives included charges and countercharges; it also included a one-hour television documentary produced by AIM entitled "Vietnam: The Real Story," which was broadcast over PBS in 1985 (see Chapter 2). Following AIM's program, PBS supporters, AIM supporters, and various "experts" engaged in a debate wherein objectivity emerged as a key issue. Could Vietnam be treated as history? If so, could the conflict be confined to objective versus subjective reporting? Embracing objectivity, AIM supporters argued that their version was more accurate, the "true" story, and, going one step further, called the PBS series un-American "propaganda." A year later, AIM called for a Congressional investigation of PBS's programming practices and denounced PBS' series as "leftist and blatantly procommunist" ("AIM calls," 1986).

That the debate over PBS's "Vietnam" goes much deeper than its strengths or weaknesses as a television documentary becomes apparent when we move beyond questions of historical fact to consider the ideological content of AIM's response. Accordingly, in this chapter we will take up the following questions: What world view is AIM attempting to promote through its interpretation of Vietnam? How does this world view relate to political struggle in the United States? What sort of world view does AIM appear to be attacking? And, finally, to what extent can PBS's "Vietnam" be said to embody such a world view?

What is the world view communicated by AIM? This view may be summarized as follows: We live in a world divided into two camps, with communists on one side and the free world on the other. Freedom-loving peoples want open societies and peaceful relations with their neighbors. Communists are people who have become puppets of the Soviet Union. When communists appear in other countries, their objective is to take over and align that country with Russia. People attracted to communism in these countries are duped. Communists and the people they overwhelm lose their homelands. When people of the free world oppose such takeovers, they are engaged in a noble cause. Those in such countries who want freedom must be protected from natives who have become the tools of Moscow. When the free world loses such a struggle, those who fought for freedom—the natives and the military—should be shown in a good light. When the media fail to portray "freedom fighters" in a good light, they play into the hands of communists and undermine the ability of the United States to meet its obligations and to protect its national interest.

Historically, the story informing AIM's response finds its origins in this country in a broad-based political movement known as "McCarthyism." The name is misleading. "McCarthyism" suggests a movement built around, motivated, and mobilized by a personality. Our focus, as a consequence, is directed not at a movement that enjoys the support of one-third of the American people, but at an alcoholic Senator from Wisconsin, who was exposed as a liar and a bully in the Army-McCarthy hearings and is now safely in his grave. The myth of "tail-gunner Joe" thus obscures the long-term political significance of the anticommunist movement.

When we resist the temptation to personify the anticommunist movement in the late 1940s and early 1950s as "McCarthyism," we discover that this movement, which had considerable mass appeal, led to the removal of people with "subversive sympathies" from the government, the unions, the legal and teaching professions, and the mass media. It promoted a number of laws pertaining to "national security," loyalty oaths being the most famous. It promoted the growth of what critics now call the "military-industrial-educational complex" designed to insure the external security or "defense" of the United States. And it fostered the development of agencies—the FBI, CIA, military intelligence, and so on—for the purpose of gathering "intelligence" and countering a communist menace at home and abroad. This system we shall call the "Security Industry."

Understood as an established and ongoing system, the Security Industry involves much of the United States' economy. It receives tens of billions of dollars annually from the national budget. What binds this vast coalition of intelligence and law enforcement agencies, the military, defense contractors and subcontractors is an ideological formation making claims about the nature of the world—the world of nations, in particular—and about the adequacy of anticommunism as a moral guide and a theoretical base for directing foreign policy.

This ideological formation grew out of and makes factual claims about historical events. Vietnam—then, in the 1950s, called by its designation in the French empire, "Indochina"—had a part in the origins of this formation. Along with the "loss" of China and the attempted "takeover" of Korea, the anticommunist movement looked upon France's war in Indochina as further evidence of a global Soviet threat. The Truman and Eisenhower administrations underwrote France's efforts to reconquer her colonies. Thus, the claimed existence of a communist menace, with its theory of Soviet expansion, provided a rationale not only for billions of dollars in foreign aid during this period, but also for the use of nuclear weapons to prevent a French defeat. With fear as a base and France's military actions as evidence, Senate Majority Leader William F. Knowland (1969, p. 106) began his advocacy of a policy of "massive retaliation" on May 16, 1954. When any country falls behind the Iron Curtain, he argued,

> that force becomes greater, and sooner or later we and the free world are going to have to draw a line because our own vital security is at stake. The loss of Southeast Asia would lead to the loss of the balance of Asia. That

> might mean the ultimate destruction of Europe based on Lenin's theory that the road through Paris is through Peking. And if we had the entire world pass into the Communist orbit, it would make, in effect, a continental Dienbienphu out of the United States.

This "Menace Theory," holding that countries or governments having Marxist, socialist, or communist ideas necessarily become part of the Soviet Bloc, became popular in the 1950s and continues to be a part of AIM's critique nearly 40 years later. Toward the end of AIM's "Vietnam," for example, Senator Symms argues that the problem we faced in Vietnam is the same problem we now face in Central America:

> If the United States fails to meet its obligations in Central America, we will in fact have probably somewhere between 10 and 20 million refugees pouring across our borders from Mexico very rapidly, because this war that's going on in Central America the target is Mexico. The target is not El Salvador. That's where the Soviets are trying to aim their arrow. So, it's critical to our future security, and if we as Americans fail to answer that call now to face our responsibilities, we will really have to pay for it.[1]

Underlying this rhetoric is both a well-defined theory about foreign affairs and an obligation to act on the basis of that theory. In an ideological context joining AIM, certain government agencies, the military, and a military-industrial-educational establishment, Menace Theory transcends history to affect domestic expenditures and foreign policy in the here and now.

Having identified and placed AIM's world view in the larger context, we are now in a position to ask what AIM is attacking. What kind of ideological formation, what sort of moral vision and theory of affairs is it that AIM objects to when responding to the PBS series? This is, from the standpoint of anticommunism, an easy question to answer: AIM objects to Communism. In this formulation, communism is evil. Anyone who supports it is evil. Because certain ideas may weaken our will to resist and may prompt us to provide aid and comfort to the enemy, those who object to anticommunism or to anticommunists are labeled "un-American," "pro-communist," "communist dupes," or "fellow travelers."

Consistent with this view of communism, anticommunists do not value and rarely characterize what they object to in terms that are acceptable to an opponent or to those willing to entertain a debate over the issues. When someone or some group is accused of being "pro-com-

[1] This and other quotations from AIM's rejoinder, unless otherwise noted, were taken from an off-air recording.

munist" or un-American," what they say is irrelevant. The issue becomes not the rationality or the rightness of their position in light of the circumstances, but whether they should be allowed to speak and assemble with others. The arguments of "communist dupes" do not require a rejoinder. Their words, their music, their documentaries merely evidence their ignorance and treason. Therefore, if we are to get a grip on what AIM is objecting to, and if we assume that this is a world view that challenges anticommunism at crucial points, we shall have to flush it out ourselves.

This much is obvious: AIM's alarm is not and cannot be confined to this particular program, to PBS, or to the mass media. People and events outside the media now challenge traditional anticommunism. Elements of an emergent world view critical of anticommunism, and AIM is sensitive to this, may be found in the antiwar movement, the "human rights" formulation of the Carter Administration, the Sane Nuclear Freeze, and anti-apartheid movements, and in activist groups operating inside the Catholic Church. Within this milieu are the glimmerings of global idealism and a theoretically grounded, morally informed case against military intervention, and an ideology commending such policies.

The existence of an anti-interventionist/pro-human rights position on foreign affairs and its emergence as a viable ideological alternative depends on practical matters—for example, on political organizing, on coalition building, on developing programs for domestic reform, on the realities of Soviet foreign policy. But there is one intellectual demand that has to be met: to create an alternative to the anticommunist story about the nature of the world. In order to be effective, this story must get beyond revulsion and anger, which will require discipline; for there is truth in Allen Ginsburg's (1965, pp. 43–44) response. He called it "Black Magic language," offering formulas for reality. "Communism," he went on, "was only a nine-letter word used by inferior magicians, using the wrong alchemical formula for changing earth into gold." The people who used such language were, he thought, "funky warlocks" who were only guessing, using "handmedown mandrake terminology" which failed to work in 1956. There is truth in Ginsburg's response, but the truths of poetry are not prosaic enough for the demands of politics, where anticommunism has functioned as a formula for reality, or for the demands of political rhetoric, where cliché is too often seen as a sign of stability.

In order to communicate politically viable truths, an anti-interventionist/pro-human rights position must distinguish not only among Marxist, socialist, and communist ideas, but also between those ideas and the actual reach of the Soviet Union as a nation with its own problems, objectives, and foreign policy. It must also try to explain the enduring appeal of anticommunism in American politics, as well as the possibility that it contains some truths.

The great truth of anticommunism is that just after World War II, the Soviet Union appeared to be on the brink of taking over much of the world. When Germany surrendered, Soviet armies occupied several countries in Eastern Europe. Communist parties in Western Europe (e.g., France, Italy, and Yugoslavia), because of their resistance to fascism, enjoyed considerable popularity and support after the war. Socialist governments came to power in Scandinavia. European colonies in the Near East, Middle East, Far East, and Africa revolted, with native resistance groups often espousing Marxist ideas. China fell. Korea was endangered. France was losing in Indochina. News of Stalin's purges reached the West. And in the midst of all this the Soviet Union tested an atomic bomb and, in 1954, a hydrogen bomb.

For a country recovering from a world war and for a people who had been led to believe that victory was complete, the rise of a Soviet empire and the threat of nuclear annihilation was nearly incomprehensible. The United States was no longer invincible. Out of shock and angry disbelief arose a movement arguing that this turn was the result of a world-wide conspiracy promoted, in this country, by traitors in high office. This is the genesis of anticommunism in the United States after World War II.

An anti-interventionist/pro-human rights approach acknowledging anticommunism as a response at a certain moment in history takes up a strategic position. It can evaluate Soviet and American foreign policy; more important, it can cross-examine the claims of anticommunism in light of subsequent events. Recall, for example, the predictions made on the basis of Menace Theory in the late 1940s and early 1950s. Forty years later, the world, including much of the "communist world," has not been absorbed into a Soviet Bloc. Socialist governments have been in and out of power all over Western Europe and in England. Communists have participated in coalition governments. Yet, none of these countries has slipped behind the "Iron Curtain." And where a Soviet empire may be said to exist—in Eastern Europe, for example—there is a history of rebellion. The invasion of Afghanistan hardly signaled a world-wide Soviet advance. As for "Red China," a cornerstone of Menace Theory, the People's Republic of China opposes the Soviet Union and has entered into a variety of economic, cultural, and political agreements with the United States.

Having raised Menace Theory to a level where it can be debated, an anti-interventionist/pro-human rights stance is now in a position to question the moral assumptions underlying anticommunism. The ideals affirmed in anticommunism are realized in a "free world." Here, we must distinguish between utopian hopes and the world as it is, between the ideals of anticommunism and the world anticommunism has had some part in making. The "free world" in no way describes the regimes propped up by American influence over the past 40 years. In Africa, in the Middle East, in Central and South America, in the Philippines, in Indonesia, the United States has aligned itself with one military dictatorship after another. The consequence in country after country has been the slaughter of native men, women, and children—sometimes referred to as the "enemy" or, equivalently, as "communists." In Chile, Indonesia, Iran, Vietnam—overt and covert American intervention has contributed to the deaths (were such statistics collected) of millions of people. An anti-interventionist/pro-human rights perspective calls into question the reality of and the assumption that intervention is likely to create a "free world."

Because the world view embraced by members of AIM disallows debating the "enemy" (hence, the "enemy's" arguments), AIM members have failed to recognize that the world view implicit in PBS's "Vietnam" is really quite formidable. To clarify the point, the conflict between AIM and an anti-interventionist/pro-human rights perspective may be drawn up in the form of propositions. Based on its response to the PBS series, AIM would reject the following propositions:

1. Marxist, socialist, and communist governments do not automatically lead countries into a Soviet Bloc.
2. The Soviet Union has not been successful in dominating countries inside its empire.
3. Nationalism offers a theory of international affairs superior to that offered through a communist menace (i.e., Menace Theory) for understanding and predicting behaviors of other countries.
4. The term "free world" does not accurately describe governments or countries dependent on or dominated by the United States.
5. Military intervention, whether covert or overt, does not contribute to the making of a free world.
   (a) Killing native peoples contradicts such a goal.
   (b) Killing native peoples leads to the creation of military dictatorships.

Casting the matter in propositional form enables us to appreciate the sincerity and to judge the validity of AIM's critique. With a feel for what AIM rejects and with some sense of the challenge anticommunism is now facing, the question thus becomes: To what extent does PBS's "Vietnam" embody an anti-interventionist/pro-human rights world view? Further, to what extent does the PBS series call into question or withhold, at crucial points, support for anticommunist ideology?

We may begin by noting that PBS's "Vietnam" does not support the existence of a communist menace or the assumptions of Menace Theory. It is not that such views are not expressed in the series. It is that they are questioned. Even if PBS had conformed to AIM's notion of a "balanced view," questioning the assumptions of Menace Theory would still be objectionable. Thus, for instance, during the discussion following AIM's "Vietnam," Reed Irvine, AIM's founder, questioned whether we want a balanced picture of communism any more than "we want a balanced picture of Auschwitz." "Something terrible has happened to Vietnam, Laos, and Cambodia. These countries have gone under to the most—one of the most horrible totalitarian dictatorships in the world." William Duiker, an East Asian specialist from Pennsylvania State University, agreed that the PBS series had downplayed the "inner nature" of the communist movement, but he rejected a portrayal of the movement in "stark Cold War terms as the epitome or quintessence of evil."

How PBS's "Vietnam" managed this issue does, of course, reveal a particular point of view. Early in the series, for example, President Kennedy declared in a speech given on September 2, 1963, that, if we withdrew from Vietnam, the communists would soon control Thailand, Cambodia, Laos, and Malaya (*Vietnam*, 1983, Vol. 101, p. 1). Similarly, Douglas MacArthur II called the Vietminh a subversive movement deriving its support from China and Russia (*Vietnam*, 1983, Vol. 102, p. 14). Later in the series, however, two Vietnam veterans (the "common man") denounced Menace Theory. Private Bill Ehrhart, for example, recalled that during his senior year, the government was saying that "the Communists were taking over Vietnam, and if we didn't stop them there, we have to stop them in San Diego" (*Vietnam*, 1983, Vol. 105, p. 2). He then pointed to the irony (*Vietnam*, 1983, Vol. 105):

> In grade school we learned about Redcoats, the nasty British that tried to stifle our freedom, and the tyranny of George III, and . . . I began increasingly to have the feeling that I was a Redcoat. I think it was one of the most staggering realizations of my life to suddenly understand that I wasn't a good guy . . . that somehow I had become everything I had learned to believe was evil. (p. 18)

The other soldier, Charlie Sabatier, Specialist 4th class, recalled asking himself, for the first time, "What the hell is Communism? I couldn't define it, and I'm layin' here and going to die for killing a bunch of people 'cause they happen to be Communist!" He talked about American troops over there and their thinking (*Vietnam*, 1983, Vol. 105):

> And we began to realize that if somebody will actually live out here in this stupid jungle, dig tunnels for ten years just to fight us, . . . when we're there to do good, it made you start wondering. . . . The troops who were actually out there doing the killing really began to respect the people they were killing. (p. 18)

With repudiations such as this, PBS's "Vietnam" alludes to but does not support the theory of a communist menace, an evil movement controlled by the Soviet Union. Rather, PBS contrasts nationalism as a theory explaining national behavior with the theory underlying anticommunism, which sees in Marxist, socialist, and communist governments throughout the world evidence of Soviet domination.

The importance of this clash over explanations was obvious to AIM. In a "Reply" to the PBS panel discussion and documents released by WGBH in Boston, Norman Podhoretz (1985) characterized PBS's "Vietnam" as a Revised Standard Version of Vietnam: "American power ought to be used not to oppose Communism but to co-opt it, to make the world safe for 'Titoism' " (p. 23). In opposition to Menace Theory, which treats ideology as a determinant in international affairs, nationalism emphasizes the relative independence of peoples and points to "non-aligned" communist countries such as Yugoslavia and China as evidence. Particularly in the persona of the narrator, the voice of authority in the series, nationalism gains in importance over the Menace Theory in explaining the war in Vietnam: "To the Communists in Hanoi, America's presence in the south was yet another act of foreign aggression. They recalled 1,000 years of struggle against foreign invaders: Chinese, Japanese, French. And now they faced Americans" (*Vietnam,* 1983, Vol. 104, p. 3).

A similar divergence and challenge occur with PBS's "Vietnam" over the nature of the "free world." In PBS's "melodrama of heroes and villains," commented Charlton Heston, narrating AIM's program, "there is no hint that two ways of life, one based on freedom, the other on Communism, were struggling for the future of Indochina." AIM denounced the vilification of the government, society, and the army of "South Vietnam" by relying on the utopian element in anticommunism—the freedom it is supposed to secure.

To suggest that a government supported by the United States is not a government at all but a military dictatorship attacks the moral underpinnings of anticommunism. Yet, again PBS offers some support for the anticommunist position—for example, when John Foster Dulles is shown commending the Diem government: "Vietnam is now a free nation, at least the southern half of it is. And it's not got a puppet government. . . . If it was that kind of a government, we wouldn't be justified in supporting it" (*Vietnam,* 1983, Vol. 103, p. 5). A short time later in the same episode the narrator commented on the Diem regime and its treatment of the Buddhists: "Buddhist groups, protesting that Diem's soldiers had killed eight worshippers while breaking up a gathering in Hue, began a series of demonstrations. . . . As the demonstrations grew, Diem rejected compromise and met the challengers with force" (*Vietnam,* 1983, Vol. 103, p. 14). The narrator goes on to show how such events could elude American observers: "Diem and Nhu struck again at the Buddhists even before [American ambassador Henry Cabot] Lodge reached Saigon. Nhu's special forces raided the temples, sealed them shut, and arrested thousands of Buddhists" (*Vietnam,* 1983, Vol. 103, p. 16).

The governments that followed were not much better. About Thieu's regime, the narrator says that it disqualified opposition candidates: "Now his police supervised the election ritual. To Thieu, like his predecessors, the election was a means to control the population and to placate the Americans. President Thieu declared that the election and his victory were an expression of civil rights in a free and democratic society" (*Vietnam,* 1983, Vol. 108, p. 11). There is no suggestion that this sham was the result of native rule. Americans were clearly implicated. Jane Barton, a civilian aide worker, noted the loss of civil liberties throughout South Vietnam: "There was no doubt whatsoever that the Americans were responsible, I feel, for the entire prison system in the province where I worked. The Vietnamese knew that. You know, they saw all the results of what happened. They were chained to their bed with Smith and Wesson handcuffs. When they were tortured it was either by Americans in the latter sixties, or in the early seventies there would be American advisers there" (*Vietnam,* 1983, Vol. 108, p. 14). American aircraft, comments the narrator, dropped six times more bombs on the South than on the North, creating more than three million refugees and killing hundreds of thousands. PBS's "Vietnam" did not suggest that the United States was trying to defend freedom; nor did it portray South Vietnam as an exemplar of a free world.

PBS also offered little support for the view that the American military in Vietnam was an instrument for the defense of freedom. Failure to do so, coupled with other images, led AIM members to charge that PBS's "Vietnam" had portrayed the American soldier as a drug addict, a racial bigot, a man who murdered his officers and NCOs almost at will. This is not an image commending the military's ability to create and defend free societies. Defending freedom is a noble cause. Showing undisciplined troops killing natives places the nobility of the cause in doubt. Presenting Vietnam veterans, like Bill Ehrhart, who question the nobility of the cause, is potentially even more damaging: "The thing I have the nightmares about is the woman in the rice field that I shot one day because she was running—for no other reason—because she was running away from the Americans who were going to kill her, and I killed her. Fifty-five, 60 year old, unarmed. And at the time I didn't even think twice about it" (*Vietnam,* 1983, Vol. 105, p. 9). In responding to the possibility that PBS's series had painted a dark picture of the American military in Vietnam, William Hammond of the Center for Military History acknowledged that, based on taped interviews with North Vietnamese, Vietcong, and peasants, one would get the impression that American soldiers were out there killing peasants wholesale. Although peasants were killed, he did not "think that it was a wholesale sort of thing at all, and there were a lot of decent men in the military who tried very hard to be fair to those people—and who perhaps got killed themselves because of it."

AIM and the military experts discussed the image of the soldier and the killing of peasants, but they did not object to images of Vietnamese natives who lived in the North or their allies in the South—the hundreds of thousands amassed in "body-counts"—being killed. Nor did they comment on the unprecedented bombing of Vietnam—three times the tonnage that was dropped during World War II—that resulted in incredible damage and the maiming and deaths of hundreds of thousands of innocent men, women, and children. This was also revealed in the series. PBS's "Vietnam" does not suggest that military intervention results in a better life for the natives.

Rather than providing support for Menace Theory or the moral assumptions of anticommunism, then, we find that PBS's "Vietnam" provides contrary testimony and images. Yet, it is not clear that PBS intended its series as a rejoinder to an anticommunist world view. If PBS had designed its documentary as a critique, it neglected an important issue: the danger of escalation, the nuclear threat posed both by the United States (recall Senator Knowland's advice) and by the Soviet Union.

PBS' series did touch on the dangers of escalation, however. For example, George Ball, former Undersecretary of State under President Johnson, recalled that, "In explaining to the President the concern that I felt about a mounting escalation, I said to him, 'You know, once on the tiger's back, we can't pick the time to dismount. You're going to lose control of this situation and this could be very serious' " (*Vietnam,* 1983, Vol. 104, p. 17). Still, the actual escalation and the dangers it entailed (e.g., bombing Soviet ships docked in North Vietnam, the meaning of a confrontation between two super-powers) were never spelled out.

The reality is that nuclear weapons during the last 50 years have spread to Second and Third World countries. Beyond proliferation, arms manufacturers have introduced powerful "suitcase" explosives—

conventional, chemical, biological, and nuclear. New military technology, its availability, ease of delivery, and devastating impact constitute a new factor in the calculation of national interest. Relatively powerless peoples can now inflict serious damage on great powers. People we are inclined to call "terrorists," but who in their own countries are sometimes called "patriots," can create havoc. And, as Caspar Weinberger (1986), Secretary of Defense in the Reagan Adminstration, has observed, "There have been a lot of attacks made in retaliation from time to time. They haven't eliminated terrorism or terrorist attacks on people who made the immediate retaliation" (p. 12). "Terrorist," "religious fanatic," "communist," "patriot"—whatever the label, new technology calls into question the wisdom of armed intervention. Added to our original set of propositions, then, is one on which AIM was not required to take a stand in responding to the PBS series:

6. Intervention in the modern atomic age endangers our National Security:
   (a) It creates hatred against the United States among other peoples.
   (b) It encourages the procurement of conventional, chemical, biological, and nuclear weapons as a countervailing force.
   (c) It encourages "terrorist" attacks inside and outside of the United States.

PBS's "Vietnam" did not explore this threat, which an interventionist foreign policy now poses for our national security.

We do not have to endorse AIM's ideology to conclude that much of what AIM rejects does in fact appear in PBS's "Vietnam." The series did not support an anticommunist ideology. It did question Menace Theory, the reality of a "free world," and the assumption that covert or overt intervention is likely to create a "free world." Consequently, the series is and will continue to be controversial.

Yet, though the series offered scant support for intervention in Vietnam, it did not endorse an anti-interventionist/pro-human rights world view. It hints at but does not offer a clear alternative to anticommunism as a guide to foreign policy. A practical alternative capable of gaining popular political support—if it is to challenge an ideology of anticommunism—must offer a new sense of patriotism and nationalism. It might, for instance, look on the slaughter of people in other countries not only as illegal and immoral, but also as a sin against God and humanity. In any event, it will not look on the killing of natives as a positive good, a victory over the "enemy," or a practical necessity. It will argue that the realities of military intervention violate, at every conceivable turn, the ideals of a "free world," offering examples from recent world history. Finally, it will challenge the wisdom of intervention in an age of advanced weapons technology, when even poor, relatively powerless peoples can cause widespread destruction. It will go far beyond what PBS's series managed to convey about Vietnam as a place where a war once occurred.

The debate over "Vietnam" is pregnant with the future. At the very least, it reminds us that we do not as a nation have a clear vision of the future, that we have no goals we would like to or are working to achieve over the next 10 or 15 years. The one project that is officially promoted at present involves spending upwards of a trillion dollars to lift the arms race into the heavens. The reason for this project lies in checking the Soviet Union's nuclear capabilities. This project originates in and promotes fear. It does not create a new world. It constitutes one more expensive, dangerous, and dubious modern miracle. Nor does it exercise the imagination of a great nation. Dismantling world-death weapons, halting our efforts to dominate other peoples: These would be worthy goals. Pablo Neruda (1976), the Chiliean poet and diplomate, was correct when, before the United States sponsored a military coup in his country, he noted the conflict and wrote that no one in the rest of the Americas wanted to sell electric power to the United States, exploit its oil, or change its customs. The world, he thought, was changing and the time for victories with bombs and swords had passed.

Fundamental questions about our future are being raised through the ruse of righting the historical record. This is both a symptom of our paralysis and a song of hope. Whether we like it or not, failures in power politics and successes in military technology have created a new era. In this light, the clash over "Vietnam" could mark the beginning of vigorous debate over the meaning of national security now and in the future. If this debate is true to our national ideals, if it is informed by the growing threat to life on this planet, it will entertain action engendering hope—not alone to the people of this country, but to the world for all future time.

REFERENCES

AIM calls for an investigation. (1986, January 23). *San Francisco Chronicle*, p. A7.

Dulles, J.F. (1955, December 19). The new phase of the struggle with international communism. *Department of State Bulletin, 33.*

Ginsburg, A. (1965). Wichita vortex sutra. In W. Lowenfels (Ed.), *Where is Vietnam: American poets respond*. New York: Anchor.

Knowland, W.F. (1969). Our policy in the Far East: A debate (1954). In R. Divine (Ed.), *American foreign policy since 1945* (p. 106). Chicago: Quadrangle.

Neruda, P. (1976). North American friend. In M. Algarin (Trans.), *Songs of protest*. New York: Quill.

Podhoretz, N. (1985). Accuracy in media's reply to WGBH's rebuttal. In C. Rolins & J. Bernian (Eds.), Unpublished manuscript. AIM, 1275 K. Street, Washington, D.C. 20005.

Reagan, R. (1984, April 7). Speech. *New York Times*, p. A5.

Vietnam: A television history. (1983). WGBH Transcripts, Vol. 101–113, 125. Western Avenue, Boston, MA 02134.

Weinberger, C. (1986, January 17). Interview. *San Francisco Chronicle*, p. A12.

Part II

Vietnam and the Shaping of Popular Imagination

4

The American Idea of National Identity: Patriotism and Poetic Sensibility Before and After Vietnam

Adi Wimmer

Institut fur Anglistik und Amerikanistik, Universitat fur Bildungswissenschaften, Austria

> Where shall we turn to find a parallel to our progress, our energy, and our increasing power?
>
> (James Fennimore Cooper, 1835)

> And we Americans are the peculiar, chosen people.
>
> (Herman Melville, 1851)

> America is the apotheosis of all that is right.
>
> (Samuel Gompers, 1925)

> We must recognize that the evil is in us, that it springs from some dark, intolerable tension in our history. It is almost as if a primal curse has been fixed on our nation. We are a violent people with a violent history.
>
> (Arthur M. Schlesinger, 1968)

In his study, *The Great War and Modern Memory*, Paul Fussell (1975) points at the undisputed semantics of concepts such as honor, duty, and glory prior to World War I. Everyone knew what these words meant, Fussell argues, because, for example, everyone had read Tennyson's poems, most notably *The Charge of the Light Brigade*, which celebrated a foolish and costly cavalry charge in the Crimean War (1854). But to cling to a moral landscape shaped by incidents (and their popular misapprehensions) that had happened 70 years previously was a dangerous folly. G.B. Shaw (1919) was quite right, therefore, when he compared his complacent pre-war English society with an old-fashioned company that had been afforded the luxury of "long credits and reckless overdrafts," resulting, inevitably, in unexpected disaster. It was not until a decade after the Armistice that the sudden appearance of outspoken literary critics (e.g., Graves, Sassoon, Blunden, Tomlinson, Aldington, to name but a few) thoroughly discredited all traditional patriotic notions and effected an equally thorough restructuring of a whole moral landscape. In 1929, Ernest Hemingway (1935, p. 144) observed that "abstract words such as glory, honor, courage, or hallow were obscene beside the concrete names of villages, the numbers of roads, the names of rivers." It is quite a parallel, then, to find exactly the same sentiment expressed in a love poem that William D. Ehrhart (1984a, p. 1) dedicated to his wife:

> *Duty, honor, country:*
> *rubbish.*
> *I am a citizen only*
> *of your heart. You*
> *are the only land*
> *I'll ever love.*

Wars have an ironic effect on those who wage them because each war is costlier and longer than anticipated, thus leading to disillusionment and the loss of innocence. Something like this must have been on the mind of the soldier who penned the wry graffiti—"America lost her virginity in Vietnam. (And she caught the clap, too.)"—on a Saigon latrine wall (Pratt, 1984, p. 638). To this we might add that the English lost theirs in what they called the "Great War," the Germans lost theirs (and a good deal more) in the war 21 years after the "war to end all wars," and America suffered a comparable loss of moral credibility in the Vietnam debacle.

A quick look at relevant United States public opinion polls yields some useful evidence. In 1964, a massive 76% majority expressed an a priori trust in the federal government. Twelve years and more than 58,000 American war fatalities later, this figure had dwindled to a mere 35%, less than half the 1964 level. Largely responsible for the swing, one suspects, was the military intervention in Indochina. In 1964, only 27% of those polled said the United States should stay out of Vietnam. Over the next eight years this percentage steadily rose to reach 57% in 1972 and 77% in 1983 (Clymer, 1985).

When America's Public Broadcasting Station (PBS) launched its controversial 13-part "Vietnam: A Television History" (1983), many Americans were shocked to learn of some very dubious reasons why this war had been fought, as well as to hear some rather unconventional views voiced by those who had done the fighting (see Chapters 2 & 3, this volume). When asked what the war had taught him, William D. Ehrhart replied: "It has taught me never to trust my government again." Of course, Ehrhart was not the first to confess such a lack of faith. Caputo (1977) had written that he would "never again allow [himself] to fall under the charms and spells of political witch doctors like John F. Kennedy" (p. 315). Kovic (1977a, p. 224) cited not only Kennedy but also John Wayne as the two main influences that seduced him to fight for his country in an attempt "to make the world safe for democracy."[1] Emerson (1985) quotes what she thinks is a typical reaction to having lived through the horrors of Vietnam:

> There is no way I'll buy the American dream again. I've seen what we've done to people. I see what we do to people in prisons, I've seen it in Vietnam, I've seen it in the civil-rights movement. I mean you're never going to sell me that shit again. . . . That's never going to be purged; it has a carry-over that is never going to be taken away from [me]. (p. 374)

Statements such as these, coming as they do from ex-combat soldiers turned writers, possess a great deal of moral authority. They recall one of the most famous incidents of antiwar protest—the throwing away of war medals by members of Vietnam Veterans Against the War in April of 1971. Dozens of decorated veterans hurled their decorations against the marble building where Congress had approved the war, thus symbolically tarnishing its white surface. This must have been a very confusing time for Americans, for they had been led to believe in nothing less than a singularly powerful moral position in the world. America was not only "the beautiful," it was "God's own country." To this day, the American dollar is the only paper money (that I know of) that proclaims "In God We Trust." Such references to the divinity reflect the belief (originally held by the Puritan settlers) that the civilization of America's wilderness was of particular interest to God, was intended by Him to lead to the creation of a second Jerusalem (Bercovitch, 1975). There has been considerable interest recently in establishing links among American mythology, the Vietnam War, and the imaginative literature coming out of that war (e.g., Lewis, 1985; Hellmann, 1986). This chapter traces some historical roots of that faith through its manifestations in literary and cultural documents.

A RHETORICAL TRADITION?

De Tocqueville was perhaps the first critic of American culture to note that the democratic nature of the early Republic, with its attendant spirit

[1] It is a mark of the Kennedy mystique that Kovic wrongly attributes President Wilson's words to John F. Kennedy.

of hopeful utopianism, encouraged Americans to contemplate their collective political self (see Chapter 9, this volume). This observation helps us to understand why Americans, despite the massive influx of fresh immigrants throughout the 19th and 20th centuries, have held fast to the idea of a common American identity, to the notion of a mythical "melting pot." One important aspect of this identity is moral superiority.

Viewed historically, the notion of a national moral superiority is not the sole province of Americans. Moral superiority gained credence in various European countries also, but only towards the end of the 19th century, when it was used to justify the status of these nations as colonial powers. However, we also find it already at an earlier stage, when it was usurped by the rising middle class in its struggle for emancipation from the aristocracy. To the bourgeoisie in England, France, and Germany, the corrupt aristocrat was what Europe represented to America. The parallel nature of such resentment was not lost on Europeans. For them, the "Declaration of Independence" and the "Bill of Rights" were inspiring documents in the struggle for democracy, particularly so after the revolutionary year of 1848. However, their political (and moral) struggle was, socially speaking, an internal one (see Chapter 9, this volume); whereas in America, the idea of national moral superiority transcended national boundaries, thus resulting in an "Idea of Mission" (Burns, 1957) or the notion of America as a "Redeemer Nation" (Tuveson, 1968). A typical exposition of such views is to be found in the 1896 address to the United States Senate by statesman and historian Albert T. Beveridge (Tuveson, 1968):

> God has. . . . made us master organizers of the world to establish system where chaos reigned. He has given us the spirit of progress to overwhelm the forces of reaction throughout the earth. He has made us adept in government so that we may administer government among savage and senile peoples. Were it not for such a force as this the world would relapse in barbarism and night. And of all our race He has marked the American people as His chosen nation to finally lead in the redemption of the world. (p. vii)

In a similarly hopeful vein, the apostle of the Protestant Home Missionary Movement, Josiah Strong, announced the coming of a new Millennium, a near-paradisical age to be ushered in by America (Tuveson, 1968):

> Anglo-Saxon civilization is more favorable than any other to the spread of those principles whose universal triumph is necessary to that perfection

of the race to which it is destined; the entire realization of which will be the kingdom of heaven fully come on earth. (p. 138)

That such ideas were not only to be found with the zealous few, but were held by a great many ordinary people, is plausible if we refer to de Tocqueville's findings once more. Discussing the areas of general interest for Americans, he asserts that "it is about themselves that they are really excited" (1966, p. 452). Leaving aside for the moment the legitimate objection that self-contemplation need not automatically result in self-praise, we can argue nevertheless that the effect of the successful War of Independence was to keep a long-lasting check on American self-criticism. Moreover, the American Puritans had traditionally thought of themselves as "Redeemers" fighting against the Satanic forces of "Red Indian" tribes (Slotkin, 1973). Nor were European immigrants likely to inject national self-criticism into American culture, for they had given up something bad in the hope of something much better and therefore tended to identify strongly with the national purpose of their new fatherland.

Throughout the 19th century the national spirit was predominantly optimistic and forward-looking, something that not even the Civil War would alter. On the contrary, the outcome of that war reaffirmed liberal American opinion that their new and still budding nation was to achieve great things in the spreading of freedom, democracy, and brotherliness throughout the world. "Americans," as Burns (1957) noted with reference to a tradition going back to the early Republic, "have conceived of their nation as ordained in some extraordinary way to accomplish great things in the world" (p. vii). In de Tocqueville's (1966) words, Americans "gladly start dreaming about the future, and in that direction their imagination knows no bounds" (p. 453).

Emerson, Thoreau, and Whitman, though occasionally critical of their society, shared these dreams. Here is Whitman celebrating the American frontier spirit:[2]

---

[2] From Whitman's long poem *Pioneers! O Pioneers!* stanzas 2 and 4. I do not want to imply that Whitman was an uncritical devotee of American culture. Occasionally, he could be profoundly critical of American life, as in his *Democratic Vistas*. And, of course, there were the nay-sayers among American writers from the beginning. By and large, however, 19th-century American writers persisted in seeing more good than bad in their society, which they were confident would emerge as the most powerful ameliorating force in the world. This sets 19th-century American writing apart from 19th-century European writing, as well as from American imaginative literature of the 20th century. Melville's credo—"God had predestined, mankind expects, great things from our race," "We bear the ark of liberties of the world," and "this country is the great charity of God to the human race" (*White Jacket*, ch. 36)—was shared by a majority of his contemporaries.

For we cannot tarry here,
We must march my darlings, we must bear the brunt of danger,
We, the youthful sinewy races, all the rest on us depend,
Pioneers! O Pioneers!

Have the elder races halted?
Do they droop and end their lesson, wearied over there beyond the seas?
We take up the task eternal, and the burden and the lesson,
Pioneers! O Pioneers!

Whitman's pledge to "take up the burden and the lesson" is a curious premonition of Kennedy's inaugural speech in which he, too, vowed to "pay any price, bear any burden, meet any hardship . . . to assure the survival and the success of liberty."[3] While striving for liberty is surely no evil intention, the ensuing campaign in Vietnam, taking the side of liberty against anything that smacked of socialism, led to great evil. It would be a mistake, though, to think of Kennedy's rousing words merely in terms of anticommunist propaganda. His speech restated a long-standing claim for moral and cultural superiority as integral parts of the American identity; it is reminiscent of President Wilson's assertion that "America [was] intended to be a spirit amongst the nations of the world," and of the exaggerated claim, also made by Wilson in 1917, that "nothing less than the liberation and salvation of the world" depended on the decision to go to war against the Axis (Tuveson, 1968, p. 175).

The same fervor is to be found in editorials written in 1939 by Henry Luce, editor of *Life*, and in various essays written by Walter Lippmann, who suggested that America would be to the 20th century what Rome had been to the ancient world and what Britain had been to the 19th century. Most likely, Lippman was unaware of the *double entendre* of his claim, which was given an ironic twist by a number of poetic responses to a war in which American troops are likened to those of Imperial Rome. Thus, Barry (1976, p. 117) imagined the rows of American bomber planes as "Roman legions traveling in phalanx,/ with a clatter of midnight chariots." Bly (1973), charging that America is abusing its power in Vietnam to suppress defenseless civilians, created an image in which "excellent Roman knives slip along the ribs" (p. 20). Ehrhart (1984b) portrayed the Vietnam War as a fight between "barbarian tribesman" and "Roman officers" (p. 39). On the other side, Henry Luce's essay, entitled "The American Century," proposed a future with

[3] These are the words by which many Vietnam veterans remember President Kennedy. W.D. Ehrhart refers to them in his memoir *Vietnam—Perkasie,* as does Philip Caputo in his *A Rumour of War,* as do a number of veterans in oral histories (Santoli, 1982).

"America as the dynamic center of ever-widening spheres of enterprise, America as the training center of skilled servants of mankind, America as the Good Samaritan," and "America as the powerhouse of the ideal of Freedom and Justice." Elements such as these, he concluded, would be required to fashion a vision of the 20th century—"the first great American Century" (Karnow, 1983, p. 14).

Understandably, these views gained even more popularity after 1945, when America had contributed in large measure towards the rescue of Europe from Nazi despotism. At the 1952 Democratic Party convention, Harry S. Truman saw America as having finally "stepped into the leadership that the Almighty God had intended it to assume" (Burns, 1957, p. 14). Kennedy, as I have noted, was ready to shoulder any burden connected with leadership in the "Free World," and Vice President Johnson similarly spoke of America's God-given role to "bring peace and hope to all peoples of the world."

AMERICA'S REDEMPTIVE ROLE IN THE 20TH CENTURY

This was the teleological scenario in which the "Vietnam generation" grew up. That God was always on the side of America was a self-evident truth. In Lewis's (1985) words, the post-World War II generation "shared a common belief system" that was part of a "world-taken-for-granted" (p. 68). Rarely, if ever, were the claims of the "common belief system" challenged by any of the socializing agencies of family, school, or church. Teenage Americans in the early 1960s could not escape the ever-present war movies, which helped to reinforce the effect of the equally ubiquitous war stories told by fathers or similarly acceptable older family members. All spoke of bravery, of the necessary fight against evil, of America's intrinsic savior role.

When Ehrhart's parents raised objections to their son's wish to enlist in the Marine Corps in order to fight in Vietnam, he silenced them with the simple argument that such a refusal would run counter to all the underlying assumptions of his upbringing as well as the schooling he had received so far; and "that ended the discussion" (Ehrhart, 1983, p. 10). Tim O'Brien (1978) recalls that it was primarily his father (a veteran of World War II) who made it impossible for him to resist the draft. His small Minnesota town was not like

> Minneapolis or New York, where the son of a father can sometimes escape scrutiny. . . . The town, my family, my teachers, a whole history of the prairie. Like magnets, these things were physical forces weighting the

problem, so that, in the end, it was less reason and more gravity that was the final influence. (p. 27)

Every generation, or so a popular belief insisted, had to fight its own war. War was inevitable, and visible proof was to be found in the all-American family. Fathers had fought in World War II, older brothers in Korea, grandfathers in World War I. In Webb's (1978) novel, *Fields of Fire*, the heroic protagonist Hodges (a literary self-portrait, the author told me in a private interview) has no choice but to volunteer for the fighting in Vietnam. He is obligated to a whole lineage of battling forefathers—from his "great-great-great-grandaddy," who fought in the war of 1812, to "Grandpa, who breathed the gas for Pershing," and finally to his own father, who "died in glory . . . in a town in France he could not pronounce, much less spell." And all of them, his grandma keeps telling him, had been "fighting mean." Young Hodges comes to acquire the "ingrained" belief that heroism is part of his nature, a challenge to carry on a hallowed tradition: "It was a continuum, a litany . . . an inherited right to violence." Continuing in this strangely fascist mode, Hodges accepts his cultural self as an integral part of a tradition in which heroes are forever "glorying in the fight like unmuzzled sentry dogs, bred to it, for the benefit of the ravishers who owned and determined the reasons," and he determines that "it is the fight that matters, not the cause" (pp. 31–33).

In truth, a whole generation was "bred" for war in this way; the film documentary *The Atomic Cafe* has demonstrated it. The school drills in anticipation of nuclear war, the daily morning assemblies with the singing of the National Anthem, right hand clasped over the heart, the historical panorama of American wars, all ending in victory: These provided the lessons to accept war as an important aspect of the American heritage. (Only a context such as this explains the naked fear of both Johnson and Nixon to go down in history as "the first American president to lose a war.")

It was equally clear against whom the next war would be fought. The Vietnam generation received its political initiation during the McCarthy hysteria, when communism (which was generally perceived as a monolithic power) came to succeed Nazism (a comparable monolith) as the apotheosis of Satanic evil (see Chapter 3, this volume). One did not have to *reason* for the view of communism as an intrinsically wicked ideology, just as one needed no proof that the earth was round. There were no socializing factors in the lives of that generation to encourage a challenge to the notion that, in terms of global politics, America was the "good guy," and communism was the "bad guy." If communism was evil, it followed that to kill communists was a necessary, maybe even desirable goal. As one soldier said, "You see the baddies and the goodies on TV and at the movies. I wanted to get the bad guy . . . I could have given a fuck for the country then. I wanted to kill the bad guy" (Baker, 1983, p. 23). Caputo (1977) similarly recalls his moral position while in combat: "There was nothing we could not do because we were Americans, and for the same reason, whatever we did was right" (p. 66).

An additional, possibly even more powerful agency of cultural initiation that helped to generate an American autoperception as the intrinsically generous power was the World War II movie, particularly in conjunction with one actor, who was elevated to a cultural hero status already in his lifetime: John Wayne. The name crops up in almost each war narrative of such important anthologies as *Nam*, *Everything We Had*, *Conversations With Americans*, and *Bloods*, which point to Wayne as the deadly seducer of boys hungering for heroism; he was an ideal who was impossible (and lethal) to emulate in the jungle warfare conditions of Vietnam. It is quite possible that this actor is "responsible for more combat casualties in Vietnam than any other American, civilian or military" (Lewis, 1985, p. 41). "With all my terror of going into the Army," remembers one veteran, "there was something seductive about it, too. I was seduced by World War II and John Wayne movies" (Baker, 1983, p. 10).

Conceivably, John Wayne was every Vietnam soldier's cultural hero, even for some blacks. As O'Brien (1978) recalls, he and his friends in their early teens played war games that were fashioned on screen images: "Then we were our fathers, taking on the Japs and the Krauts along the shore of Lake Okabene" (pp. 20–21). Kovic (1977b), too, remembers the trips to the movies that were a regular feature of Saturday afternoons, and specifically mentions *To Hell and Back* starring Audie Murphie and, inevitably, *The Sands of Iwo Jima*, perhaps John Wayne's best war movie. Afterwards, whenever he would hear the marines' hymn from the latter film, Kovic "would think of John Wayne and the brave men who raised the flag on Iwo Jima that day" (p. 55). Webb (1978) also thought of John Wayne as "at least a prophet, if he was not God incarnate" (p. 34). An endless series of structurally identical movies "fed a generation a consistent diet of war images from which Americans might learn to interpret the nature of armed conflicts" (Lewis, 1985, p. 22; see also Chapters 5, 6, & 7, this volume).

It is not surprising, therefore, that so many veterans recall initially behaving in Vietnam as if they had been in a film called *The Vietnam War and How I Won It*. One such veteran describes his arrival aboard the carrier USS Boxer in the following words: "Everyone saw the movies going on in their heads," and "it was the movies, except it was real."

When for the first time subjected to the experience of enemy artillery, another veteran recalls with astonishment that "it was just like the movies, except it was real" (Santoli, 1982, pp. 22, 35). Behaving like John Wayne was a foolishness common amongst the "fucking new guys," as the "in-country" terminology was at the time; but it was also common amongst troop commanders, who would order the most insane John Wayne type operations at the mere sight of a TV camera crew.[4] This syndrome Michael Herr (1978) calls the "John Wayne wet-dream"— "We'd all seen too many movies, stayed too long in Television City, years of media glut had made certain connections difficult" (pp. 20, 209). The connection is certainly present in "Cobra Pilot" by Don Receveur (1972), one of the earliest Vietnam war poems, which, in characterizing the background of a fighting American, closes with the lines: "He hunts/ the Indian-gooks/ in the Wild West/ of his mind." Even more explicit is Harrison Kohler's (1972) poem, "The Cheerleaders," which pillories the warmongering efforts of actors or entertainers and specifically singles out John Wayne, Georgie Jessel, Martha Raye, and Bob Hope. Its last stanza brings to mind the war poetry of Siegfried Sasson, condemning as it does the facile views of civilians, who, from their position of safety, portray war as good fun, urging the young to fight:

War
Is
A paunchy worn out movie hero
A tired old man
A menopaused hag
A grotesque comedian
Parading
Patriotic
Obscenities.

The record industry, never totally detached from the film industry, also did its share in stirring up patriotic fervor. As Terry Anderson (1986) has shown, antiwar songs (despite popular misperceptions) never dominated the music industry, not even during the hey-day of popular protest. In all, an equal number of pro-war and antiwar songs (about one hundred each) were popular, and the best selling record of the field was not *Eve of Destruction* or *Fixin' to Die Rag*, but Barry Sadler's *The Ballad of the Green Berets*, which sold a staggering seven million copies in the middle 1960s. The success of the record resulted in a flood of volunteers for the Special Forces and in an enduring "Myth of the Green Berets" as a subdivision of the great American myth. This is what Alasdair Spark

[4] As recalled by war journalist Michael Herr (1978, p. 14).

(1984) has claimed; in his view the Green Berets, "alone of all the many US Army and Marine units . . . secured and have sustained a place in the popular imagination." As I have attempted to show elsewhere (Wimmer, 1989), Sylvester Stallone's success as "Rambo" (who is a particularly gifted member of the Special Forces) seems to support this argument (see also Chapters 5, 6, & 7, this volume).

As a result of the triadic socializing agencies (the father, the cultural father or fatherland, and the John Wayne movie), American soldiers in Vietnam shared certain assumptions concerning themselves and their culture. In Caputo's (1977) words, they were "American to a man, idealistic, insolent, generous, direct, violent, and provincial in the sense that they believed the ground they stood on was now forever a part of the United States simply because they stood on it" (p. 26). Strewn amongst the negative epithets of this list are two characteristics that we should not overlook: generosity and idealism—arrogant generosity, yes, and idealism tinged by hubris, but still generosity and idealism. Vietnam was something of a quest and was successfully marketed as such by the opinion makers, if we take into account that opinion polls indicated support for the American war effort until after the TET offensive of 1968.

Kolko (1971) observes that Americans saw themselves as representatives of a chivalresque tradition in Vietnam, that their blind faith in this role was acting as a shield against embarrassing realities. Arthur Miller, writing at the same time, observes that there was not so much evil intent at work as ordinary cultural self-centeredness (see Chapter 9, this volume). These are typical 1960s aspects of self-criticisms, embodying perhaps excessively uncharitable views. For we must not overlook that the International Volunteers Service (IVS) had sent its first contingent of helpers to Vietnam in 1957, a full eight years before the arrival of combat troops. The same cultural optimism that led to an ugly and racist war also spawned quite genuine humanitarian efforts, including those of the immensely idealistic IVS and a number of private organizations sponsored by charities or religious groups (e.g., the Quakers). Not for all Americans was Vietnam "a heroic and almost painless conquest of an inferior race," as FitzGerald (1973, p. 492) has charged. Emerson's observation that he would run for his life if he knew for certain that a man was coming to his house with a conscious design of doing him good is perhaps of relevance in the Vietnam context. After the withdrawal of American troops, Turner (1974) drew the lesson not to scuttle idealism, but to match it with knowledge:

> We seem like some benign blind Polyphemus who gropes in utter darkness toward expression of good will. And let no one mistake this: American good will is a reality, whatever the rest of the world may call it, racism,

> genocide, callous economic opportunism. These are but the ghastly blunders of a giant doomed to commit them out of ignorance and fear. (p. 4)

Even though a European reader might worry to hear Turner argue for the existence of American idealism, "whatever the rest of the world may call it," his reference to collective ignorance is on target. Few Americans were able to find Vietnam on a map at the beginning of the war, and, if recent newspaper reports are correct, the original ignorance about Vietnam has been compounded by a new ignorance about even the most basic facts of the Vietnam War itself.[5] "We are the ones you sent to fight a war/ you did not know a thing about" is the accusation and didactic starting point in one of Ehrhart's (1984b, pp. 17–18) earliest poems, "A Relative Thing." In a later poem, "The Teacher" (1984b), this line is continued as he vows to spare his students at Sandy Springs School the "rocks of ignorance/ and malice honorable men/ call truth," and to make them question a value system that causes information to be suppressed if it clashes with these values. After all, he darkly promises, he knows "things/ worth knowing" (p. 48).

THE POETIC RESPONSE TO THE CRISIS OF THE VIETNAM WAR

Writers and poets have always known "things worth knowing," but, usually, few people were willing to lend them their ears. For the brief period of the Vietnam protest years, that was different. In those years, when a majority of Americans opposed their elected leaders, the poet was something of an "unacknowledged legislator of the world," as Percy Bysshe Shelley had so confidently asserted in 1812. When Woolf and Bagguley launched their project, *Authors Take Sides on Vietnam* in 1967, which was modeled on W.H. Auden's writers' opinion poll on the Spanish Civil War, they found, even at this early stage, only a small minority of American writers who supported the American presence in Vietnam.[6]

The fiercest opposition came from the poets. Allen Ginsberg's Viet-

---

[5] According to several news reports, 30% of American high school students do not know on which side the U.S. fought. For comparable evidence, see Lelyveld (1985).

[6] Of 64 American authors, 54 condemned the American presence in Vietnam, three chose to sit on the fence, and seven were in favor of it (among them: John Updike, Paddy Cheyefsky, and Marianne Moore). Objections to the war, however, were raised also on purely tactical grounds: the war was considered "too costly," "unwinnable," or simply "the wrong sort of war" (Woolf & Bagguley, 1967).

nam rally and mass sit-in in Berkeley (October, 1963) in protest against the visit of the notorious Madame Nhu was the first antiwar demonstration on the West Coast. Poets found it easier to turn against the war, for their poetic rebellion against American reality "had been growing steadily over the previous two decades, spurred by such polar influences as Charles Olson's *Projective Verse* essay and Ginsberg's *Howl* (Mersmann, 1974, p. 23). Such rebelliousness had caused the poets of the Beat Generation to "drop out" 10 years earlier. Typical for their alienation from mainstream America was Paul O'Neal's (1959) advice: "The only way a man can call his soul his own is by becoming an outcast." A decade later this was considered to be a sterile attitude. In 1967, at the "Angry Arts Week" in New York City, Harold Rosenberg expressed the anguish of many writers when he declared: "You cannot go about your business these days, especially if you're an artist." And Denise Levertov (1971) expressed a sense of national paralysis in the face of war in her poem *Tenebrae,* which opens with the unforgettable lines: "Heavy, heavy, heavy, hand and heart/ we are at war, bitterly, bitterly at war."

Their complaint was echoed by more and more poets as the war deepened. Neutrality, objectivity, and a disciplined tone increasingly lost their currency. The distance between the poem and the world shrunk, as did the distance between poet and society. The idea of the lyrical persona, that pet child of the New Criticism, was condemned as a sinister plot to deprive poetry of its political validity. Peter Whigham (1967, p. 10), one of the San Francisco poets, expressed the new content-oriented mode of writing poetry in suitably unpoetic fashion:

> *We do not seek safety in Art.*
> *We recognize Art as a serious business.*
> *Art has "sociological concerns." [. . .]*
> *What we are a witness to, and do not prevent, we are responsible for.*
> *Every act we make, of dissent or otherwise, is a part of what is happening. [. . .]*
> *Being a part of it, I bear responsibility for its character.*

Protest poetry of the Vietnam era took many forms and addressed itself to a multitude of issues. But one of its most potent themes was the scrutiny of cultural mythology. If this mythology made it feasible for Americans to view themselves as a chosen people incapable of ever doing wrong, then it had to be critiqued. Thus, Robert Bly's long poem, *The Teeth Mother Naked At Last* (1980, p. 21), likens Americans not to the children of Zion, but to their oppressors, the Pharaohs. The opening passage sets itself the task of examining all the national myths with which the nation grew up: "Now the time comes to look into the past-tunnels/ the hours given and taken in school." And what he finds—the myth of an early Republic that threw off the shackles of a land-owning class; of George Washington, who could not tell a lie, thus setting an example for all future American politicians; the purity of the pioneer settlers in their Conestoga wagons—he attacks. The poem conjures up an oppressive view of a nation engulfed by untruthfulness:

> *The ministers lie, the professors lie, the television lies, the priests lie . . .*
> *These lies mean that the country wants to die.*
> *Lie after lie starts out into the prairie grass,*
> *like enormous caravans of Conestoga wagons.*

More frightening still is Bly's vision of books shying away from a tainted America:

> *I know that books are tired of us*
> *I* know *they are chaining the Bible to chairs.*
> *Books do not want to remain in the same room with us anymore*
> *New Testaments are escaping . . . dressed as women . . . they go off after dark.*

Such anguish is shared by former U.S. marine Samuel Hazo (1987, p. 17) in his poem *To a Commencement of Scoundrels*. Beginning with the flat assertion, "My boys, we lied to you," the poem goes on to offer a writer's nightmare in which "books break down their bookends,/ Paintings burst their frames." It is a near- apocalyptic vision that calls for the courage of spiritual honesty:

> *I wish you what I wish*
> *myself: hard questions*
> *and the nights to answer them,*
> *the grace of disappointment*
> *and the right to seem the fool*
> *for justice . . .*

When Robert Duncan (1968, p. 81) opens his protest contribution *Up Rising: Passages 25* with three lines conjuring up a vision that has President Johnson going up "to join the great simulacra of men,/ Hitler and Stalin, to work out his fame/ with planes roaring out from Guam over Asia," he is not merely slinging dirt in an hysterical and politically myopic fashion. It goes without saying that Johnson never was in the same league as Hitler or Stalin, but that is beside the point. The point is that the hyperbole of the comparison seems to be the only way of adequately expressing such bitter disappointment and shame with one's nation. Years before liberal lawyers and other concerned citizens began to call for a revival of the Nuremberg Court (in order to try American atrocities of the Vietnam War), the poems and songs of the protest movement mentioned Auschwitz and Majdanek and saw America as threatened by a spiritual holocaust.[7] It is a shame that couples Vietnam with other contemporary issues: the Civil Rights Movement, the treatment of Native Americans, the devastation of nature. Vietnam is the fall from grace, the loss of a paradise, the loss of a glorious past, in whose name America pretends to wage this war, too. As Starck (1967, p. 130) so aptly put it:

> *Imagine!*
> *The American Revolution!*
> *Bunker Hill, the long winter of '77, Washington*
> *crossing the Delaware . . .*
> *It's all over.*
> *Now we are crossing the Red Sea—we,*
> *the Egyptians.*

Such drastic revision of the *Myth Americana* also brought about imaginative new perspectives on the war itself. Surely what was happening in Vietnam was only a replay of older American sins? The devastation of the Vietnamese countryside, the poisoning of crops and water—all in an attempt to deny the enemy sustenance and protection—was only an "improved" version of the "scorched earth policy," which was so effective in the war against the "Red Indians."[8] Was there something in the American past that forced the nation to repeat its insane brutalities over and over again? Were there some "unacknowledged, unrepented crimes" (Duncan, 1968)? Poets see some condemning evidence. In Marge Piercy's (1968) words, coupling nostalgia with horror, "this nation is founded on blood like a city on swamps/ yet its dream has been beautiful and sometimes just/ that now grows brutal and heavy as a burned out star." Her image of a cosmic implosion as a consequence of the violation of a national idealism finds a parallel in Hayden Carruth's (1969, p. 32) poem *The Event Itself*. Here, the willful scuttling of an ideal ("We, having betrayed our fathers and all our silent grandfathers") leads to an apocalypse of storms, earthquakes, erupting volcanoes, and rampant diseases.

Protest poetry anthologies published during this time often reissued

[7] Some examples are provided by Tom Paxton, Olga Cabral, and Millea Kennin in protest poetry anthologies (see Dane & Silber, 1969; Lowenfels, 1967, 1969).

[8] Significantly, VC-controlled territory was nicknamed "Indian country," while helicopters were called "the cavalry." The saying "only a dead gook is a good gook" likewise is reminiscent of the Indian wars.

poems by older writers who had prophesied what had come to a terrible fruition. Kenneth Rexroth, Thomas Merton, and Lawrence Ferlinghetti often found themselves side-by-side with Walt Whitman, Ezra Pound, or Robert Lowell. They were felt to be the last remaining representatives of an American ideal that had been betrayed by those in power. In its place, Robert Duncan (1968, pp. 82–83) sees a "black bile of old evils arisen anew," the center of which he mercilessly locates in the White House:

> *. . . and the very glint of Satan's eyes from the pit of the hell*
> *of America's unacknowledged, unrepented crimes that I saw in*
> *Goldwater's eyes*
> *now shines from the eyes of the President*
> *in the swollen head of the nation.*

The conservative rollback of the 1980s has made poems such as these very unpopular. Now the war is often interpreted along lines provided by films like *Rambo II* or *Missing in Action* (see Chapters 5, 6, & 7, this volume). Nor do more realistic films, such as *Platoon* or *Full Metal Jacket*, which at least do not subscribe to the ridiculous stereotyping of the *Ramboesque* genre, engage in what Mitscherlich and Mitscherlich (1975) have called "the labor of mourning." This is owed partly to the peculiarities of all realistic modes, which favor the presentation of direct action rather than the analysis of national policies or a cultural past. However, it is surely also a reaction to the catastrophic financial failure (because of an effective film distributors' boycott) of Peter Davies' film documentary, *Winning Hearts and Minds* (1974), which transcended ground-level issues, attempted a cultural critique of America's role in Vietnam, and did not get an audience. Thus, too, Vietnam war novels have not yet provided an adequate critique: Most are imbued with a pent-up sense of having to tell terrible stories, are too wrapped up in naturalistic detail in order to engage in a discourse of the broader historical and cultural perspectives. So, it was left to the soldier-poets to continue this debate, as I will attempt to show.

Psychoanalysts Alexander and Margarete Mitscherlich (1975) have argued that collective psychoses can be traced to the same causes as those of the individual. In particular, they note that an individual guilty of a crime will truly reform only if that individual not only acknowledges guilt, but also admits to shame and empathy with the victims of his actions. This is a painful and difficult process—hence, the "labor" of mourning. On a collective level, they argue, large segments of German society plus a succession of post-World War II German governments never tackled the "labor of mourning" regarding the victims of the holocaust. Without some publicly identifiable form of mourning there can be no complete recovery from the disease of Nazism. Evidence for the correctness of their theory was provided by the outcome of the 1986 presidential elections in Austria. After the World Jewish Congress documented how Dr. Kurt Waldheim had lied about his past during the Nazi regime, the conservative party backing his campaign unleashed a series of obliquely antisemitic election posters. Waldheim won by a comfortable 7% margin.

Though a critique of post-war Germany, the "labor of mourning" thesis advanced by Mitscherlich and Mitscherlich lends itself to a similar critique of American society after Vietnam. No Senator or Congressman, and certainly no President or general, has ever publicly expressed sorrow and sympathy with the victims of America's awesome power in Vietnam. Thus, for example, President Carter declared in 1977 that America owed Vietnam no debt because "the destruction was mutual." Five years later, President Reagan took the process one step further by declaring that American involvement in Vietnam had been "in truth a noble cause" that not only justified the slaughter of more than 58,000 Americans, but also carried a condemnation of all Vietnamese victims as supporters of an "ignoble" cause. A collective American "inability to mourn" manifested itself in an unwillingness to face the after-effect of Vietnam. Veterans were not listened to, reports on them and anything to do with the war were ignored (see Chapter 1, this volume). For years Vietnam was simply gone, taken "off the air," unavailable either in the media or in that "other clearing-house of information, the university" (Berg, 1986). Nor was it any longer present even in mainline American poetry and fiction.

While the war was being fought with Americans actively participating, there was hardly a poet who did not contribute to the flood of war protest poetry in one way or another. With the signing of the Paris agreement in January of 1973, however, Vietnam quickly became a non-topic. Why this was so continues to baffle critics. The ambiguous status of the returnee in the war-weary society to which he or she returned—oscillating between "victim and executioner" (Lifton, 1973)—was one hindering factor; but the role of a collective unconscious trying to salvage a badly dented notion of *America the Redeemer Nation* has not been examined so far. The war, having never been started by an official declaration, was declared "finished" by President Ford on April 23, 1975. What made the public so eager to accept such a recommendation from a leader whose caretaker role condemned him to public indifference? Haines' (1986) answer is that "administrative acknowledgment of America's first military defeat took form as an attempted reconciliation [of a divided nation], an appeal to prewar memories, a plea for national consensus based on the reassurance of strength and purpose," resulting in America's readiness "to follow the lead of administrative power in a strategic forgetting of the war" (p. 2).

In 1976, 50 distinguished American poets were invited by poet Alberta T. Turner to contribute a recently composed poem to an anthology. Each poem was to be selected, as Turner (1977) explained in her introduction, with the purpose of demonstrating "the poet's *strongest contemporary concern*" (emphasis added); in turn, each poet was to comment on his or her poem's context. Surprisingly, not one of the poems mentioned Vietnam or its aftermath as an important thematic issue. David Ray, who had combined with Robert Bly to edit a volume entitled *A Poetry Reading Against the War,* was the only contributor to make an oblique three-line reference to Vietnam in a poem of more than 250 lines. The war had been given a quiet burial.

Yet, the war somehow refused to be dead and buried. Out of the 3.4 million American men and women who had served in Vietnam, several hundred attempted to "tell how it really was" in poetic form: the noise, heat, and smells of Vietnam; the frustration, pain, and horror of battle; daily incidents; vignettes of military life. The first wave of combat poetry found an outlet in the anthology *Winning Hearts and Minds,* which was reviewed rather unfavorably by critics such as Philip Beidler (1982) and Jeffrey Walsh (1982) for its "dogged concreteness," its "inappropriate [ness] to communicate the character of the Vietnam war," or its alleged "imperviousness to an aesthetic." This is standard *New Criticism* fare—ignoring the message of an implicit moral vision. However, this unpretentious anthology sold 42,000 copies, even though it was cold-shouldered by the commercial publishing industry.[9]

While some of the former criticism may be partly accurate for early war poetry, it would be grossly unfair to apply these tenets to those poets who continue to expand their poetic range and who have emerged "with a broader mediating perspective, negotiating between the extremes of concreteness and artifice, quotidian and universal" (Smith, 1986). Those poets who continue to articulate the message have courageously taken up the unpopular task of examining the *Myth Americana* where mainstream American poetry dropped it in the early 1970s. Since Vietnam as a thematic concern was abandoned together with many other forms of *literature engagé* (ushering in the contemporary preponderance of the introspective poetic mode), Vietnam veteran poets have emerged as the true heirs of prophetic and political poetry.

This is not to say that protest is the only redeeming feature in veter-

---

[9] For a detailed history of *Winning Hearts and Minds* and its publishing house, see Slocock (1982).

ans' poetry. But what seems to be its common ground is the maturity of having painfully grown out of a mythic American bond. *Demilitarized Zones* (Barry, 1976), for instance, is a valuable collection documenting just that maturity, despite its qualitative unevenness. At the 1985 Asia Society conference on the literature of the Vietnam War, Ehrhart praised the unique ability of Vietnam War poetry to "present a complete thought in a snapshot whereas historians, oral historians and novelists have to trace their thoughts through full-length movies" (see Lomperis, 1986, p. 49). Ehrhart might have added that this more mature poetry is especially laudable as moral discourse (and I point here particularly to Ehrhart's own poetry) in light of the fact that contemporary (i.e., postmodernist) discourse has largely withdrawn from the ethics debate.

In combining the personal epistemology of "direct experience" with the larger issue of debating the *conditio humana,* Vietnam War poetry is a useful antidote to political mystification and xenophobia. When Jan Barry (1976) calls Vietnam his "foster, second home," acknowledging a pedagogical role of an enemy country in a personal development, where he is "not just a man/ but a human being," he implies that his first home has in some way failed him (p. 173). We find a strong "Us versus Them" opposition throughout the anthology, an alienation between the veteran and his or her environment bordering on downright hostility (in a different context, see Chapter 8, this volume). Bereft of a common mythical identity and, at the same time, disinherited by their protesting peers, veteran poets find themselves in a cultural "no-man's land." Like their Beat Generation counterparts and the "Lost Generation" writers of the 1920s, the only role he or she can assume is that of an outcast: "[I] can never live with the dwarfs/ of my hometown in quiet middle age" (Smyth, 1976, p. 172) is a typical sentiment. Another is the fear that Vietnam and the Vietnam veteran will be erased from America's collective memory: "What does not perish here by forgetting/ survives only in the occasional bad dream" writes Mark Osaki in his poem "Amnesiac" (in Ehrhart, 1985); "we wake up each morning to a new history./ We don't know if we remember" (p. 215).

Charles Purcell's poem "Coming Home" (in Barry & Ehrhart, 1976, pp. 64–66) is more radical in its expression of social alienation. Here, we follow an angry veteran on his coast-to-coast journey; we observe how his happiness to be "back in the world" gives way to an astonished realization of an all-pervading atmosphere of seediness, corruption, and evil. Observing a car with a sticker patriotically proclaiming "This is my country," Purcell wistfully responds: "I'm happy about that/ I was afraid/ it might be mine." Finally, he escapes an unbearable reality, momentarily at least, by joining the drug-dealing underworld, no longer "looking for America." The veteran is indeed another "vanishing American." The place he or she used to call home is no longer there, having been deprived of its identity-giving mythology. "Home won't be there anymore," as poet and novelist Gustav Hasford (1980) grimly prophecies, "and we won't be there either. Upon each of our brains the war has lodged itself, a black crab feeding" (p. 176).

Painfully apt, considering the high cancer rate among veterans who were sprayed with Agent Orange, the cancer metaphor is not entirely negative. The cancer of rebellion produces visions of corruption that were previously inaccessible. G.V. Driscoll's poem, *Crossing New York Bay* (in Barry, 1976, p. 116), deprives the Statue of Liberty, that unassailably powerful symbol of American idealism and charity, of its mythical qualities:

> *hunger hate death*
> *for these they make us toil*
> *we poor we tired we masses*
> *herded on the shore—*
> *old lady liberty the whore,*
> *gift from one deceived people*
> *to another*
> *(. . .)*
> *but she's gone green*
> *green as the scum on the water*
> *in the bombcraters of Hanoi*

Such lines are indicative of a national identity crisis in the minds of many veterans; the "bomb craters" of the last line serve as an objective correlative. Hellmann (1985) has argued that a similar identity crisis took place in the minds of nonveteran protesters—pointing particularly to Mary McCarthy's "shocked sense that Vietnam is the America that no longer exists" and to Susan Sontag's "confession" that North Vietnam is a place that deserves to be idealized, having the mythic quality of a vanished American pastoral landscape (pp. 84–86). Though this perspective may simply transfer a benign myth from America to the "enemy" nation, from the oppressor to the victim, some veteran poets have created new, mature landscapes. One of the best poetic attempts to do this is found in Philip Appleman's gripping poem "Waiting for the Fire" (in Barry, 1976). First comes what we might call "conventional" sorrow about the "wreckage/ of our unnatural acts." Such sorrow is darkly supplemented by a biblical reference that works both as a symbol for self-inflicted punishment and as a contemporary metaphor for the nuclear apocalypse: Sodom. It is a stunning reference. "God's own country" is suddenly its own antonym, threatened by the wrath of an avenging

God. "Where are the volunteers/ to hold back the fire?" asks the poem, for in Sodom not even 10 good people could be found that would have stopped the rain of fire and brimstone. In finding the answer to avert future catastrophes, Appleman seems to have in mind the thesis advanced by Mitscherlich and Mitscherlich:

> *the only wash that purifies is tears,*
> *and after all our body counts,*
> *our rape, our mutilations,*
> *nobody here is crying; people who would weep*
> *at the death of a dog*
> *stroll these unburned streets dry-eyed.*
> *But forgetfulness will never walk*
> *with innocence; we save our faces*
> *at the risk of our lives, needing*
> *the wisdom of losses, the gift of despair*
> *or we could kill again.* (p. 164)

"Nothing will ever be the same again" is the leitmotif also of John Balaban's (1974) poem *After Our War,* which similarly begins with an ironically detached enumeration of human war waste, reminiscent of Remarque's famous "litany" of possible combat wounds (*All Quiet on the Western Front,* 1929, ch. 10):

> *After our war, the dismembered bits*
> *—all those pierced eyes, ear slivers, jaw splinters,*
> *gouged lips, odd tibias, skin flaps, and toes—*
> *came squinting, wobbling, jabbering back.*
> *The genitals, of course, were the most bizarre,*
> *inching along roads like glowworms, and slugs.* (p. 37)

Balaban's poetry is the kind that goes both back to Vietnam and beyond to collective war memories; it possesses that forward-looking quality that is so absent from the earlier poets and that has only recently entered the works of Ehrhart and of Bruce Weigl. Balaban's reference to the "ancient tales" may well be expressive of a suspicion that these mythic tales had been wrong all along and that the Vietnam "experience," as the new sanitized terminology goes, was merely the straw that broke the camel's back, the collective eye-opener, the necessary heave-ho into the trash can of naive idealism. As Michael Herr (1978) put it in his fragmentation grenade style,

> Anyway, you couldn't use standard methods to date the doom; might as well say that Vietnam was where the Trail of Tears was headed all along, the turnaround point where it would touch and come back to form a con-

taining perimeter; might as well lay it on the proto-Gringos who found the New England woods too raw and empty for their peace and filled them up with their own imported devils. (p. 46)

Rarely before have fiction and poetry played such an important role for "truth telling" in an important period in the history of the United States, particularly since Vietnam is not yet a closed chapter or even a digested event of American history. At the 1985 Asia Society conference on Vietnam War literature, writers, critics, journalists, and historians alike agreed that imaginative literature (rather than factual histories) would serve best as a guideline for future generations in their understanding of that era. And this is largely so because imaginative writing creates a dialogue between the merely temporal and that vast area of cultural assumptions, self-perceptions, and epistemological patterns that make up the grand American Mythology. In its ability to provide short cuts through the jungles of official obfuscations, imaginative writing plays a role of paramount importance in obtaining a real understanding of the cultural implications of the war by rendering sympathetic what it means *to the individual.* Attempts like these, which aim at "signification," seem the more important in the presence of forces that would challenge their knowledge and insights, for these are the forces that would rid us of an embarrassing "Vietnam syndrome" (some kind of disease, apparently), which they see as detrimental for future military actions, such as those in Nicaragua.

We are now witnessing a political process that attempts to erase both the memory of the war and the moral conclusions that a vast majority of Americans drew in the early 1970s, all in the name of a resurging "pride" and a reconstituted belief in America's infallibility. If many Americans refuse to embrace what has been called the "revisionist" view of the war, then a large measure of the credit must go to Vietnam veteran writers. Their radical examinations of national myths have so far prevented a total backslide into complacency and righteousness. If we provide them with the attention they deserve, then Ehrhart's (1984b) appeal—"please/ do not let it all come down/ to nothing" (p. 35)—will provide a cornerstone of a new and more mature mythology.

REFERENCES

Anderson, T. (1986). American popular music and the war in Vietnam. *Peace and Change, 9*(2), 51–65.

Baker, M. (Ed.). (1983). *Nam: The Vietnam war in the words of the soldiers who fought there.* New York: Berkeley Books.

Balaban, J. (1974). *Blue Mountain*. Greensboro, NC: Unicorn Press.

Barry, J. (1976). Christmas in Hanoi. In J. Barry & W.D. Ehrhart (Eds.), *Demilitarized zones* (p. 117). Perkasie, PA: East River Anthology.

Beidler, P. (1982). *American literature and the experience of Vietnam*. Athens, GA: University of Georgia Press.

Bercovitch, S. (1975). *The Puritan origins of the American self*. New Haven, CT: Yale University Press.

Berg, R. (1986, Spring). Losing Vietnam: Covering the war in an age of technology. *Cultural Critique, 3*, 92–125.

Bly, R. (1973). The teeth mother naked at last. *Sleepers joining hands*. New York: Harper & Row.

Burns, E.M. (1957). *The American idea of mission*. New Brunswick, NJ: Rutgers University Press.

Caputo, P. (1977). *A rumour of war*. New York: Ballantine Books.

Carruth, H. (1969). The event itself. In H. Lowenfels (Ed.), *The writing on the wall* (p. 32). Garden City, NY: Doubleday.

Clymer, A. (1985, March 30). What Americans think now. *New York Times Magazine*, pp. 34–43.

Dane, B., & Silber, I. (Eds.). (1969). *The Vietnam Songbook*. New York: Guardian Books.

De Tocqueville, A. (1966). *Democracy in America* (G. Lawrence, Trans.). New York: Harper & Row.

Duncan, R. (1968). Up rising. *Bending the bow* (pp. 81–83). New York: New Directions.

Ehrhart, W.D. (1983). *Vietnam—Perkasie: A combat marine memoir*. Jefferson, NC: McFarland.

Ehrhart, W.D. (1984a). Patriotism. *Art: MAG Original Series, 1*, 1.

Ehrhart, W.D. (1984b). *To those who have gone home tired*. New York: Thunder Mouth Press.

Emerson, G. (1985). *Winners and losers*. New York: Viking Penguin.

FitzGerald, F. (1973). *Fire in the lake: The Vietnamese and the Americans in Vietnam*. New York: Random House/Vintage.

Fussell, P. (1975). *The great war and modern memory*. Oxford: Oxford University Press.

Gompers, S. (1925). *Seventy years of life and labor, an autobiography*. New York: E. P. Dutton.

Haines, H. (1986). 'What kind of war?': An analysis of the Vietnam Veterans Memorial. *Critical Studies in Mass Communication, 3*, 1–20.

Hasford, G. (1980). *The short timers*. Toronto: Bantam Books.

Hazo, S. (1987). To a commencement of scoundrels. *Nightwords* (p. 17). Riverdale-on-Hudson, NY: The Sheep Meadow Press.

Hellmann, J. (1986). *American myth and the legacy of Vietnam*. New York: Columbia University Press.

Hemingway, E. (1935). *A farewell to arms*. Harmondsworth, England: Penguin.

Herr, M. (1978). *Dispatches*. London: Pan/Picador.

Karnow, S. (1983). *Vietnam. A history*. New York: Viking Press.

Kohler, H. (1972). The Cheerleaders. In L. Rottmann, J. Barry, & B. T. Pacquet

(Eds.), *Winning hearts and minds: War poems by Vietnam veterans* (p. 43). Brooklyn, NY: First Casualty Press.

Kolko, G. (1971). On the avoidance of rality. In R. Falk, G. Kolko, & R. Lifton (Eds.), *Crimes of war: A legal, political documentary, and psychological inquiry into the responsibility of leaders, citizens, and soldiers for criminal acts in wars* (pp. 11–16). New York: Random House.

Kovic, R. (1977a). On the eve of the tet offensive. In L.R. Obst (Ed.), *The sixties* (pp. 224–226). New York: Rolling Stone Press.

Kovic, R. (1977b). *Born on the fourth of July*. New York: Simon & Schuster.

Lelyveld, J. (1985, March 31). The enduring legacy. *New York Times Magazine*, pp. 28–43.

Levertov, D. (1971). Tenebrae. *To stay alive* (p. 17). New York: New Directions.

Lewis, L. (1985). *The tainted war: Culture and identity in Vietnam war narratives*. Westport, CT: Greenwood Press.

Lifton, R. (1973). *Home from the war: Vietnam veterans—neither victims nor executioners*. New York: Simon & Schuster.

Lomperis, T. (1986). *'Reading the wind': The literature of the Vietnam war*. Durham, NC: Duke University Press.

Lowenfels, W. (Ed.). (1967). *Where is Vietnam? American poets respond*. Garden City, NY: Doubleday.

Lowenfels, W. (Ed.). (1969). *The writing on the wall: 108 American poems of protest*. Garden City, NY: Doubleday.

Mersmann, J. (1974). *Out of the Vietnam vortex*. Kansas: University of Kansas Press.

Miller, A. (1971). The age of abdication. In R. Falk, G. Kolko, & R. Lifton (Eds.), *Crimes of war: A legal, political documentary, and psychological inquiry into the responsibility of leaders, citizens, and soldiers for criminal acts in wars* (pp. 473–475). New York: Random House.

Mitscherlich, A., & Mitscherlich, M. (1975). *The inability to mourn*. New York: Grove Press.

O'Brien, T. (1978). *If I die in a combat zone*. New York: Dell/Laurel.

O'Neal, P. (1959, November 30). The only rebellion around. *Life*, p. 126.

Osaki, M. (1985). Amnesiac. In W. D. Ehrhart (Ed.), *Carrying the darkness: American Indochina—The poetry of the Vietnam war* (p. 215). New York: Avon.

Piercy, M. (1968). The peaceable kingdom. *Breaking Camp*. Middletown, CT: Wesleyan University Press.

Pratt, J.C. (1984). *Vietnam voices*. New York: Viking Penguin.

Receveur, D. (1972). Cobra pilot. In L. Rottmann, J. Barry, & B. T. Pacquet (Eds.), *Winning hearts and minds* (p. 49). Brooklyn, NY: First Casualty Press.

Santoli, A. (Ed.). (1982). *Everything we had*. New York: Ballantine Books.

Schlesinger, A. M. (1921). America 1968: The politics of violence. In T. E. Kakonis & R. J. Shereikis (Eds.), *Scene seventy. Recent nonfiction* (pp. 269–282). Boston: Houghton Mifflin.

Shaw, G.B. (1919). *Heartbreak house*. London: The Bodley Head.

Slocock, C. (1982). *Winning Hearts and Minds:* The first casualty press. *Journal of American Studies, 16*, 107–117.

Slotkin, R. (1973). *Regeneration through violence: The mythology of the American frontier, 1600–1800*. Midletown, CT: Wesleyan University Press.

Smith, L. (1986, November-December). A sense-making perspective in recent poetry by Vietnam veterans. *The American Poetry Review*, pp. 13–18.

Smyth, S. (1976). Back home. In J. Barry & W. D. Ehrhart (Eds.), *Demilitarized zones* (p. 172). Perkosie, PA: East River Anthology.

Spark, A. (1984). The soldier at the heart of the war: The myth of the green berets in the popular culture of the Vietnam era. *Journal of American Studies, 18*(1), 29–48.

Starck, C. (1967). On a clear day. In W. Lowenfels (Ed.), *Where is Vietnam?* (p. 130). Garden City, NY: Doubleday.

Turner, A.T. (Ed.). (1977). *Fifty contemporary poets: The creative process*. New York: David McKay.

Turner, F.W. (Ed.). (1974). Introduction. In *The portable North American reader*. New York: Viking Press.

Tuveson, E.L. (1968). *Redeemer nation: The idea of America's millennial role*. Chicago: University of Chicago Press.

Walsh, J. (1982). *American war literature, 1914 to Vietnam*. London: Macmillan.

Webb, J. (1978). *Fields of fire*. New York: Bantam Books.

Whigham, P. (1967). Vietnam peace poem. In The Community Council to end the war in Vietnam (Eds.), *A poetry reading for peace in Vietnam* (pp. 10–11). Santa Barbara, CA: Unicorn Press.

Wimmer, A. (1989). Rambo: American Adam, Anarchist, and Archetypal Frontier Hero. In J. Walsh & J. Aulich (Eds.), *Vietnam images: War and representation* (pp. 184–195). London: MacMillan Press.

Woolf, C., & Bagguley, J. (1967). *Authors take sides on Vietnam*. London: Owen.

5

Images of the Warrior Returned: Vietnam Veterans in Popular American Film

George N. Dionisopoulos
Department of Speech Communication, San Diego State University

> I keep thinking about all the kids who got wiped out by seventeen years of war movies before coming to Vietnam to get wiped out for good.
>
> (Michael Herr, 1978)

> Castiglia and I saw *The Sands of Iwo Jima* together. The Marine Corps hymn was playing in the background as we sat glued to our seats, humming the hymn together and watching sergeant Stryker, played by John Wayne, charge up the hill and get killed just before he reached the top. . . . John Wayne in *The Sands of Iwo Jima* became one of my heroes.
>
> (Ron Kovic, 1976)

The war in Vietnam tore at the very soul of American society. The "longest, saddest, baddest war America ever fought" (Morganthau, Willenson, Wallcott, Horrock, & Lubenow, 1985, p. 34), it continually frustrated efforts to produce a satisfactory resolution. Even today, more than a decade after tanks of the victorious North Vietnamese Army rolled into the conquered city of Saigon, traces of the war are everywhere (Chace, Kennedy, Luttwak, Fitzgerald, Marin, Phillips, & Gilder, 1985).

For a period following the end of the war, American society "indulged in a remarkable exercise of recoil and repression" (Morrow, Kane, Stacks, & Taylor, 1985, p. 23). Gradually, this sense of societal amnesia has given way to a need to make sense out of our experience in Vietnam. Indeed, much of the "cultural legacy" of Vietnam has been an attempt to give form to an acceptable public memory and consciousness regarding our experience in Southeast Asia. In many respects this attempt has proved to be as frustrating as the war itself.

Popular American film is a particularly intriguing medium for analysis of the cultural legacy of Vietnam. Like speeches, movies are agencies of temporal and societal time, serving as "devices for societal consensus" and "instruments for education and enlightenment" (White & Averson, 1968, p. 3). As such, films provide data concerning cultural values and collective images. Since the 1967 release of *The Green Berets,* Hollywood has presented archetypical images as an instantiation of our need to make sense of Vietnam (see Chapters 4, 6, & 7, this volume).

In this chapter I offer some observations concerning the role of popular film in society, and suggest how that role is related to our conception of the Vietnam veteran. Second, I examine popular American films from three periods and suggest that the portrayal of Hollywood's "Vietvet" has changed over time. Finally, I offer some observations concerning Hollywood's portrayals of the Vietnam veteran and the current "new generation" of Vietnam-oriented films. Since the latter two are dependent on a deeper appreciation of the first, I will begin by discussing concerns pertaining to Hollywood's treatment of Vietnam veterans.

HOLLYWOOD AND WAR

The role of the mass media in modern society would seem to defy any definite codification aimed at identifying *the* relationship between the two. However, it is safe to conclude that at least part of our "modern" view of the world is due to the information provided by mass media (Berg, 1972). In addition to this educational function, media possess an ability to alter or challenge "many of the values and doctrine of powerful social and cultural forces in American society, providing alternative ways of understanding the world" (Sklar, 1975, p. 316). Thus, the collective images offered by various elements of the mass media affect much of the scope and quality of understanding of our complex environment.

Popular film, in particular, influences and is in turn influenced by the society in which it is created. American movies are "made by people who are part of their culture and the time they live in. They cannot escape telling stories that say something about America" (Nimmo & Combs, 1983, p. 105). A film "projects collective images, fantasies, and values of the culture in which [it] is created." Cinema "often dramatizes symptoms of particular societal needs of an era." "[F]ilms give tangible structure to social phenomena" and "reinforce societal trends" (Rushing & Frentz, 1978, pp. 64–65). Movies possess an ability to "report, educate [and] persuade" (Pitts, 1984, p. 2), and thus serve as a "potent vehicle for symbolizing socio-political change" (Rushing & Frentz, 1978, p. 64), for "expressing archetypes" (Rushing & Frentz, 1980, p. 406), and for helping to define or refine certain images within society.

Obviously, the complex entity labeled herein as "Hollywood" has some very pragmatic institutional concerns—such as profit—that weigh heavily upon the selection of material and the production of films. But a film's success is dependent, in part, "on its resonance with a popular audience. The success of a movie depends on the meshing of the fantasy of a small group of people (the moviemakers) with the fantasies of sometimes hundreds of thousands of people (the audience). In that sense the movies really are "a democratic art" (Nimmo & Combs, 1983, p. 105).

But it is the cultural role of film as "story" that is of interest here. As Jarvie (1978) has observed, the teller of tales has always offered stories that "served to explain, order, and . . . process the confused flux of experience." In essence, then, movies—as narratives—serve to give "shape to the totality of human experience" (p. x) by "fashioning [that] experience into a form assimilable to structures of meaning" (White, 1981, p. 1). Movies have become a modern technological version of the story teller. As Gerbner observed, the creation and distribution of these stories help transform "selected private perspectives into broad public perspectives, and bring mass publics into existence;" it helps to create a type of "visual public consensus" (Jowett & Linton, 1980, p. 75) by "flesh[ing] out what's in, and on, the minds of the American mass public" (Nimmo & Combs, 1983, p. 105).

During both World War II and, to a much lesser extent, Korea, movies offered a visual public consensus that "served the goals of national policy makers and promoted mobilization and patriotism" (McInerney, 1979–1980, p. 23). "Americans did not go into, or out of, World War II cynically, there were ideals for which to fight and, if necessary, for which to die with courage and vision," and the movies of the period "depicted commitment" (Nimmo & Combs, 1983, p. 113). After these wars had ended, Hollywood was "complacent about motives and destiny" (McInerney, 1979–1980, p. 23), offering images concerning the reassimilation of returning soldiers and the problems faced by disabled veterans.[1]

But Vietnam was very different from World War II or Korea, and Hollywood's treatment of the Vietnam War did not follow any pattern established previously. In Vietnam, many of the old stereotypes simply did not apply. As Adair (1981) observes, during Vietnam "the nation found itself denied the reassurance of a broad consensus of opinion; decisions of urgent matter were openly, violently contested—in the streets, on campus—as they were being taken; history, as never before, was re-

---

[1] For example, pictures like *The Pride of the Marines, The Men,* and the Oscar-winning *The Best Years of Our Lives* all concerned the difficulties faced by men who had been maimed in WWII or Korea (see Corliss, 1978, p. 66).

vised as it was being written" (p. 45). That is, a majority of Americans were confused about our collective "Vietnam experience." Much of that confusion remains to this day, as we struggle to make sense out of, and draw lessons from Vietnam. This is a situation in which the mechanisms of mass culture are supposed to help ease our confusion, helping us to "purge [our] devils by naming them" (Turner, 1978, p. 63).

Movies, as narratives, provide a method of helping Americans assimilate Vietnam into experience. They afford a mechanism that allows us to make sense retrospectively by storytelling in the present, drawing on events in the past. To the extent that the meanings shaped by the stories become widely accepted, they function to make the past not only understandable but usable (Commager, 1967; Melanson, 1983; Neustadt & May, 1986; Fromkin & Chace, 1985). Indeed, Koning (1979) wrote that popular culture offers a "quintessentially American way for our society to come to grips with its Vietnam experience" (p. 1).

One way popular films have helped us interpret our Vietnam experience is through portrayals of the Americans who fought the war. This chapter advances the idea that Hollywood has offered the "Vietvet" as a metaphoric representation of America's need to make sense out of our Vietnam experience. To illustrate this idea more fully, this chapter examines images of the Vietnam veteran from American films made during three time periods. The first period includes the years 1968–1976 and, thus, includes films made during the war and immediately following American disengagement. The second period covers the "Vietnam genre" films of 1977—1980. The final period covers the "revisionist" films of 1981–1985.

HOLLYWOOD'S VIETNAM VETERAN DURING THE WAR: 1968–1976

The first popular films relating to Vietnam were produced before the major American troop build-ups in 1965–1966. Films like *Saigon*, in 1948, could be considered precedents for "Vietnam films" (McInerney, 1979–1980, p. 23). But John Wayne's 1968 film, *The Green Berets*, was the first that actually proclaimed itself to be dealing with American soldiers in Vietnam.

In December of 1965, Wayne wrote to President Johnson expressing concern that it was "extremely important that not only the people of the United States but those all over the world should know why it is necessary for us to be [in Vietnam]." In the same letter, Wayne also stated that the motion picture medium was "the most effective way" to accomplish that task (Suid, 1979, p. 20). The only "Vietnam movie" made during the war with the full cooperation of the Department of Defense, *The Green Berets* was a blatantly partisan film aimed at winning the hearts and minds of American audiences. It was unabashedly Manichaean in its presentation of the reasons underlying United States military involvement in Southeast Asia.

Although *The Green Berets* was a commercial success, it was less of a public relations victory for the war effort. Richard Schickel (1968) observed that the film was "just as stupid—ideologically speaking—as you were afraid it would be and far worse—as an action film—than you suspected it could be" (p. 8). Reviewers suggested that the film "could not be simpler" in the presentation of its "message" (Morgenstern, 1968, p. 94; see also, "Far from Vietnam," 1968; Gilliatt, 1968), and New York Democratic Congressman Rosenthal quipped that "this alliance of Hollywood and the Pentagon seems to have brought out the worst in both institutions" (Madden, 1969, p. 23).

The Green Berets was also the first popular movie to offer a portrayal of the men who were serving in Vietnam. Unfortunately, that portrayal proved to be about as simplistic as the rest of the movie. A key indicant of this image is offered during the film's opening sequence, where a group of visitors is being given a demonstration of Green Beret expertise. During a question and answer session, a reporter named Beckworth asks some pointed questions concerning United States military involvement in Vietnam. The answers given by the Green Berets conducting the demonstration are, at best, simplistic: "What's involved [in Vietnam] is Communist domination of the world." At worst, they are patently ludicrous. For example, there is an effort to dismiss concerns about South Vietnamese political repression by drawing an analogy between the Thieu government and the United States constitutional convention in 1787.[2]

Notwithstanding this attempt to make President Thieu the first "moral equivalent of the founding fathers," the important point here concerns the images of the soldiers themselves. The film's opening sequence carried a message established explicitly in an exchange between Beckworth and John Wayne's character, Colonel Kirby:

Beckworth: Your brainwashed sergeant didn't sell me.
Kirby: Didn't sell you what?
Beckworth: Didn't sell me on the idea that we should be involved in Southeast Asia.
Kirby: Have you ever been to Southeast Asia?

[2] This propagandistic opening to the film was eliminated from several prints of the film distributed to the European market (see Adair, 1981, p. 48).

Beckworth: No, I haven't.
Kirby: Uh huh.

Here, Kirby terminates discussion by walking away. The clear message is that only those who had been "over there" could know what Vietnam was "really" like or about, and that those who had been "over there" were unanimous in their support of the war effort. Even Beckworth's skepticism vanishes as he comes to see firsthand the justification of U.S. intervention. As the film's press kit synopsis states, Beckworth, a "former skeptic about the war," "leaves [Vietnam] to write about the heroic exploits of the American and South Vietnamese forces" (Adler, 1968, p. 49).

The soldiers depicted in *The Green Berets* display no antiwar attitude, nor is there even a hint that some of them might be apolitical. These were America's finest, out to stop "communist domination of the world." These were men not only highly skilled in the execution of their mission, but articulate in defense of government policy, moving with ease from being warriors in Vietnam to being policy diplomats in the United States.

The film's portrayal of American fighting men bore more resemblance to characters in other war movies (or "westerns") than to actual Vietnam veterans (see Chapter 4, this volume). These were the same kinds of heroes who had gone off to fight in World War II and Korea. Besides their unquestioning belief in the justness of their cause, the soldiers under Wayne's command did not exhibit any of the countercultural elements evident among troops in Vietnam. There was no hint of any "orientation toward drugs, rock music [or the] generalized subversion of authority that significantly changed the public image of the American Army in the late 60s" (Adair, 1981, p. 51; see also Herr, 1978). Instead, these men were tough and resourceful, but also "kind and paternal towards the South Vietnamese" (Spark, 1984, p. 37; see also Jeffords, Chapter 7, this volume).

The obvious trouble with this image is that by the time the movie was released, a great deal of the opposition to the war effort was coming from men who had been "over there" and did not like what they had seen. In fact, 200 members of Vietnam Veterans to End the War staged a protest at a New York theater that was showing *The Green Berets* ("Glory," 1968, p. 84). Still, the soldiers portrayed in this film represented the perspective that a great many Americans had adopted concerning Vietnam. Indeed, the collective conscious of Richard Nixon's "silent majority" "thought U.S. motives in Vietnam benevolent" (Nimmo & Combs, 1983, p. 117), applauded the righteous endeavor of stopping communist domination of the world, and felt sincerely that our efforts in Vietnam were done to "help" the South Vietnamese, who were fighting for their freedom.

In spite of the limited financial success of *The Green Berets*, for years following its release there were no other "Vietnam" films. However, images of Vietnam veterans were hardly absent from the screen during this time. This period was highlighted by the "drought" of films concerning Vietnam and by the use of Vietnam as a kind of subtext or pretext within popular movies.

By the end of the 1960s and by the beginning of the 1970s, Vietnam war movies were conspicuous by their absence. They were considered to be "unbankable" by the major studios, and a "profound silence about Vietnam pervaded the American film industry" (Edelman, 1979, p. 539). There were documentaries, such as the award-winning *Hearts and Minds* and *Year of the Pig*, but major studios did not want to handle a situation in which America "seemed to be neither winning nor right" (McInerney, 1979–1980, p. 23). Peter Davis, whose documentary *Hearts and Minds* played to near empty theaters, explained the movie makers' dilemma during this time: "I don't think our country has really come to grips with the Vietnam experience. It's very hard to do that; and a movie that's just going to make people feel guilty is bound to fail" (Turner, 1978, p. 62; see also Chapter 4, this volume).

This was a period in which the industry censored itself, and the country "had to pause, wipe the sweat off its brow, and take a deep breath before accepting cinematic explorations of [Vietnam's] meaning" (Edelman, 1979, p. 539; see also Auster & Quart, 1979). Several writers have argued, however, that films made during this "drought" period were making statements related to the American experience in Vietnam (Smith, 1975; Kerr, 1980; Turner, 1978).

In part, filmic statements about the Vietnam experience during this period were confined to a subliminal questioning of "the kind of values that put us in Vietnam" (Turner, 1978, p. 58). Images of Vietnam veterans were very evident, but they were found primarily in low-budget films about motorcycle gangs, and usually portrayed the Vietnam veteran as deeply disturbed by the war. In these pictures Vietnam is used as a subtext or pretext for the behavior of a protagonist. Most of the movies of this type followed the theme that returning veterans were disturbed or, in some cases, antisocial to the point of being psychotic. In "B" pictures such as *Angels From Hell* (1968), *The Angry Breed* (1968), *The Big Bounce* (1968), *Satan's Sadists* (1969), *Chrome and Hot Leather* (1971), *Welcome Home Soldier Boys* (1972), and the feature film *Taxi Driver* (1976), the protagonist's experiences in Vietnam are used as a pretext for all manner of violent behavior.

Spark (1984) observes that in some of these movies the veteran is portrayed as having been driven to violence as a result of the war, while in others the violence is portrayed as "part of [his] training and experience" (p. 40). Either way, the filmic image of Vietnam veterans in these movies suggests that the returning veteran is a "human frag bomb," an "all-purpose all American villain" (Corliss, 1978, p. 65). Interestingly, most of these films never provide any detail concerning the main character's experiences in Vietnam that served to produce such antisocial behavior. Instead, service in Vietnam becomes "a narrative function, a plot device which enables other textual troubles to be explained or elided" (Kerr, 1980, p. 72), or, more simply, just "a convenient excuse" that serves "to explain someone's bizarre behavior" (Canby, 1978, p. B13).

Though most of these movies were not widely seen, the image of the "deranged Vietvet" became a "stock character in American culture" (Freedman, 1985, p. 55). Edelman (1979) observes that even prime time television portrayed the veteran as either "a sadist who rapes and carves up women" or "an operating room technician who mutilates nurses" (p. 541). Thus, the Vietnam veteran as "junkie, emotional cripple or ticking time bomb" became a staple in mass-mediated culture.

But this representation was, again, a metaphor for an American society that was trying to make sense out of an experience that defied all attempts. That this image was offered, and implicitly accepted, in such a widespread manner suggests that it achieved some "resonance with a popular audience" (Nimmo & Combs, 1983, p. 105). Vietnam demonstrated much of the darker side of American society. The conflict "produced a large body of young men who practiced or witnessed at first hand the sanctioned use of violence—not surprisingly, film and television writers and producers have assumed the mass audience will accept the portrayal of veterans as constantly violent" (Smith, 1975, p. 155).

As Morrow et al. (1985) suggest, until Vietnam, Americans held an almost romantic view of war. It "was an essentially knightly exercise—a man riding out in resplendent armor . . . to rescue the innocent from the wicked. . . . But when the knights somehow seem monstrous, killers risen out of a black id, perpetrators of My Lai, then the entire chivalric logic collapses" (p. 24). As our darker side was demonstrated night after night on the evening news, we began to fear the living representation of that image—the Vietnam veteran.

Previously, movie images had characterized war veterans as going "over there" to "get the job done," but they could somehow "turn it off" and return to "normal" when they came home. As Vietnam veteran Robert Santos notes, "In World War II films the all-American G.I. Joes kissed their sweethearts goodbye, fought the noble war, and came home to cheers" (Edelman, 1979, p. 541; see also Smith, 1975, pp. 170–171). But after Vietnam, American veterans were portrayed as threatening to society. This image was undoubtedly as insulting as it was unrealistic.[3] However, judging from the number of movies that used the "deranged Vietvet" theme, Hollywood assumed that the American public would readily accept this image.

As stated above, a constant in these early movies is that they provide little background concerning the characters' experiences in Vietnam—possibly because the Vietnam veteran, like Vietnam itself, was considered "unknowable." Vietnam appears as being outside the narrative, important only insofar as it serves to explain the characters' otherwise inexplicable behaviors. Such a lack of orientation toward Vietnam suggests, then, that there were no "real Vietnam" films between 1968 (*The Green Berets*) and 1976. By 1977, however, there were signs that Hollywood's self-imposed restrictions about Vietnam were being re-evaluated. The Vietnam "drought" was about to end.

THE "VIETNAM GENRE"—1977–1980

At the end of the 1970s there was still a sense within the film industry that Vietnam was "a turnoff for the public" (Gelman, 1978, p. 86). But Hollywood gradually became more willing to produce movies concerning America's "Vietnam experience." Initial efforts were viewed as a gamble, and most of the marketing techniques carefully avoided promoting these new ventures as being "about Vietnam."

There were several reasons for Hollywood's hesitation. The Vietnam War had no satisfactory conclusion, it had been on television every night for years, and there were still a great many cultural wounds connected with America's experience in Southeast Asia. As Morrow et al. (1985) have observed, during "a long period in the '70s, the nation indulged in a remarkable exercise of recoil and denial and amnesia about Vietnam. Americans did not want to hear about it, to think about it" (p. 23). Eventually, however, Hollywood apparently decided that people were "willing to leave their homes and pay good money to relive an experience commonly thought to be so nightmarish and bewildering, so painful and guilt-ridden, that no self-respecting American would bring it up, much less expect to be 'entertained' by it" (Turner, 1978, p. 65; see also Canby, 1978).

But by 1980, McInerney (1979–1980) was able to list eight films that had been released between 1977 and 1980 that he felt certified "the conclusion that there is a Vietnam genre" (p. 22). The films in this genre suggest that

---

[3] Thomas Bird organized the Vietnam Veterans Ensemble Theatre Company after seeing *Taxi Driver*. He was angry that the De Niro character, Travis Bickle, was developed only enough so that the audience knew he was a Vietnam veteran (see Freedman, 1985, p. 55).

popular images of the men who fought in Vietnam had changed. Moving away from the Vietnam veteran-as-psychopath, Vietnam genre films attempt to use the war as "the villain which scarred individuals and the nation" (Suid, 1979, p. 22). The central characters in these films had "problems," but now they were the problems of an entire society; the image of the veteran trying to make sense of his "Vietnam experience" became a metaphoric representation. Two films that are particularly illustrative of Vietnam genre films are *Coming Home* and *The Deer Hunter*.[4]

Coming Home (1978), which is a film about disabled Vietnam veterans, was panned by some reviewers for being "at least ten years too late" (Suid, 1979, p. 23), for having "too many suicides for anything except Shakespeare" (Canby, 1978, p. B13), and for being really about "Ms. Fonda's orgasms" (Wilson, 1982, p. 84). Yet, in a 1980 survey by the Veterans Administration, Vietnam veterans rated *Coming Home* as one of the two films that portrayed them most favorably; the other, interestingly, was *The Green Berets*. As Freedman (1985) has pointed out, the fact that these two apparently incompatible films were highly rated can be explained by the fact that both celebrate heroism: "For all the political differences in the two films, the veteran in *Coming Home* could well have been the soldier in *The Green Berets*" (p. 54).

For example, in the opening sequence of *Coming Home*, a group of disabled veterans discussing their inability to discern a reason or justification for their being crippled is juxtaposed with images of a Marine officer preparing himself for his impending tour in Vietnam. The officer, played by Bruce Dern, is Captain Bob Hyde, who embodies "every misguided impulse that got us into the War" (Corliss, 1978, p. 68). He is preparing as though he were an athlete getting ready for a competition. There is no talk of securing freedom for the South Vietnamese, no question of his refusing to go. He is a noble career serviceman going to the war, which he refers to as "combat city," because that is what a career serviceman does. His tour in Southeast Asia is just part of his job, the "ticket" to promotion and a successful career.

Dern plays the character with integrity and a heroic quality that is all the more dramatic when contrasted with Jon Voight's character, Luke Martin. Both men are portrayed as products of a pre-Vietnam society,[5]

---

[4] Other films within the "Vietnam genre" include *Heroes* (1977), *Rolling Thunder* (1977), *Who'll Stop the Rain* (1978), *Go Tell the Spartans* (1978), and *Apocalypse Now* (1979).

[5] Several writers have offered interesting observations concerning how certain cultural images—such as the "John Wayne hero" or a sense of involvement as one of "Kennedy's children"—were "important part[s] of the folk culture of the young Americans who [fought] the war in Vietnam" (Mohr, 1968, p. 49; Herr, 1978; Van Devanter & Morgan, 1983; Kovic, 1976).

and both are irreversibly altered by their experiences overseas. Martin comes back crippled in body, but "a lot smarter now than when I went." Refusing to give in to the bitterness of being confined to a wheelchair, Martin finds a rebirth in seeking, through antiwar activism, to help others avoid the mistakes he has made. Hyde, however, exhibits "a set of values which were later destroyed by the realities of an unconventional war and his wife's infidelity" (Crane, 1982, p. 41).

Vietnam changed both men, but it also formed a bond between them that only another "brother" could understand, a bond that is exemplified when Hyde and Martin refuse to compete with each other for the affections of Sally (Fonda). Hyde goes so far as to go to Martin's apartment to warn him that the FBI has him under surveillance for antiwar activities. Even in the film's dramatic confrontation scene, Martin is able to defuse the situation by relating to the Vietnam experiences he and Hyde shared: "I'm not the enemy," Martin exclaims. "Maybe the enemy's the war. But you don't want to kill anybody here. You've enough ghosts to carry around." When Hyde responds by surrendering the captured weapon—his "trophy" from the war—he realizes that everything he has held onto has been stripped away by Vietnam: "I just want to be a hero, that's all. . . . One day in my life, one moment. I just want to go out a hero."

Coming Home is a statement directed toward America's "cultural amnesia" of the war and toward our silence about the Americans who fought it. On one level, the movie suggests the need for America to come to terms with its "Vietnam experience." Producer Bruce Gilber and actress Jane Fonda both stated that one of the reasons they became involved in the project was a mutual feeling that "there would be a cultural battlefront in the future to determine what the lessons of the war were" (Turner, 1978, p. 63). But this movie was also an indictment of how American society had reacted toward Vietnam veterans, in general, and toward crippled veterans, in particular. In one of the film's most powerful scenes, Sally attempts to get some of the officers' wives to express an interest in the men at the Veterans hospital; she is unsuccessful. In another scene, a disabled veteran complains about his inability to get answers to simple questions concerning how he is to live with his crippled body. Both scenes, and the movie as a whole, challenge society's ability to ignore veterans, to treat them as an invisible entity. Still, because *Coming Home* did not offer the audience any visual images of the war itself, it continued Hollywood's practice of treating Vietnam as unfathomable. The horrors of the war are simply insinuated through their effects on the film's central characters.

Another "Vietnam genre" film, *The Deer Hunter*, was partially filmed in Southeast Asia, though producer, director, and author Michael Cimino argued that his film was not about Vietnam (Suid, 1981, p. 142).[6] Because the movie focuses on the relationships and bonding rituals of three men involved in war, Cimino claims that "it could just as easily have been about the Civil War or any war" (Auster & Quart, 1979, p. 9); it concerns "the ordinary people in this country who journeyed from their home to the heart of darkness and back" (Kent, 1977, p. B23).

Although critics attacked the film for its racism and its lack of historical accuracy, *The Deer Hunter* presented a story of interest, for my purposes, precisely because it focused on people instead of politics. Michael, Nicky, and Stevie, the three main characters, are steel workers from the fictitious town of Clairton, Pennsylvania; they represent the traditional values of working-class America. Theirs was a world embodying "the communal codes and rituals of ethnic American labors" (Wilson, 1982, p. 84) in which male bonding and successfully facing a challenge are of primary importance (Mills, 1979). These are young American men responding to what their culture has told them is their duty, and it is on them that the odious burden of Vietnam has fallen. As Krantz (1980) puts it, Cimino's careful construction of the three central characters insures the audience's sympathy so that by the time they get to the war, "anything they do, including lose, is all right with us" (p. 19).

Cimino's portrayal of the Vietnam veteran through the characters of Michael, Nicky, and Steven is, again, representative of our attempts to make sense out of our collective experience of Vietnam. Michael's emergence from the war as a stronger, more sensitive person, and the collective singing of "God Bless America" in the final scene constitute Cimino's ode to what "we once were and will be again" (Harmetz, 1979, p. C15). But Cimino's characters also offer some disturbing elements. The central characters respond to the call to arms and want to go where "the bullets are flying," but, like Hyde in *Coming Home*, they do so with *no* sense of political consciousness. Their Vietnam is so devoid of any historical or political sensibilities that it exists "in a historical vacuum," "a world where the war has become merely an arena for existential and personal dramas of courage, fear, and breakdown" (Auster & Quart, 1979, p. 9). Here, again, the mysterious aspects of Vietnam are highlighted, suggesting that Vietnam cannot be understood by Americans; it can only be survived (Spark, 1984, p. 41), and our survival makes us stronger.

[6] Rushing and Frentz (1980) concurred that *The Deer Hunter* is not primarily about the Vietnam War. However, other writers (Koning, 1979; Wilson, 1982) have maintained that the emotions engendered by Vietnam predisposed Cimino's audiences to perceive the movie as being a commentary on the war.

Even the film's central "Russian roulette" metaphor—although "extremely effecti[ve] and harrowing on a visceral, emotional level" (Auster & Quart, 1979, p. 8)—rings false and actually tends to diminish the sacrifice of American soldiers in Vietnam. "However misguided," Wilson (1982) observes, "Americans died in Vietnam for definite political and historical reasons." The Russian roulette "metaphor implies that Vietnam was only a fatal game: random, meaningless, nihilistic" (p. 88).

Films belonging to the Vietnam genre continued to offer the veteran as a metaphor for an America trying to make sense of its Vietnam experience. Within this metaphor veterans are portrayed as having been through an ordeal that changed them, yet from which they would emerge stronger; and we get the sense that American society would be stronger for their metamorphosis. A rather different kind of image is offered by a third group of Vietnam films, which represent Hollywood at its revisionist best.

WE WIN—1981–1985

Commenting on Vietnam films, such as *Uncommon Valor, Rambo,* and *Missing in Action,* Stanley Karnow, author of *Vietnam: A History,* suggests that these movies can "turn a defeat into victory; you can achieve in fantasy what you didn't achieve in reality" (Zoglin, 1985, p. 73). Like those that preceded them, these films suggest a perspective from which to view Vietnam veterans, and are metaphorically suggestive of America's attempt to analyze the "experience" of Vietnam.

Because the plot of *Rambo* is almost interchangeable with *Uncommon Valor* or *Missing in Action,* we may sensibly handle them as a group. The storyline is basically this: an individual "super-veteran" or a group of "super-veterans" go "back to the Nam" to rescue American prisoners of war who are still being held captive. The heroes successfully complete their mission by operating much like their former adversaries did in the jungles. Along the way, they are harassed by authorities of the United States government who, for various reasons, don't want the public to know about the fate of the missing Americans (see Chapter 1, this volume).

These movies offer a number of messages. One seems to be that the Vietnam veteran is a victim of a brutal war, a hostile public, and an uncaring government; he is the soldier who "fought under insane conditions in Vietnam and then rebuilt his life in an ungrateful America" (Freedman, 1985, p. 51). For example, Kauffman (1985) observes that Sylvester Stallone's character, Rambo, is "strong, taciturn, self-reliant, and *wronged*." He personifies "the slighted Vietnam veteran" (p. 16; see also O'Brien, 1985).

In the 1982 film *First Blood*, Rambo is introduced as a former Green Beret, "the soldier at the heart of the war," who represents all "wronged" veterans of that conflict (Spark, 1984, p. 40). When the authorities of a small town harass him, we see the neglect and abuse of American society toward the returning veteran. This "veteran-as-victim" theme—a continuation from the previous era—is particularly emphasized in *Rambo: First Blood Part II* when Rambo says that he wants what every guy who fought in Vietnam wants: for "our country to love us as much as we loved it." This message would be satisfactory if it stopped with a self-examination of the raw deal that returning veterans received from an uncaring society. But movies of this sort also carry some rather simplistic messages concerning the "lessons" we should draw from that war, lessons that are all the more disturbing given recent events in Central America.

Such movies offer the viewing public a group of "revenge fantasies," as celluloid heroes "win back a measure of U.S. prestige and self-confidence" (Saltzman, 1985, p. 47). As *New York Times* film critic Vincent Canby notes, the stories are "not about the war as it was fought and as it came to an end ten years ago, but as it has come to look to the macho mind of today." They offer, and at the same time reflect, a perspective "toward the war that, in the 1970s was seen as a harrowing American disgrace" (Saltzman, 1985, p. 47) and has subsequently been revised as a moral defense of U.S. intervention (Herring, 1987). From this perspective such films suggest that American defeat was the result of some kind of government conspiracy of silence and/or ineptness (usually personified by a middle-level bureaucrat), and offer a collective fantasy that suggests that "the lowly grunts would have won if left to their own devices" (Kopkind, 1985, p. 77; see also Zoglin, 1985).[7] This also hints at the possibility that if "Vietnam" has to be fought again—in Nicaragua? El Salvador?—we will win. What is not clear is whether we will win *because* of the government or *in spite* of the government.

While trying to elevate the character of the Vietnam veteran by portraying him as a "super-warrior," these films tend to cheapen the sacri-

---

[7] If box office receipts are any indication, the American movie audience was receptive to this revisionist message. In the early 1980s, the "Rambo" character became an important part of American folk culture—"shorthand for a whole lot of issues"—in much the same way that John Wayne had earlier. In fact, President Reagan "helped to catapult the movie onto the front pages of newspapers around the world" when he made this remark after a hijacking: "I saw *Rambo* last night, and next time I'll know what to do" (Farley, 1985, p. 109).

fices and accomplishments of those who actually fought in Vietnam. The Stallone/Norris "super-veteran" accomplishes more in two hours than the entire U.S. military did in 10 years, and the impression is that, if we would have had enough soldiers like these, we could have beaten the Vietcong at their own game.

SUMMARY AND OBSERVATIONS

Before beginning work on *Apocalypse Now,* producer/director Francis Ford Coppola hired President Carter's pollster, Pat Caddell, and media advisor Gerald Rafshoon to survey "why people went to the movies and what their feelings were about the war" (Turner, 1978, p. 57). This survey suggested that people were "curious" about the war itself and the reasons for it. Films help satisfy that curiosity by offering images for collective sense making, and, thus, a "good deal can be learned about the . . . fantasies of any age by examining and interpreting the popular movies of the time" (Nimmo & Combs, 1983, p. 109). One image that emerges from films about Vietnam has been Hollywood's portrayal of the veteran as a metaphor for our societal struggle to make sense out of our experience in Southeast Asia.

Having evolved over three societal and temporal periods, the initial image was of the veteran as either a hero, unhesitant in his commitment to his task, or a representative of the darker side of our nature, a man to be feared. Then came films that portrayed the veteran as scarred by the war but as having emerged stronger for his experiences in Vietnam. The third image portrayed the Vietnam veteran as a victim who could have won the war if only he had been allowed to do his job. More than merely a filmic shift in focus, the evolution of the image of the Vietnam veteran mirrors concomitant changes in America's interpretation of Vietnam.

As of this writing, studios are manifesting a revival of interest in Vietnam, spearheaded by Vietnam veteran Oliver Stone's movie *Platoon.* As John Wheeler, Chairman of the Vietnam Veterans Memorial Fund, points out, *Platoon* is "a new statement about Vietnam veterans." It "makes us real" (Corliss, 1987, p. 57). If *Platoon* is an indication of the new genre of "Vietnam movies," perhaps movie makers are finally attempting a positive, realistic portrayal of Vietnam veterans; perhaps they are beginning to tell the "human" story of "what happened to the people who fought there" (Goodgame, 1987, p. 58).

On the other hand, one element of the post-Vietnam political landscape is still absent in Hollywood's treatment of Vietnam. With the exception of the cartoon-like portrayal of *Green Berets* in 1968, Hollywood seems unable or unwilling to address in a serious manner the underlying political policy questions surrounding U.S. involvement in Southeast Asia. Even the most recent "realistic Vietnam" films ignore the submerged political questions. The Vietnam War was a different kind of war for Americans. It was America's first military defeat, and the only rewards of defeat, apparently, are the lessons learned that may produce victory in the next war (Church, Jackson, & Munro, 1985). There is also in Hollywood a lingering fear of "making old cultural wounds bleed afresh;" so, films sanitize Vietnam to the point that it is recognizable only through its technology and its elements of counterculture. One significant consequence of this is that Hollywood's persistent failure to address the political questions emerging from America's involvement in Vietnam strips veterans of the context that makes their sacrifices both understandable and meaningful.

Here, again, the movie industry's inability or unwillingness to address underlying questions of policy may be indicative of American society as a whole. At this point there appears to be a public consensus to recognize and reconcile with Vietnam veterans, to acknowledge their collective sacrifice; but there is still little public consensus concerning the political "lessons" of the war these veterans fought (Chace et al., 1985; Fromkin & Chace, 1985; Wheeler, 1985; see also Chapters 1 & 8, this volume). Even now, more than a decade after the fall of Saigon, our experience in Indochina divides the country, posing "fundamental questions about the nation's role in the world, about the uses of military force, and about the power of public opinion in shaping—and restraining—U.S. decision making" ("The war that won't go away," 1985, p. 32; Morganthau et al., 1985). Perhaps, then, it is unreasonable—given the potential constraints posed by institutional and political concerns—to suggest that Hollywood *should* provide serious presentations of fundamental policy questions posed by Vietnam before there is a more demonstrable public consensus.

However, if film is a mechanism for giving structure to social phenomena and for dramatizing societal needs, it may be that this is precisely what is called for before we can truly understand the veteran or the war. The soldiers who served in Vietnam fought this country's most divisive foreign war. What they endured, who they are, and what they represent is integrally bound up with that war in all its elements, including its "lessons." Possibly, the next generation of Vietnam films will include a more realistic or provocative assessment of the war itself.

REFERENCES

Adair, G. (1981). *Vietnam on film: From "The Green Berets" to "Apocalypse Now."* New York: Proteus.

Adler, R. (1968, June 20). Screen: *Green Berets* as viewed by John Wayne. *New York Times*, p. 49.

Auster, A., & Quart, L. (1979). Hollywood and Vietnam: The triumph of the will. *Ceneaste*, *9*, 4–9.

Berg, D.M. (1972). Rhetoric, reality, and mass media. *Quarterly Journal of Speech*, *58*, 255–263.

Canby, V. (1978, February 19). Hollywood focuses on Vietnam at last. *New York Times*, *II*, 1, 13.

Chace, J., Kennedy, P.M., Luttwak, E.N., Fitzgerald, F., Marin, P., Phillips, K.P., & Gilder, G. (1985, April). What are the consequences of Vietnam? *Harpers*, pp. 35–46.

Church, G.J., Jackson, D.S., & Munro, R.H. (1985, April 15). Lessons from a lost war. *Time*, pp. 40–42, 45.

Commager, H.S. (1967). *The search for a usable past: And other essays in historiography*. New York: Knopf.

Corliss, R. (1978, March 20). Guns and buttered popcorn. *New Times*, pp. 65–68.

Crane, W. (1982). Creative conflict: Bruce Dern and the making of *Coming Home*. *Post Script*, *1*, 27–45.

Edelman, R. (1979, November). Viet vets talk about Nam films. *Films in Review*, pp. 539–542.

Far from Vietnam and Green Berets. (1968, June 21). *Time*, p. 84.

Farley, E. (1985, August 26). The U.S. has surrendered–now *Rambo* is taking the world by storm. *Business Week*, p. 109.

Freedman, S.G. (1985, March 31). The war and the arts. *New York Times*, pp. 50–51, 54–57.

Fromkin, D., & Chace, J. (1985). What *are* the lessons of Vietnam? *Foreign Affairs*, *63*, 722–746.

Gelman, D. (1978, February 13). Vietnam marches home. *Newsweek*, pp. 85–86.

Gilliatt, P. (1968, July 6). The current cinema. *New Yorker*, pp. 44, 46.

Glory. (1968, June 29). *New Yorker*, pp. 24–27.

Goodgame, D. (1987, January 26). How the war was won. *Time*, p. 58.

Harmetz, A. (1979, April 26). Oscar-winning *Dear Hunter* is under attack as "racist film." *New York Times*, p. C15.

Herr, M. (1978). *Dispatches*. New York: Avon.

Herring, G.C. (1987). America and Vietnam: The debate continues. *American Historical Review*, *92*, 350–362.

Jarvie, I.C. (1978). *Movies as social criticism: Aspects of their social psychology*. Metuchen, NJ: Scarecrow Press.

Jowett, G., & Linton, J.M. (1980). *Movies as mass communication*. Beverly Hills: Sage.

Kauffman, S. (1985, July 1). Now about Rambo. *New Republic*, p. 16.

Kerr, P. (1980). The Vietnam subtext. *Screen*, *21*, 67–72.

Kent, L. (1977, December 10). Ready for Vietnam? A talk with Michael Cimino. *New York Times*, pp. B15, B23.

Koning, H. (1979, May 27). Films and plays about Vietnam treat everything but the war. *New York Times*, *II*,1, 23.

Kovic, R. (1976). *Born on the Fourth of July.* New York: McGraw Hill.
Krantz, R.C. (1980, October). *Apocalypse Now* and *The Deerhunter:* The lies aren't over. *Jump Cut,* pp. 18–20.
Madden, R.C. (1969, June 27). John Wayne and the Army under fire. *New York Times,* p. 23.
McInerney, P. (1979–1980). Apocalypse then: Hollywood looks back at Vietnam. *Film Quarterly,* pp. 21–32.
Melanson, R.A. (1983). *Writing history and making policy: The Cold War, Vietnam and revisionism.* Lannam, MD: University Press of America.
Mills, N. (1979). Memories of the Vietnam war. *Dissent, 26,* 334–337.
Mohr, C. (1968, June 20). U.S. Special Forces: Real and on film. *New York Times,* p. 49.
Morganthau, T., Willenson, K., Wallcott, J., Horrock, N.M., & Lubenow, G.C. (1985, April 15). We're still prisoners of war. *Newsweek,* pp. 34–37.
Morgenstern, J. (1968, July 1). Affirmative? Negative! *Newsweek,* p. 94.
Morrow, L., Kane, J.J., Stacks, J.F., & Taylor, E. (1985, April 15). A bloody rite of passage. *Time,* pp. 20–26, 31.
Neustadt, R.E., & May, R.E. (1986). *Thinking in time: The uses of history for decision makers.* New York: Free Press.
Nimmo, D., & Combs, J.E. (1983). *Mediated political realities.* New York: Longman.
O'Brien, T. (1985, September 20). Saving humors: The aftershock of Summer. *Commonwealth,* p. 449.
Pitts, M.R. (1984). *Hollywood and American history: A filmography of over 250 motion pictures depicting U.S. history.* Jefferson, NC: McFarland.
Rushing, J.H., & Frentz, T.S. (1978). The rhetoric of *Rocky:* A social value model of criticism. *Western Journal of Speech Communication, 41,* 63–72.
Rushing, J.H., & Frentz, T.S. (1980). *The Deer Hunter:* Rhetoric of the warrior. *Quarterly Journal of Speech, 66,* 392–406.
Saltzman, J. (1985, September). Apocalypse again. *USA Today,* p. 47.
Schickel, R. (1968, July 19). Duke talks through his green beret. *Life,* p. 8.
Sklar, R. (1975). *Movie-made America: A cultural history of American movies.* New York: Vintage.
Smith, J. (1975). *Looking away: Hollywood and Vietnam.* New York: Scribner.
Spark, A. (1984). The soldier at the heart of the war: The myth of the Green Beret in the popular culture of the Vietnam era. *Journal of American Studies, 18,* 29–48.
Suid, L. (1979, September/October). Hollywood and Vietnam. *Film Comment,* pp. 20–25.
Suid, L. (1981). Hollywood and Vietnam. *Journal of American Culture, 4,* 136–148.
Turner, R. (1978, March 20). The worst years of our lives. *New Times,* pp. 54–58, 62–65.
Van Devanter, L., & Morgan, C. (1983). *Home before morning.* New York: Warner.
The war that won't go away. (1985, April 15). *Newsweek,* pp. 32–33.
Wheeler, J. (1985). Coming to grips with Vietnam. *Foreign Affairs, 63,* 747–758.
White, H. (1981). The value of narrativity in the representation of reality. In

W.J.T. Mitchell (Ed.), *On narrativity* (pp. 1–23). Chicago: University of Chicago Press.
White, D.M., & Averson, R. (1968). *Sight, sound, and society: Motion pictures and television in America.* Boston: Beacon.
Wilson, J.C. (1982). *Vietnam in prose and film.* Jefferson, NC: McFarland.
Zoglin, R. (1985, June 24). An outbreak of Rambomania. *Time,* pp. 72–73.

6

The Pride is Back: *RAMBO, MAGNUM, P.I.*, and the Return Trip to Vietnam

Harry W. Haines
Department of Communication Studies, California State University, Sacramento, CA

David Rabe's 1972 play, *Sticks and Bones*, foreshadowed the Vietnam combat veteran's initial postwar fate. Manipulating the familiar symbols of television situation comedy, Rabe focused directly on the returning soldier as pariah. Three members of a stereotypical family (Ozzie, Harriet, and Ricky) convince David, a Vietnam veteran, to commit suicide, to omit himself as a destabilizing reminder of the war's shattering effects on the national story. But David "only nearly dies," and the play's final scene reduces his presence to an extreme close-up of his face, projected on a color slide. Identified as "somebody sick," the projected image signifies both David's removal from discourse and the veteran's decontextualized maladjustment. The veteran "dies" in the sense that he no longer speaks, although Rabe's play also foreshadows the actual suicides attempted at the Vietnam Veterans Memorial almost 15 years later. Silenced, David's troublesome memories become products of his own psychosis, disconnected from any sociological or political realities. He stops conjuring up the image of his Vietnamese lover referred to by Ozzie as "some yellow fucking whore." More important, he stops identifying the ideological contradictions of American policy (see Chapter 1, this volume).

Sticks and Bones locates the combat veteran's peculiar anthropological knowledge of Vietnam—his knowledge of the foreign Other—specifically in the breakdown of administrative explanations of the war. The veteran's radical political potential resides in the self-reflexive position as participant-observer in a lived ideological crisis, the only context within which to understand David's behavior and speech. David's speech implies a critique of military containment, the anticommunist policy operationalized so disastrously in Vietnam (Gibson, 1986). Rabe's play claims legitimacy for the combat veteran's antiwar or oppositional voice by linking the family's internal conflicts to the hypocrisy of American foreign policy. Ozzie rebukes David for showing a "home movie" of war atrocities "so you can bring them home like this house is a meat house." Harriet explains that David simply wants "to speak to those he loves," and David responds:

> Yes! That's right; yes. What I mean is, yes, of course, that's what I am—a young . . . blind man in a room . . . in a house in the dark, raising nothing in a gesture of meaning toward two voices who are not speaking . . . of a certain . . . incredible . . . connection! (Rabe, 1972, p. 38)

David is silenced not only because his speech threatens the complacency of the situation comedy family, but also because he presumes to identify ideological contradictions. The play is politically volatile because it challenges "official" explanations of the war generated by administrative power, or what Gramsci (1971) defines as the "historical block" (p. 377). Rabe positions the Vietnam veteran as a sign of ideological contradictions. Significantly, CBS cancelled and then rescheduled a televised adaptation of *Sticks and Bones* when the original broadcast time coincided with the 1972 release and homecoming of American prisoners of war (Kolin, 1988). The CBS decision focused explicitly on the appropriate representation of the Vietnam veteran. Rabe's play interpreted the veteran's social experience in terms inconsistent with the conventional view of the POW as an heroic figure whose sacrifice was rational and necessary (see Chapter 1, this volume). Rabe's play demonstrates an explicit challenge to the political limitations revealed by the CBS decision. *Sticks and Bones* struggles against the process whereby the Vietnam War experience is defined by administrative power as "a noble cause" gone awry, a war justified by traditional American values. David understands that the structural and historical relationships that produced his dysfunctional and politically numbed family also produced the ideological crisis of the Vietnam War.[1]

Rabe predicted in 1972 the price that combat veterans would pay once the nation entered its "trance of collective amnesia" (Butterfield, 1983, p. 8), forcing the lived experience of Vietnam combat veterans into a politically safe black hole. Al Santoli (1981), a Vietnam veteran, recalls: "Before I went over, I knew a couple of friends who came back. And

[1] Rabe served in an Army medical unit in Vietnam from February of 1966 to January of 1967. He recalls: "When I first came home . . . I found that not just my family but *nobody* wanted to hear about what actually happened over there. People were only interested in the debate on the war, not the war itself, or any evidence of it" (Brockway, 1972). Kolin (1988, pp. 29–43) provides a stage history of *Sticks and Bones*.

when I came back I ended up the same way. Almost mute" (p. 132). The national attempt to forget Vietnam positioned veterans as a nondiscursive segment of society. Removed from discourse, the combat veteran was simultaneously removed from politics where his presence was potentially more volatile and less manageable than that of previous war veterans (see Chapter 8, this volume).

Symbolically, the image of the veteran had far less political currency than the image of the veteran in other wars (Ehrenhaus, 1986, 1987). We should remember that while the returning soldiers experienced no homecoming parades, neither were they helped by the war managers, the politicians, or the antiwar activists who had used them as political symbols throughout the war. No longer usable in the postwar period, the combat veteran was abandoned by hawk and dove alike. Vague administrative messages of the veteran's special "burden" and "inner conflict" (Carter, 1982, p. 1268) substituted for recognition of what Lloyd Lewis (1982) identifies as the veteran's experience of a shattered belief system in Vietnam, the sociological explanation of what Hellmann (1986) describes as a loss of national myths. Media representations of the veteran's special "burden" developed the image of troubled victim or violent psychotic, variations on the theme of repression (Berg, 1986; see also Chapters 5 & 7, this volume). The Vietnam combat veteran's lived social role developed as the embodiment of contradictions, demonstrated by the narrow range of representation in cultural forms, which required him to adapt to the repression of ideological crisis by remaining silent about the war.

Quite suddenly in the mid-1980s, cultural forms offered the combat veteran a new role. Mass media representations of the veteran's combat experience sent him on a series of imagined "return trips" to Vietnam, enacted in films and television series. Encouraged by media events surrounding the televised introduction of the Vietnam Veterans Memorial, representations of the "return trip" interpreted the veteran's initial removal from discourse as a social effect of postwar conditions, mysteriously disconnected from the combat experience itself. The combat veteran reemerged as a politically potent symbol, usable in the reconstruction of consensus. The veteran silenced in *Sticks and Bones* regains limited power of speech in *Rambo: First Blood, Part II*, Sylvester Stallone's 1985 sequel to the film adaptation of David Morrell's (1972) adventure novel in which Vietnam veteran John Rambo obliterates an American town. *First Blood* "touched a nerve with audiences in the summer of 1982" (Broeske, 1985, p. 32), and encouraged the production of a sequel that might explore Rambo's anger more fully.

This chapter examines the ideological significance of *Rambo* as an important interpretation of the Vietnam War's meaning and of the combat veteran's role in postwar society. Additionally, this chapter looks at the "return trip" as it appears in an important two-part episode of *Magnum, P.I.*, a crime-adventure television series focused on a Vietnam veteran's postwar life. To understand the pivotal position of the "return trip" in the ideological struggle to assign meaning to the Vietnam War, it is useful to locate *Rambo* and *Magnum, P.I.* in the broader context of the war's lived social drama.

THE VIETNAM WAR AS A SOCIAL DRAMA

Anthropologist Victor Turner (1982) explains the ritualistic enactment of "social dramas" through four phases: breach, crisis, redressive, and reintegrative. The concept of social drama provides a way of thinking about and describing how societies represent their ideological struggles within the rituals enacted by cultural forms (dance, religion, etc.). Although Turner focused on less technological societies than our own, his concept is especially useful in examining the ways in which mass media assign meaning to ideologically contested events, such as the Vietnam War. The concept of dramatistic enactment, a ritualized form of conflict management in which cultural forms process the meaning of events in ways consistent with the continuing national story, implies ideological struggle to the extent that disputes are resolved in somebody's interest, an interest that reflects a coherent and hierarchical world view.

A social drama originates in the interruption of "norm-governed social life," or a "breach," and proceeds to the "crisis" stage when the community splits "into contending factions and coalitions" (Turner, 1982, p. 92). The Vietnam War rendered problematic an array of interrelated salient relationships. Both the nature of the breach and the ensuing crisis developed as matters of vitriolic dispute, prompting the curious argument that Americans are now incapable of learning anything from the experience (Fromkin & Chace, 1985). Nothing less than our sense of national identity—how, and in whose interest, to define "America"—emerged as the objective of ideological struggle, demonstrating Hall's (1985) observation that no "guarantees" exist as ideas "fracture along certain lines and in certain directions" (p. 94; see also Gramsci, 1971, p. 327). As the oral histories now suggest, many combat soldiers experienced the crisis phase in the "lie" of Vietnam:

> Vietnam taught you to be a liar. To be a thief. To be dishonest. To go against everything you ever learned. It taught you everything you did not need to know, because you were livin' a lie. And the lie was you ain't have no business bein' there in the first place. You wasn't here for democ-

racy. You wasn't protecting your homeland. And that was what wear you down. (Terry, 1984, p. 133)

Despite the connotations of remedy and compensation, Vietnam's redressive phase developed as an extraordinarily painful social experience, profoundly influencing the postwar position of combat veterans. A broad range of publicly performed rituals, experienced as mass media representations, suggested Turner's (1982) use of "sacrifice, literal and moral," as the central metaphor of the "adjustive" redress (p. 71). For example, the publication of the *Pentagon Papers,* the forced resignation of President Nixon, the public humiliation of administrative power in the Watergate hearings, the passage of the War Powers Resolution, and the swift, ignominious collapse of South Vietnam all contained elements of ritual sacrifice for the "sin" (or ideological contradictions) of Vietnam. The redressive phase coalesced in the silence ritualized by Rabe's (1972) bitter play. For example, Ozzie, who is "possessed with astonished loathing," slaps David and tells him:

> You did what you did and I was no part of it. You understand me? I don't want to hear anymore about her [David's Vietnamese lover]! Look at him. Sitting there. Listening. I'm tired of hearing you, Dave. You understand that? I'm tired of hearing you and your cry-baby voice and your cry-baby stories. And your cry-baby slobbering and you—LOOK . . . AT . . . HIM! YOU MAKE ME WANT TO VOMIT! (p. 48)

In another section of the play Harriet actually *does* vomit after learning that David had a Vietnamese lover and risked the birth of what Ozzie calls "little bitty yellow puffy creatures for our grandchildren." David's darkly humorous role as a quintessential pain-in-the-ass rests on his challenge to the family's racism and commitment to Cold War bromides.

Sticks and Bones and the poetry of antiwar Vietnam combat veterans (Rottmann, Barry, & Paquet, 1972; Barry & Ehrhart, 1976) bear witness to the sacrificial nature of the redressive stage, at least as it was experienced by many Americans (see Chapter 4, this volume). In the redressive phase, the soldier's lived ideological crisis recedes into the background like a fade-out in a silent movie. American cultural forms, unaccustomed to a rhetoric of defeat, employed a rhetoric of avoidance that associated further explanation of the war with unnecessary debate (Karnow, 1984). Adjustive mechanisms mystify the war, strategically forgetting or, at best, psychologizing the men who fought and sacrificed. It is here in the redressive phase of the social drama, and not on the battlefield, that American society "abandons" the combat veteran, demonstrated by the failure to process his lived social experience of ideological crisis adequately (Berg, 1986; Clark, 1986; Ehrenhaus, 1987). Most important, cultural forms, including the political speech, fail to assign a meaning to the war dead consistent with the national story.

The Vietnam Veterans Memorial in Washington, D.C. signifies a return of the repressed to discursive practice and the movement of the social drama into its final, so-called "reintegrative" phase in which the wounds of Vietnam are healed (see Ehrenhaus, 1987, 1988; and Chapter 10, this volume). The reintegrative phase originates in the attempt to assign meaning to the sacrifice of American lives in Vietnam, a process inspired in this instance by Vietnam combat veterans (Scruggs & Swerdlow, 1985). Providing a site for the ritualized enactment of complex relationships among pilgrims and casualties, the Memorial also develops as a politically volatile sign of the citizen's relationship to others and to the state (Ehrenhaus, 1988) and does not, as Griswold (1986) incorrectly argues, "separate war and politics" (p. 55). On the contrary, the Memorial emerges as a locus of ideological struggle (see Chapter 10, this volume), revealing the political nature of the reintegrative phase. As Kaplan (1987) observes in his recent review of newly published analyses of the war, "what we choose to remember, and how, is part of the process by which we become what we are" (p. 29; see also Hammer, 1987; Hung & Schecter, 1987). The reintegrative phase is characterized by ideological struggle to assign particular meanings to the Vietnam War experience and thereby to interpret the war in ways consistent with particular visions of the "nation" (Hall, 1988) and its proper role.

THE PRIDE IS BACK

The Memorial punctures the silence of the redressive phase and, by giving the combat veteran an opportunity to speak, generates a new symbolic field for media representations of the war. Paralleling the healing rituals observed at the Memorial, mass media attempt the reintegration of the Vietnam War experience into the continuing American story. But the combat veteran returns to discourse in a revisionist period, as evidenced on several fronts. For example, elite policy-planning organizations,[2] fearing a loss of American global power, develop a research agenda and propaganda strategy aimed at reasserting the failed policy of military containment (Peschek, 1987), a project anticipated by right-

[2] Peschek (1987) discusses the strategies of the Brookings Institution, Trilateral Commission, American Enterprise Institute, Heritage Foundation, and Institute for Contemporary Studies.

wing polemicists (Lewy, 1978; Berger, 1980; Podhoretz, 1983). The news media undergo a kind of organizational and ideological adjustment to what Hallin (1986) describes as "the new patriotism" of the Reagan era. Managers reassert their dominance in news organizations (Boylan, 1986), restoring order among young reporters "radicalized" by the Vietnam experience. Network television news, identifying itself with a "new national mood," helps generate an emerging consensus, which Hallin (1986) calls the "We're Number One" theme, also used in advertising.

In 1985, for example, the Chrysler Corporation Plymouth division deployed an extensive campaign around the slogans "The Pride is Back" and "Born in America"—both suggesting and misunderstanding Bruce Springsteen's recording "Born in the USA." Aimed at Japanese imports, the advertisement also suggested that Chrysler, like the rest of the country, was undergoing regeneration and a return to basic values; its advertising copy took the form of a political manifesto: "The Pride is back. The confidence in America is back. The good feeling about what we can accomplish is back" ("The Pride," 1985). The three-page color fold-out advertisement appeared in nationally distributed magazines and included a celebratory collage of pluralist ideology. The images are classic representations of American nationalism, not unusual in advertising. Their significance emerges in their widespread dispersal throughout the Spring of 1985. The development of the Vietnam veteran as a warrior hero (see Chapter 5, in this volume) thus occurs within a field of representation dominated by the signs of nationalism and the memory of social relationships that predate the Vietnam War.

New York City's homecoming parade (May 7, 1985), which preceded *Rambo*'s wide release by just 15 days, solidifies the Vietnam combat veteran's position within the reintegrative phase of the social drama. "Disciplinary power" (Foucault, 1979, p. 187) produces the veteran on Broadway, imposing his "compulsory visibility" as a World War II memory. While the Chrysler advertisement repositions the American-made automobile within a system of reimagined social relationships, reports from New York reposition the Vietnam veteran in the reenactment of V-J Day, prompting Michael Clark (1986) to observe that "the curiously perverse occasion of a decade-old defeat lent the festivities an air of historical surrealism" (p. 47).

The revisionist strategy that "hails" (Althusser, 1971) the Vietnam veteran as a hero—every bit as "good" as a World War II veteran—of course subsumes the lived experience of ideological crisis, giving meaning to the war dead, without questioning the specific context of their sacrifice, and serving the political interests of those who support the "domino theory" and its response—containment policy (see Chapter 3,

this volume). The revisionist strategy "contains" the Vietnam War dead in the memory of World War II. Simultaneously, this strategy "contains" the veteran's oppositional voice. For example, an Associated Press report reveals what Foucault (1979) calls "the power of normalization," imposing homogeneity on the Vietnam War experience, while individualizing the veteran, "making it possible to measure gaps" between normalized and unnormalized individuals, "rendering the difference [politically] useful" by marginalizing the opposition (p. 184). The revisionist strategy includes a therapeutic component. It offers the Vietnam veteran the opportunity to reenter public discourse through ritualized recognition of sacrifice, but only if the veteran poses as a World War II participant. Veterans who refuse this role are not merely bitter. By their own choice they remain "burdened" by the war. The report ("Belated welcome," 1985), part of the emerging revisionist consensus that sets the stage for *Rambo*, identifies opposition as "bitterness," unreasonable criticism of the clearly therapeutic positioning of the veteran, a stubborn unwillingness to put the war behind us: "Jerry White, 35, of Manhattan, a former Marine who said he served in Vietnam '13 months, 23 days and 6 hours,' agreed" with New York Mayor Ed Koch's statement that the parade should have come several years earlier "and was bitter that the nation's approval was so long in coming." The veteran "did not march, saying he came out of respect for those who died." " 'I don't consider this a thank you and it's not a parade. It's just a mob, it's more like a political convention or something. Ten years is too late for anything,' he said" (p. 2).

In the reintegrative phase of the social drama, cultural forms provide the veteran a measure of political rehabilitation, contingent on his acceptance of the offered role. Oppositional veterans identify the revisionist strategy as the "Honor the Vietnam Vet Movement," originating in a 1973 New York City parade sponsored by the Department of Defense (Delano, 1987, p. 11). The strategy's therapeutic nature is suggested in the reaction of a Home Box Office (HBO) representative to a telephone inquiry about the distribution of funds raised by an HBO produced "Superstar Tribute to Welcome Home Vietnam Veterans," an edited cable television version of a July 1987 Washington gala. The HBO representative "brushed off [the] question and ended up attacking [the caller] as another ungrateful Vietnam vet. 'That's the trouble with you guys. You're so cynical you don't know how to let someone help you' " (Delano, 1987, p. 12).

Given the therapeutic nature of the revisionist strategy, oppositional veterans are easily contained as unreasonable, stubbornly unrehabilitated malcontents. The oppositional voice is especially vulnerable to Ozzie's accusation of "cry-baby" since it necessarily declines the role of warrior hero, as in W.D. Ehrhart's (1986) response to the 1985 homecoming parade:

ten, fifteen, twenty years
too late for kids not twenty
years old and dead in ricefields
brain-dead, soul-dead, half-dead
wheelchairs; afraid to share,
afraid to sleep, afraid of trees,
and alien, invisible; forgotten;
even the unmarked forever AWOL.
You'd think that any self-respecting
vet would give the middle-finger
to folks who thought of it
ten years and more too late—
yet there they were: the sad
survivors, balding, overweight
and full of beer, weeping, grateful
for their hour come round at last.

Ehrhart, a Marine combat veteran, laments the historical moment within the reintegrative phase in which the Vietnam veteran is "subjected, used, transformed and improved" (Foucault, 1979, p. 136) through disciplinary and therapeutic measures. *Rambo* and *Magnum, P.I.* deploy the strategy more widely.

THE RETURN TRIP AS REINTEGRATIVE

In the reintegrative phase of the Vietnam War's social drama, media representations move beyond themes of repression and focus instead on the veteran's abandonment. Participating in the rituals of reintegration originating at the Vietnam Veterans Memorial, film and television enact the war's meaning in a series of "return trips" to Vietnam by combat veterans on unfinished business. These return trips interpret the veteran's initial removal from discourse as part of the war experience itself, not as a social effect of postwar conditions. They enact the veteran's initial role of pariah while simultaneously contributing to the historical revision of the Vietnam crisis. The combat veteran reemerges as a political symbol, usable in the reconstruction of consensus and consistent with other ideological adjustments evident throughout mass media. Just as the 1985 Chrysler advertisement proclaims "the pride is back" in American automobile manufacturing, *Rambo* proclaims a regeneration of pride in the Vietnam combat veteran and—like the New York City homecoming parade—hails him as a warrior hero.

By removing the Vietnam War experience from a temporal and historical context, *Rambo* (and films like it) functions ritualistically to offer the combat veteran a measure of social reincorporation without the necessity of examining his lived social experience of ideological crisis. By providing a "dramatization of victory in Vietnam" (Hoberman, 1986, p. 44), *Rambo* supplants one postwar denial with another; nonrecognition of the war changes to nonrecognition of defeat. The combat veteran reemerges as a speaking person within a narrowly defined discourse of inexplicable abandonment, underscored by John Rambo's climactic speech: "I want what they want," Rambo says, referring to the POWs he has released. "And what every other guy wants—for our country to love us as much as we love it. That's what I want." Less than two weeks after its release (May 22, 1985), *Rambo* generated a debate over "fascist aesthetics."[3] Denby (1985) suggested "it's possible we're seeing the stirrings of incipient fascism," an American variation of paranoia, military fantasy, and pathological individualism (p. 10). Wood (1986) described film trends as "entertainment that a culture ready for fascism might be expected to enjoy" (p. 41).

A structuralist position emerged, and Pally (1986) linked *Rambo* and other movies in the return trip cycle to the film industry's ideological adjustment to Reagan foreign policy and to a new sense of militarism (p. 33). Pally also saw the adjustment as a marketing response to a "crisis in self-image," insisting that "any ad exec could've told you back in 1980 that this was the way the media would go" (p. 33). Jeffords (1986) focused on industrial sources (the Cannon Group, Golan-Globus) of films in the return trip cycle and stressed *Rambo*'s Vietnam victory as "a reaffirmation of the American male and the values of masculine war experience"—all geared to prepare Americans for the next war (p. 188; see also Chapter 7, in this volume).

Rambo's popularity does not signify a fascist political movement but, rather, a "cult of domination" (Egendorf, 1985, p. 282) organized

[3] Pally (1986) places *Rambo* in a genre including *Red Dawn, Invasion U.S.A., Eleni,* and *Rocky IV*. Jeffords (1986) includes *Rambo* among *Red Dawn, Uncommon Valor, Missing in Action, I* and *II,* and *The Killing Fields*. Pally stresses simplistic anticommunism, and Jeffords stresses antifeminism as major ideological characteristics identifying the genre. Several critics (e.g., Sarris, 1985; Kaul, 1985; Kauffmann, 1985) focus on the "heart of darkness" theme developed in *Apocalypse Now*. Crook (1985) concludes that "*Rambo* is the darkness itself, unilluminated and unilluminating, a pathos of what might have been" (p. 10E). *Rambo* opened on May 22, 1985, in a record-setting 2,074 theaters, and the film's total domestic gross surpassed $260 million. The film achieved international success, including a favorable review in *People's Daily* (Wimmer, 1986). In America, the May release date helped assure a strong competitive position in the mix of youth-oriented films. *Rambo*'s debut came less than one month after several network television specials and other media events marked the 10th anniversary of the war's end.

around media consumption and fired, at least in part, by a hostile reaction to feminism (Jeffords, 1986). This is not the first time that American films have demonstrated alignment with identifiably fascist qualities (Hoberman, 1986); nor are the return trip movies the first Vietnam War films discussed in terms of a fascist aesthetic (Wander, 1983). Although the introduction of fascist themes in postwar films warrants explanation, this critical emphasis tends to shift attention away from what these films facilitate. The important question here is not *Rambo*'s fascist qualities, but how the film uses the veteran's estrangement.

ESTRANGEMENT

Administrative reluctance to recognize widespread readjustment problems (Keller & Atchison, 1984) solidified the veteran's political and social isolation during the redressive phase of the social drama. As Lewis (1982) shows, American soldiers experienced a disconfirmation of meaning in Vietnam, forcing them to construct an entirely new "cognitive map" to explain why Americans fought wars. Vietnam provided a social context in which "the final repository of meaning and value became sheer physical survival" (p. 160), making Vietnam different from other American wars in the crucial sense that ideological explanations and belief systems collapsed. Reports indicate that veterans of the Soviet war in Afghanistan occupy a similar position and are called "Afghansti" in the Soviet press, recalling Lifton's (1973) very early identification of a "counterfeit-reality" among American troops in Vietnam. Lewis (1982) explains the veteran's postwar isolation in terms of social reference group theory, concluding that "nonrecognition devalued the Vietnam War identities to which the vets were habituated" (p. 227). The soldier's sense making required for physical survival prepared him for a postwar identity crisis in which the construction of "self" became problematic, prompting Egendorf's (1985) estimation of a "subclinical malaise" affecting as many as two million veterans (p. 36). The lived experience of ideological crisis left the combat veteran extraordinarily vulnerable as a sign of loss, not merely the loss of Vietnam but also the loss of the American "story." The war produced the combat veteran as a continuing, tramatizing social effect, necessarily avoided by political strategists attempting to reconstruct the consensus shattered by the war.

In the reintegrative phase, the combat veteran returns to public discourse, but the specific conditions of revisionism inscribe his postwar identity, which is made necessary by virtue of his otherwise anomalous ideological position. The strategy submerges Vietnam's ideological contradictions and provides a therapeutic position for the veteran, whose

reintegration becomes contingent on the *source* of his estrangement. The ritualized return trip is not "about" Vietnam; it is about the veteran's postwar struggle to reenter civilian life.

Rambo gives expression to the veteran's discontent while decontextualizing its origin. John Rambo's sense of betrayal goes beyond a mere "stab in the back, self- pitying alibi" (Sarris, 1985, pp. 38–39). More than any film in the return trip cycle, *Rambo* represents an intense, pathological estrangement[4] from American society, prompting Hallin (1986) to suggest that Rambo represents a "significant break" from characters in earlier war films: "The machismo of John Wayne was always bounded by a sense of connection to a human culture—usually symbolized by the nuclear family Wayne could not be a part of—and an ideological vision of political order. Rambo's violence is profoundly antisocial" (p. 22).

Imprisoned for his single-handed destruction of an American town (in the 1982 film, *First Blood*), Rambo wins release from a rockpile when an unspecified Congressional committee returns him to Vietnam on a secret mission. Murdock, a representative of American interests, which presumably "lost the war," instructs Rambo to photograph an alleged POW camp where sadistic Vietnamese and Russian troops keep American captives. The POWs work as slaves, moving from one isolated area to another. The film explains that American authorities know about the POWs but do nothing to rescue them. The Vietnamese keep the Americans as slaves because the American government reneged on President Nixon's secret agreement to provide war reparations. During the war Rambo had escaped from this camp, a point that explains his familiarity with the jungle terrain and provides an additional element of retribu-

---

[4] Parodies of *Rambo* focus on estrangement. As the 1985 deer season opened, cartoonist Dan Piararo's *Bizarro* feature included "Bambo: First Fawn, Part II, Chapter III, Book IV, Verse V, Stanza VI, Paragraph VII, Line VIII." An enraged Bambo stands in a forest fire and holds a meanacing club. "Finally," the caption reads, "violence the whole family can feel *good* about!" Mimi Cotter (1985) imagines "Rambo: The Formative Years," and social isolation results from his violence and narcissism well before his graduation from G. Gordon Liddy High School. Jaroslovsky (1987) reports a joke circulating in Washington, D.C., which places the Iran-Contra arms deal in the context of *Rambo*: "Some wags suggest the ultimate Ronald Reagan movie: *Iranbo*" (p. 1). Bjerager (1987) reported that a response to *Rambo* apparently inspired the development of "the Danish Underground Consortium," young persons who "try to make the place less boring" by enacting various dramatistic events, including a mock Indian raid on a railway station." Bjerager also reports that "the 200 or so members of the underground consortium can't say exactly how it emerged. All they recall is that its first escapade was carried out one August night by two young Danes at Copenhagen Airport. Stealing through the dark to an airport fence, they cut their way through and sneaked up to the private Boeing 727 of Mr. Stallone, who recently married a Danish woman. Then, in blood-red paint, they labeled Rambo's plane, 'Ho Chi Minh Air' " (p. 1).

tion. When released to the media, the photographs will prove that no POWs exist, thus quieting citizen groups who insist that American prisoners remain in Vietnam (see Chapter 1, this volume).

Returning to the jungle, Rambo ignores orders and rescues the Americans he finds in a bamboo cage. The rescue and subsequent struggle against Vietnamese and Russian troops provide a well-paced, state-of-the-art adventure movie. Rambo's central conflict develops with Murdock, whose decision to "abort the mission" leaves Rambo and a rescued POW atop a hill surrounded by Vietnamese troops. On Murdock's orders, a hovering American helicopter refuses to take them aboard, despite their certain capture. Rambo's decision to free the POW makes the mission too controversial and seals his fate of abandonment—again. The film represents the combat veteran's postwar silencing with a powerful image of abandonment atop a dangerous hill. America betrays Rambo and the POW for purposes of political expediency, verifying what Rambo reveals to indigenous agent Co: "I'm expendable."

Following his capture, Rambo is strung-up and lowered into an open cesspool filled with leeches, and is then tied to a bedspring used by a sadistic Russian who tortures Rambo with electric shocks. Escaping his torturers, Rambo informs Murdock by radio that "I'm coming after *you*!" The film develops as a quest within a quest; Rambo seeks the rescue of American POWs, while he seeks Murdock who remains at a jungle outpost equipped with high technology communication gear, a sign of voyeurism (Wimmer, 1986, p. 8) and decadent authority. The conflict locates Rambo between two threatening polarities: the Vietnamese-Russian pursuers and the ambiguous American bureaucracy. The film represents a brutal configuration of power that attempts to silence and constrain Rambo because the revelation of POWs (Vietnam's "reality") will threaten everyone who holds authority. The film develops a sense of managed affairs in which powerful strategies manipulate Rambo, leaving him no alternative but to function as a mutated World War II hero in an utterly hostile and ahistorical environment.

Rambo's sense of betrayal suggests an undercurrent of opposition, identified in one of the few positive journalistic reactions to the film. Wragg (1985) implies an element of class conflict in *Rambo*: "The Commies are incidental. This movie is about being fed up with the smug bureaucrats, the prep school boys who would use a decent working-class man—use him up, in fact, and then discard the remains." Wragg then suggests an oppositional scenario in which the American troops maintain support for traditional American values—"He's loyal, honest, trustworthy, a Boy Scout with Eagle honors in guerrilla warfare" (p. 14)—while the war managers sell out the war effort as a matter of political expediency, accounting for Rambo's distrust of all authority. Before embarking on the return trip, Rambo asks his former commanding officer, "Do we get to win this time?"

But the film misses its radical potential by reasserting Rambo as a fighting machine (more effective than John Wayne) and by obscuring the lived combat experience of Vietnam by placing it within the conventions of a World War II movie. *Rambo* demonstrates why cultural forms struggle unsuccessfully with Vietnam, why they avoided representing Vietnam combat, and why the single notable exception, *The Green Berets*, lapses into "epistemological drama" (Berg, 1986, p. 111). Vietnam's combat experience was lived by men who often did not picture the enemy as *Rambo* portrays them, by men who learned to distrust authority because power *placed* them in Vietnam, not because power restricted their ability to fight there effectively. *Rambo* coopts Vietnam's radical potential by representing the veteran's distrust of power in terms consistent with potential reassertions of military containment. Like the New York City homecoming parade, *Rambo* offers a therapeutic option, an opportunity to serve power as a sign of an emerging consensus characterizing the reintegrative phase of the social drama. *Rambo* signifies the veteran's political rehabilitation by demonstrating his potential victory—if only the war managers' ideological commitment to containment had not failed. Benjamin (1969) observes that "fascism sees its salvation in giving" the "masses not their right, but instead a chance to express themselves" (p. 241). *Rambo* dislocates the veteran's source of estrangement, while expressing his lost sense of Vietnam War identity. The film helps inscribe a postwar identity consistent with the requirements of revisionist strategies, and this angered oppositional veterans.

The fear that *Rambo* might "glamorize" war for young people, for example, promoted Vietnam veterans to picket the film in several American cities. A Salt Lake City affiliate of Never Again/Vietnam Veterans Peace Action Network picketed a theater showing *Rambo* in August of 1985. The group distributed handbills with the warning, "Don't Be Fooled! This Movie is a Lie!" The handbill also included "An Open Letter to Sylvester Stallone," which asked:

> First, we want to know where you were in 1968 when we needed you. What right do you have to make this kind of movie and allow people of this country who have never been to war to believe that this is how wars are fought?
>
> Many of our brothers went to their graves because they believed that you fought wars the way John Wayne did in his movies. Are you prepared to accept responsibility for the deaths that may happen in future wars as a result of the youths who believe?

The message implies a struggle over rights of ownership of the Vietnam "Story" and the appropriate way to represent lived experience (see Chapter 8, this volume). The group demanded that Stallone donate a certain percentage of the film's profit to help distressed combat veterans and their families. The handbill echoes the war's ideological crisis through its reference to John Wayne, whose image functions more importantly as a sign of political consensus than as a model for actual combat technique. The Vietnam War literature makes numerous references to John Wayne's World War II films as powerful political experiences in the childhood memories of the men who fought in Vietnam. By repudiating John Wayne the group repudiates the political consensus that produced him as a powerful figure, and the group clearly sees *Rambo* as an attempt to reassert that consensus.[5] Additionally, the group responds to the actual emergence in Salt Lake City of a teenage "Rambo" cult. During the first few weeks of the film's release, adolescents wore Rambo costumes and highly accurate Vietnam-era uniforms when they attended the movie. Local theaters showing *Rambo* and other films in the return trip cycle encouraged the development of a cult-following by dressing their male employees in jungle fatigues. Although the practice waned (in part, perhaps, a result of mixed reactions to the costumes by Vietnam veterans attending the films), the phenomenon was not limited to Salt Lake City. Boston and San Antonio SWAT teams responded in the autumn of 1985 to complaints about young men on simulated reconnaissance missions through suburban residential areas.

Although John Rambo makes limited contact with Vietnamese villagers, the film naturalizes the destruction of village life, a painful and controversial aspect of the war's history. In each encounter he is on the run and barely has the chance to outmaneuver his enemies. His contact with villagers develops as accidental collisions, unfortunate encounters between the warrior hero and the village social system. Pursued by Rus-

[5] In February of 1986, Harvard University's Hasty Pudding Theatricals named Stallone "Man of the Year." During the award ceremony about 60 Vietnam veterans (members of the Major General Smedly D. Butler Brigade, a Boston-based unit of Veterans for Peace) demonstrated against recognition of Stallone. The protesters "centered their objections around . . . the *Rambo* movies, which they said demeaned Asians and created a false sense of the Vietnam War" (Haygood, 1986, p. 1). Paul Atwood (personal interview), one of the protesters, said that working-class "street kids" greeted the protesters with a counterdemonstration. A young woman grabbed Atwood's shirt and shouted angrily, "He's my hero!" Atwood recalled that "a young fellow, about 15 years old, stood across the street from us, daring us to fight with him and actually believing that *he* was a badass when *we* were the ones who had done the fighting in Vietnam. It was pathetic, and it was frightening to see these youngsters succumbing to the blandishments of this faker, this man who would have puked his guts out if he had actually experienced the events portrayed in the movie."

sian and Vietnamese troops, Rambo abruptly happens upon the villagers and, through no apparent fault of his, brings destruction and suffering to them, suggesting the well-known remark of an American officer in Vietnam: "We had to destroy the village in order to save it."

In one sequence, Rambo flees through a hillside village and tricks the pursuing troops to follow him into a nearby field of tall, dry grass and bamboo. Here, he traps them with a wall of fire that moves rapidly across the field and chases the troops toward the hillside village. The action develops as a visual reminder of incendiaries, napalm strikes, and self-immolations. The scene suggests Broyles' (1984) widely quoted article in which he celebrates war's erotic appeal and dramatic grandeur, revealing that he "preferred white phosphorus, which exploded with a fulsome elegance, wreathing its target in intense and billowing white smoke" (p. 62). Rambo's fireball culminates in the destruction of the village itself—incinerated by Rambo's well-placed explosive arrow to prevent the enemy troops from reaching safety. Two walls of fire trap Rambo's enemies. The villagers pay the seemingly reasonable price of destruction (the price they were expected to pay by American war managers) for stopping the Vietnamese and Russians—a rational, albeit regrettable, process of war.

And it is precisely here that the film attempts the repositioning of American invincibility and innocence. The viewer is apparently expected to understand this sequence as confirmation of American capability and as a verification of explicable, rational violence—the only position from which Rambo's action makes sense. The villagers remain curiously absent as their homes explode in imagery depicting "the haunting and disturbing beauty of the portrayal of violent action and the ease with which it can be made to appear necessary and natural" (Wander, 1983, p. 71). The film offers a vague suggestion that the villagers may actually approve of Rambo's action, or that they understand the process of war well enough to escape the village before Rambo burns it.

Earlier in the film, as the Vietnamese and Russians chase Rambo into the village, a small boy recognizes the "meaning" of the American's return. The boy runs through the village proclaiming Rambo's presence. An extreme close-up of an old man—whose stereotypical representation suggests "an ancient Chinese" rather than a Vietnamese, thus underscoring the film's pervasive racism—communicates fear, but no one in the village tries to stop Rambo. The sequence implies the villagers' approval of Rambo's destruction of their homes, as if they uncritically accept the reassertion of American pride and its strategy of pacification. (Americans interact similarly with Vietnamese peasants in an episode of the CBS television series *Tour of Duty*. The episode romanticizes the relationship between an American soldier and a member of the National

Liberation Front, a "VC." The relationship unfolds within the context of the strategic hamlet program, a disastrous effort that uprooted millions of villagers in the South, turning them against the Americans and the Saigon government [Gibson, 1986]. The episode shows the relocation as a rational effort that the villagers accept with little dispute.)

Rambo makes additional contact with villagers while he pilots a damaged helicopter filled with freed POWs. His Russian enemy pursues him in a giant, well-armed helicopter. The action suddenly erupts over an isolated village. At first, Rambo refuses to fire at the Russian while the two helicopters fly over the fearful villagers. When the Russian demonstrates his callous disregard for the Vietnamese by firing his guns, Rambo returns a carefully aimed shot that damages a section of the Russian's craft, causing a sheet of armor to fall on the village. The armor bounces on the Vietnamese terrain, threatening the villagers who seek uncertain cover, and it finally smashes a tree, setting it and a nearby home on fire. The brief event occurs within the much longer aerial chase sequence and remains embedded within Rambo's sadomasochistic relationship with the pursuing Russian. The event signifies the veteran's ritualized reintegration by absolving him of responsibility for civilian suffering, which it simultaneously projects upon the hated Russian, who is portrayed in the conventions of a wartime German Nazi. Rambo makes contact with Vietnamese village life in a context of rational, necessary sacrifice—of the villagers.

Rambo's remarkable achievement is not merely the revision of history; the film employs a revised Vietnam experience to dislocate the soldier's loss of cognitive structure, suggesting that all was well until he made the mistake of going home. Rambo's estrangement results not from the ideological crisis of the war's lived experience, but from an inexplicably hostile civilian population. Back in the "world" Rambo experiences "a quiet war, a war against all the soldiers returning." He tells Co, "It's the kinda war you don't win."

Rambo also inverts historical roles. Not only does Rambo "become war," as he says, he becomes the resourceful guerrilla fighter struggling against numerically superior, mechanized forces. Throughout the recurring chase scenes, Vietnamese and Russian forces move in large numbers through the jungle, announcing their presence the way American military units sometimes did in Vietnam. Russian advisors appear as vague recollections of what American advisors sometimes became in Vietnam, and this is even suggested by the Vietnamese-Russian power relations represented in the movie. The Vietnamese defer to Russian leadership on how best to handle Rambo. The revision of history requires an extensive role inversion if John Rambo is to function as a warrior hero. The Vietnam combat veteran is transformed into a Viet Cong guerrilla to communicate the veteran's heroic self- sacrifice and ingenuity. "Born 7-6-1947 in Bowie, Arizona," Rambo's Indian-German descent proves to be "a hellova combination" in outwitting the Vietnamese and Russian troops. His Indian origins enable him to move deftly through the jungle, using the natural environment as a weapon; his German origins explain his superior command of technology and strategy. He tells Murdock, "I always thought the mind was the best weapon."

Rambo's box office success encouraged the appearance of numerous return trip clones throughout the 1985–1986 network television season. The theme worked its way through the crime-adventure genre, especially in series representing the lives of combat veterans. *Matt Helm*, the story of a Vietnam veteran who works as a private detective, included at least one return trip, as did *The A Team*, a series that explicitly represents Vietnam veterans as a marginalized outlaw group. *Miami Vice* reversed the formula by bringing Vietnam's unfinished business to Miami in the form of Southeast Asian drug dealers, intelligence agents, and combat veterans. But in network television, the return trip cycle reached its peak in an ambitious two-part episode in the series *Magnum, P.I.*, "All for One," which aired on CBS during the winter audience sweeps and was seen on January 31 and February 7 of 1985.[6]

MAGNUM'S RETURN

It would be difficult to overestimate the significance of *Magnum, P.I.* within the mass media rituals of the reintegrative phase. The series explores the limits of its genre (Newcomb, 1985) by focusing on the process of recollection. The audience follows the postwar reconstruction of a veteran's identity in the weekly coping of its lead character, Thomas Magnum. Formulated as a "cumulative narrative," *Magnum* is "about" history, and Newcomb concludes that the series is therefore "about Vietnam" (p. 25). The viewer understands that Thomas Magnum attempts to cope with his position in history, his role as a Vietnam combat veteran. Magnum, disillusioned, attempts to make sense of his unspecified war experiences. Magnum is not merely what Fenichell (1983) describes as the well-adjusted veteran; he is the well-adjusted veteran who works at *remaining* adjusted, and the series deploys a therapeutic strategy in which the viewer experiences the inscription of his postwar identity. Magnum's self-reflexive sense making emerges in his continuing

---

[6] *Magnum, P.I.* completed its final network season in 1988. Currently, the series is seen widely in off-network syndication.

voice-over comments on the action. The series psychologizes the Vietnam veteran to the extent that Magnum consciously reflects on the condition of his condition, sharing moments of insight with his buddies, Rick and T.C., who often assist in investigations.

Like Rambo, Magnum is a military outcast, although he maintains unspecified and informal contacts with former colleagues in Naval Intelligence. Magnum's estrangement is less dysfunctional than Rambo's, and his sense of betrayal less specific. Doubtless, the episodic nature of network television and the genre's current focus on humane collectivities (friendship groups organized around work) give Magnum's estrangement a softer, less psychotic edge than Rambo's. Still, Magnum remains curiously isolated and, like Rambo, has no continuing relationships with women (Flitterman, 1985). Somewhere back in Vietnam something snapped, but the series never makes it clear just why Magnum has turned his back on a promising military career. Oddly, the program's final episode (broadcast in May of 1988) concluded the series with Magnum's return to service in Naval Intelligence but provided no clear indication of why Magnum "returned" to the Navy.

In "All for One," Magnum and his buddies return to Southeast Asia, ostensibly to rescue a captured American, but they learn that the mission actually centers on rescuing the "George freakin' Washington of Cambodia," the leader of what eluded American policy makers for a decade: the democratic Third Force. The episode reveals the wartime relationships of Magnum's collectivity and introduces a new character—Tyler Peabody McKinney—who convinces the series characters to go on "one more diddy-bop" before the onset of middle-aged complacency. War emerges as a boyhood game. Tyler's sense of adventure allows Magnum and his friends to pursue a more rational objective: freedom.

Within the episode's framework, freedom emerges as a highly ambiguous value. Tyler admits that he lied about the captured American in order to get Magnum and his buddies to help rescue "the Provisional President of a Confederation of Democratic Resistance Groups," which now fight the Vietnamese and the Khmer Rouge. But Tyler explains his lie in terms of freedom: "I think it's about time we stopped puttin' conditions on the words freedom and commitment. You live 'em or you don't. That's why we're here." The clandestine mission, although conducted by civilians, has the tacit approval of the American government. The subtext of Tyler's explanation suggests a removal of constraints, the "freedom" to do whatever is required to assert American objectives. Like *Rambo,* the episode inverts historical roles by placing the Vietnamese and the Khmer Rouge on the *same side* in Cambodia's continuing war, suggesting the revisionist ploy of associating the Khmer Rouge genocide in Cambodia with the communist victory in Vietnam (Berger, 1980). The Vietnamese occupation of Cambodia, a result of complex political, military, and ideological struggle (Chanda, 1986), is reduced to one explanation: The Vietnamese force the Cambodians to cultivate poppies as a cash crop. The Vietnamese use poppies to produce opium, a source of international currency, presumably American dollars. The Provisional President reinforces Tyler's use of "freedom" as a euphemism for military containment, and he explains to Magnum why Tyler's lie was necessary:

President: But the lying itself was based on a truth. And I think that that truth is one that you and he and your friends ultimately share.
Magnum: What truth is that?
President: The most basic one of them all. The belief in freedom. Sometimes I think people just have to be reminded of it. And sometimes it doesn't particularly matter how. Thank you.

The President cannot be understood as representing anything remotely similar to an actual political faction in Cambodia's recent history (Gordon, 1986; Porter, 1988). Nor does his Confederation mirror any actual group that existed during the war except, perhaps, in the wishful dreams of American policy makers. But, of course, the character has less to do with generating authenticity than with facilitating the veteran's role as warrior hero and providing a rationale for American sacrifices consistent with the needs of anticommunism. The character demonstrates the surrealism required by cultural forms to represent the Vietnam combat veteran within the ideological framework of revisionism. Here, the "comedy of public safety," as Marc (1984, pp. 56–98) calls the crime-adventure genre, explicitly transposes "lie" with "truth" to generate agreement on the war's heroic nature. The "lie" of Vietnam—the soldier's experience of ideological crisis—rises up as the "truth" of freedom, if Magnum will only fill his proper role.

Magnum and his buddies rescue the Cambodian democrat and then aid Cambodian villagers in a climactic shoot-out with the Vietnamese. Throughout the two-part episode, an undercurrent of conflict develops between Tyler and Magnum. Tyler's recklessness during the Vietnam War resulted in the loss of several Americans in fighting at a place called Cam Lai. The village name alludes to Cam Ne, where a CBS film crew and correspondent Morely Safer showed American troops burning villagers' homes, the so-called "Zippo-lighter story." It also alludes to the village of My Lai, where American troops massacred Vietnamese civilians. At Cam Lai, the Vietnamese forces were led by the very officer who now pursues the returning Americans, and who also assures that oppressed Cambodians will continue cultivating poppies. "All for One" develops as a story of revenge and atonement, as Tyler seeks to pay back the Vietnamese. In the shoot-out, the Vietnamese officer tosses a grenade at two Cambodian children to deflect attention from himself, and Tyler makes the ultimate sacrifice to save them. Magnum, forced to support "freedom" by Tyler's heroic act, guns down the Vietnamese.

Tyler's heroic self-sacrifice expiates the worst memory of the war, the killing of noncombatants, and rationalizes the purpose of American policy. Americans died for freedom and to prevent Vietnamese soldiers from performing heinous acts against civilians. Tyler's death reduces the contradictions of American policy to a matter of tactics, a position similar to Lewy's (1978) argument that the Vietnam War represents no significant departure from the general rules of war or from the specific American experience of modern warfare. Rather than questioning the efficacy of military containment, the return trip represents the policy as a misapplication, an interpretation similar to the current tactical analysis (Summers, 1982) presented at the United States War College. Tyler atones for a tactical error, not for structural contradictions inherent to the intervention. Containment remains viable.

In *Magnum, P.I.*, the war's meaning is explorable but, in the end, inexplicable. Like Rambo, Magnum provides a concluding statement intended to frame the action and conflict within the veteran's need for therapeutic self-discipline. Returning to Hawaii, Magnum and his friends walk along the beach, sharing the problems they must solve as a result of their absence. Rick, his arm in a sling, stands with the Pacific as a backdrop, and asks: "What if we hadn't o' gone?" Viewers familiar with the series understand that Rick's question refers not only to the recent return trip, but also to the broader issue of the Vietnam War itself. Magnum and the other characters stop and remain silent for several seconds until Magnum provides an answer: "We did." Like *Rambo*, the episode decontextualizes the veteran's experience while expressing his estrangement and hailing his commitment to a generalized, ahistorical "freedom," as Magnum reveals in his closing voice-over narration: "We wound up going to Cham Kur and Bang Lai for that most basic truth. Freedom. But did Tyler? I don't know. Ultimately, it didn't matter. What mattered was we were faithful to that truth. And so was Tyler Peabody McKinney." What matters is the veteran's action based on his internalized commitment to the truth of freedom; Vietnam's meaning resides in the imagined history of the veteran, which displaces the history of the war.

CONCLUSION

The return trip suggests the reintegration of the combat veteran and closure to the war—in terms of rational sacrifice and necessary violence. David, the silenced combat veteran of *Sticks and Bones*, may now speak, but with a voice constrained by therapeutic measures. Developing first as the anomaly in the postwar strategy of silence, the combat veteran is now submerged in the images of former wars. In film and television the return trip provides a glimpse of what the Vietnam Veterans Memorial might have been if revisionism had prevailed in the cultural form of public architecture (see Chapter 10, this volume).

The themes of revenge and atonement converge on the object of quest in the return trip to Vietnam. The mission to free imagined POWs demonstrates a sense of loss and anger, the only reference in the cycle to a shattered national mythology. The postwar abandonment of the combat veteran is projected back upon the experience of the war itself, and we ritualistically seek him in bamboo cages. The abandonment of the veteran is represented as a malevolent bureaucratic effect. In these scenarios the veteran's reintegration depends on his position as a sign of consensus, indicating the political nature of the social drama's reintegrative phase. The combat experience of Vietnam is transformed into a World War II pose, the price of the veteran's ideological cleansing, his political rehabilitation.

The silenced protagonist in David Rabe's *Sticks and Bones* might have expected more, and he surely deserved better. Cultural forms return him to discourse in representations that constrain his speech in terms of former wars, a strategy that rationalizes loss and explains his abandonment in terms consistent with a revised history of the war. No longer the pariah, the veteran emerges in these representations as a sign of anticommunist consensus, available for use.

REFERENCES

Althusser, L. (1971). *Lenin and philosophy and other essays* (B. Brewster, Trans.). London: New Left.

Barry, J., & Ehrhart, W. (Eds.). (1976). *Demilitarized zones: Veterans after Vietnam*. Perkasie, PA: East River Anthology.

Belated welcome home lauds Vietnam vets. (1985, May 8). *Salt Lake Tribune*, pp. 1–2.

Benjamin, W. (1969). In H. Arendt (Ed.), *Illuminations*. H. Zohn (Trans.). New York: Shocken.

Berg, R. (1986). Losing Vietnam: covering the war in an age of technology. *Cultural Critique*, 3, 92–125.

Berger, P. (1980, February). Indochina & the American conscience. *Commentary*, pp. 29–39.

Bjerager, E. (1987, January 2). Is Denmark dull? Maybe, but a beacon of hope now shines. *The Wall Street Journal*, pp. 1, 10.

Boylan, J. (1986, November/December). Declarations of independence. *Columbia Journalism Review*, pp. 29–45.

Brockway, J. (1972, August). Defining the event for myself. *After Dark*, *5*, 56–57.

Broeske, P. (1985, October 27). The curious evolution of John Rambo. ("Calendar section). *The Los Angeles Times*, pp. 32–38.

Broyles, W. (1984, November). Why men love war. *Esquire*, pp. 55–65.

Butterfield, F. (1983, February 13). The new Vietnam scholarship. *The New York Times Magazine*, pp. 26–32.

Carter, J. (1982). *Public papers of the presidents of the United States: Jimmy Carter 1980–81* (Vol. 2). Washington, DC: GPO.

Chanda, N. (1986). *Brother enemy: The war after the war*. New York: Harcourt Brace Jovanovich.

Clark, M. (1986). Remembering Vietnam. *Cultural Critique*, *3*, 46–78.

Cotter, M. (1985, December 23–30). Rambo: The formative years. *People*, pp. 50–52.

Crook, D. (1985, August 25). Stallone's 'Rambo' denies horror that 'Apocalypse' illuminates. *Salt Lake Tribune*, p. 10E.

Delano, S. (1987, August). The latest production of the "honor the vet movement." *Nothing to lose* (pp. 11–16). New York: Vietnam Veterans United to Prevent World War III.

Denby, D. (1985, June 3). Blood simple. *New York*, pp. 72–73.

Egendorf, A. (1985). *Healing from the war: Trauma and transformation after Vietnam*. Boston: Houghton Mifflin.

Ehrenhaus, P. (1986, November). *On not commemorating Vietnam: Problems in the celebration of failure*. Paper presented at the annual meeting of the Speech Communication Association, Chicago, IL.

Ehrenhaus, P. (1987, November). *On Americans held prisoner in Southeast Asia: The POW issue as hostage of American foreign policy*. Paper presented at the annual meeting of the Speech Communication Association, Boston, MA.

Ehrenhaus, P. (1988). Silence and symbolic expression. *Communication Monographs*, *55*, 41–57.

Ehrhart, W. (1986). Parade rest. *Cultural Critique*, *3*, 44–45.

Fenichell, S. (1983, September/October). Prime time's Vietnam vets. *Channels of Communications*, p. 59.

Flitterman, S. (1985). Thighs and wiskers: The fascination of *Magnum, P.I. Screen*, *26*, 42–58.

Foucault, M. (1979). *Discipline and Punishment: The birth of the prison*. New York: Vintage.

Fromkin, D., & Chace, J. (1985). What *are* the lessons of Vietnam? *Foreign Affairs*, *63*, 722–746.

Gibson, J. (1986). *The perfect war: Technowar in Vietnam*. Boston: The Atlantic Monthly Press.

Gordon, B. (1986). The third Indochina conflict. *Foreign Affairs*, *64*, 66–85.

Gramsci, A. (1971). *Selections from the prison notebooks*. Q. Hoare & G. Smith (Eds. & Trans.). New York: International.

Griswold, C. (1986). The Vietnam veterans memorial and the Washington mall: Philosophical thoughts on political iconography. *Critical Inquiry, 12,* 686–719.

Hall, S. (1985). Signification, representation, ideology: Althusser and the post-structuralist debates. *Critical Studies in Mass Communication, 2,* 91–114.

Hall, S. (1988). The toad in the garden: Thatcherism among the theorists. In C. Nelson & L. Grossberg (Eds.), *Marxism and the interpretation of culture* (pp. 35–73). Urbana, IL: University of Illinois Press.

Hallin, D. (1986). Network news: We keep America on top of the world. In T. Gitlin (Ed.), *Watching television* (pp. 9–41). New York: Pantheon.

Hammer, E. (1987). *A death in November: America in Vietnam, 1963*. New York: Dutton.

Haygood, W. (1986, February 19). Stallone comes through at Harvard. *The Boston Globe*, p. 21.

Hellmann, J. (1986). *American myth and the legacy of Vietnam*. New York: Columbia University Press.

Hoberman, J. (1986, March). The fascist guns in the West. *American Film*, pp. 42–48.

Hung, N., & Schecter, J. (1987). *The palace file*. New York: Harper & Row.

Jaroslovsky, R. (1987, January 2). Washington wire. *The Wall Street Journal*, p. 1.

Jeffords, S. (1986, Winter). The new Vietnam films: Is the movie over? *Journal of Popular Film and Television*, pp. 186–194.

Kaplan, H. (1987, December). Remembering Vietnam. *Commentary*, pp. 13–29.

Karnow, S. (1984). *Vietnam: A History*. New York: Penguin.

Kauffmann, S. (1985, July 1). Now, about Rambo . . . *The New Republic*, p. 16.

Kaul, D. (1985, July 22). Liberal reflections on *Rambo II. Desert News*, p. 9.

Keller, T., & Atchison, J. (1984). Reaching out to troubled Vietnam vets: The DAV's role. In G. Baer (Photographer) & N. Howell-Koehler (Eds.), *Vietnam: The battle comes home* (pp. 31–33). Dobbs Ferry, NY: Morgan & Morgan.

Kolin, P. (1988). *David Rabe: A stage history and a primary and secondary bibliography*. New York: Garland.

Lewis, L. (1982). The thousand-yard-stare: A socio-cultural interpretation of Vietnam narratives. *Dissertation Abstracts International, 43,* 2012-A. (Univ. Microfilms No. DA8226482).

Lewy, G. (1978). *America in Vietnam*. New York: Oxford University Press.

Lifton, R. (1973). *Home from the war: Vietnam veterans, neither victims nor executioners*. New York: Simon & Schuster.

Marc, D. (1984). *Demographic vistas: Television in American culture*. Philadelphia: University of Pennsylvania Press.

Morrell, D. (1972). *First blood*. New York: M. Evans.

Newcomb, H. (1985, May/June). Magnum: The champagne of TV? *Channels of Communication*, pp. 23–26.

Pally, M. (1986, February). Red faces. *Film Comment*, pp. 32–37.

Peschek, J. (1987). *Policy-planning organizations: Elite agendas and America's right-ward turn*. Philadelphia: Temple University Press.
Podhoretz, N. (1983). *Why we were in Vietnam*. New York: Simon & Schuster.
Porter, G. (1988). Cambodia: Sihanouk's initiative. *Foreign Affairs*, pp. 809–826.
Rabe, D. (1972). *Sticks and bones*. New York: Samuel French.
Rottmann, L., Barry, J., & Paquet, B. (Eds.). (1972). *Winning hearts and minds: War poems by Vietnam veterans*. Brooklyn, NY: 1st Casualty Press.
Santoli, A. (1981). *Everything we had*. New York: Ballantine.
Sarris, A. (1985, October). The reverberations of Rambo. *Columbia*, pp. 38–39.
Scruggs, J., & Swerdlow, J. (1985). *To heal a nation*. New York: Harper & Row.
Summers, H. (1982). *On strategy: A critical analysis of the Vietnam war*. New York: Random House.
Terry, W. (1984). *Bloods*. New York: Random House.
The pride is back. (1985, December 23–30). *People*, inside front cover advertising foldout.
Turner, V. (1982). *From ritual to theatre: The human seriousness of play*. New York: Performing Arts Journal Publications.
Wander, P. (1983). The aesthetics of fascism. *Journal of Communication, 2*, 70–78.
Wimmer, A. (1986, September). *Rambo: American Adam, antichrist, and archetypal hero*. Paper presented at the conference on the effects of Vietnam on American culture, Manchester Polytechnic, Manchester, England, UK.
Wood, R. (1986, January). The leaden times. *Canadian Forum*, pp. 41–42.
Wragg, J. (1985, July 20). So what's wrong with John Rambo? *Salt Lake Tribune*, p. 14.

7

Reproducing Fathers: Gender and the Vietnam War in American Culture*

Susan Jeffords
Department of English, University of Washington, Seattle, WA

It is a key theme of U.S. films, novels, essays, and personal accounts of the Vietnam War that women are associated with life and men with death. John Wheeler (1984), former Army captain and West Point graduate, states this gendered thesis most clearly:

> I considered my commitment [to the military and his country] as a statement that there are things worth dying for. It is a masculine statement. I think it is *the* masculine statement. This is why war has tended to be viewed as a masculine enterprise. . . . Woman expresses the idea that there are things worth living for. (pp. 140–141)

These associations with life and death are most often articulated in Vietnam narratives through the images of birth and death, with reproduction and birth standing as the antitheses of the death of war. For William Broyles, Jr. (1986), Vietnam veteran and former editor of *Newsweek*, "War was an initiation into the power of life and death. Women touch that power at the moment of birth; men on the edge of death" (p. 201). But the philosophy of William Eastlake's *The Bamboo Bed* (1969) is clearest. "[E]very soldier hears death ticking off inside him . . . Not only every soldier . . . But every male human being. Not every female human being. They don't hear death ticking off inside them because they feel life ticking inside them. . . . A female would rather fuck than fight" (p. 249). Women, Eastlake's main character suggests, "don't have to go to war to prove something" (p. 85).

---

* Portions of this essay appear in *The Remasculinization of America: Gender and the Vietnam War*, and are reprinted with the permission of Indiana University Press, Bloomington, IN. Copyright © 1989.

War is, as Broyles (1984) declares, "for men, at some terrible level the closest thing to what childbirth is for women: The initiation into the power of life and death" (p. 61). Following this logic, men who don't go to war "now have a sort of nostalgic longing for something they missed, some classic male experience, the way some women who didn't have children worry they missed something basic about being a woman" (p. 56).[1] Broyles' reversal of gender and biology—that the war is basic to the "male" and reproduction to "women"—is indicative of a more comprehensive logic at work in recent accounts of the Vietnam War in which war is described as a biological necessity for the human male; without it, he is somehow only half alive. In the same way, reproduction is portrayed as a requisite for the social well-being of the human female, something for which she will feel a nostalgia for having "missed."

According to Nicole-Claude Mathieu (1984), maternity is consistently interpreted as a biological role and paternity a social one. Mathieu's statements directly contradict and reveal the motivation of Broyles' equation of the male role in combat as "natural" and woman's role in reproduction as social. If, as Broyles and other Vietnam writers want to claim, reproduction is defined as a social and not a biological activity, then it is possible for the masculine[2] to appropriate this role to itself, to encompass the feminine position of reproduction within its own sphere of control. On the other hand, to the extent that women are limited in their roles by their biologically ascribed status, they will be unable to do

[1] This is not speculation on Broyles' part. There are numerous cases of men who did not fight in combat in the Vietnam War—whether through draft deferral, draft avoidance, or having a noncombat position in the military—who state that they regret this condition. Christopher Buckley wrote in an article published in *Esquire* (August, 1983): "I didn't suffer with them [veterans]. I didn't watch my buddies getting wiped out next to me. And though I'm relieved, at the same time I feel as though part of my reflex action is not complete. . . . I haven't served my country. I've never faced life or death. I'm an incomplete person" (Wheeler, 1984, p. 124). James Fallows' now famous 1975 essay ("What did you do in the class war, Daddy?") was one of the earliest public "confessions" of having "missed" something important in life by not having served in the war. As he says elsewhere, "I don't know anyone who has changed his views about the rightness or wrongness of the war—but for some there is this feeling that a normal way station on the route to masculinity has been missed" (MacPherson, 1984, p. 180). On the other side, there are some feminist writers whose assertions about childbirth and its significance for women sound remarkably like the claims Broyles wishes to make for warfare and men. For example, Sheila Kitzinger says in her book, *The experience of childbirth* (1974), that "The experience of bearing a child is central to a woman's life. . . . It is unlikely that any experience in a man's life is comparably vivid" (p. 17).

[2] I will distinguish throughout this chapter between "men" and "masculine." Clearly, there are qualities of masculinity as it is socially defined that are not shared by all men, and individual men may choose to reject or feel ambivalent about many of those qualities, may even choose to adopt what are generally recognized as "feminine" characteristics.

the same (i.e., incorporate a masculine role). This blurring of the social and the biological in Vietnam representation takes place predominately through discussions of reproduction. It is just such confusions that enable the appropriation of gender by the masculine and the derogation of women in warfare to a biologically limited status.

Some of the reasoning behind this paradigm is explained by Judith Hicks Stiehm (1981): "Were women to enter combat, men would lose a crucial identity—warrior. *This is the only role now exclusively theirs,* the one that is as male-defining as child-bearing is female-defining" (p. 296; emphasis added). As Nancy Hartsock points out in her description of the birth of the *polis* or city-state as an extension of the warrior role, the exclusion and socialization of reproduction are not simply locally but historically linked to the role of the male as warrior.[3] For this to be masculinity's only exclusively remaining space for identification in modern times marks the reason for the insistent resurgence in Vietnam narratives of confrontations between reproduction and masculinity, confrontations that end with the exclusion of the woman/mother and the appropriation of the tasks of reproduction by the masculine.

In this chapter I want to explore in some detail how that appropriation takes place, particularly how the masculine character assumes to itself the province of reproduction—not biological reproduction,[4] but social, familial, and historical reproduction—principally by claiming for itself the tasks of "birthing" and self-sufficient parenting. Vietnam narratives here provide some of the primary material for a larger cultural argument that is at work throughout current U.S. representational productions. The fathers, both biological and social, of television programs like *My Two Dads, Full House,* and *Who's the Boss?*, or the fathering figures of programs such as *The Equalizer* or *J.J. Starbuck* are only the most

---

[3] Hartsock (1983) interprets this appropriation in terms of the masculine control of creativity and rhetoric. I am emphasizing here the much more literal appropriation of reproduction itself, rather than its metaphors.

[4] Though it would seem that an appropriation of biological reproduction by the male would be impossible, recent cultural narratives have been hinting at just such possibilities. *Enemy Mine,* a film about an "androgynous" lizard-like creature, is significant here because the actor who portrays the alien, Lou Gosset, Jr., has such a deeply "male" voice that his subsequent admission that he is pregnant seems less a sign of androgyny than of a pregnant male. That the baby is delivered by Cesarean is also in keeping with any possible male reproduction. In addition, the premier episode of *St. Elsewhere*'s 1987 season depicted a Vietnam veteran who not only believed he was pregnant—experiencing "morning sickness," for instance—but convinced some of the young doctors of this, as well. In an acted-out birthing, he "delivers" a memory of killing a child in Vietnam during the war. Neatly, his wife becomes pregnant during this time, as if she exists only to carry out "his" pregnancy. Such narrativizations of male pregnancy provide cultural testing grounds for the scientific experimentation of male reproduction through cloning.

straightforward examples of a pattern of gender relations that pervades dominant culture representations in contemporary U.S. society: fathers or father-figures are being shown as taking over and surpassing women in their roles as mothers or maternal models, and, at the same time, they are maintaining previous masculine qualities and characteristics (i.e., maintaining the power affiliated with masculinity in America). Further, the fathers we see in the domestic situations of family situation comedies are emblematic of the reappearance of strong paternal images throughout society, most obviously in the political realm, but less obviously in corporate relations, law, and international affairs. In all of these cases, the appropriation of reproduction works not only to show a masculine character who has regained control of gender definitions, but also of a masculinity able to "reproduce" itself, apart from challenges by femininity, feminists, or women.

The most logical arena within which to display this control is that over which men in the U.S. have exclusive domain—combat and warfare. The firmest basis for these arguments in recent years is found in depictions of a revived strength and commitment in characterizations of the Vietnam veteran (Jeffords, 1988a; see also Chapters 4, 5, & 6, this volume). As the television miniseries, *Amerika*, stated most clearly, it is only the Vietnam veteran who retains the values, strength, and will to stand as a fathering figure—not simply within a nuclear family too dominated by women (and, consequently, in this narrative by the invading Russian occupation forces), but also for the culture at large—as the hero (Kris Kristofferson) becomes a symbol for culture-wide rebellion against a Soviet system. In recent film productions, Vietnam veterans have been presented as marginal figures—imprisoned (as in *Amerika*, or John Rambo in *First Blood, Part II*), or Colonel Braddock as a POW in *Missing in Action*), living in a mobile home on a beach (Riggs, played by Mel Gibson, in *Lethal Weapon*), holed-up in a sculpting studio (Wilkes, played by Fred Ward, in *Uncommon Valor*), or hospitalized (Luke, played by Jon Voight, in *Coming Home*). Isolated from American culture and saved from its deterioration and feminization (Jeffords, 1986), veterans are characterized as sources of value, able to revitalize an American society that has lost or corrupted its own.

In such terms, the appropriation of reproduction that is narrated in Vietnam-oriented films, novels, television programs, and nonfiction marks the first and most significant step in furthering arguments that are oriented toward restabilizing previous relations of difference, principally the forms of difference of gender, race (Wiegman, 1988), and class. Because it is primarily through the incorporation of reproduction into the masculine character that this operation takes place, I am focusing here upon the difference of gender. As I will argue, it is principally through the oppositional relations of gender that contemporary dominant culture is redefining and reinscribing itself (Jeffords, 1989).

Reproduction is *the* repressed recognition of Vietnam representation, the topic whose eruption orients the identification of women as the mother/whore whose appearance requires such violence to control, whose entrance into combat and the masculine collective demand death and silence. This demand is met in Vietnam representation in two ways: First, by identifying the feminine with reproduction and, subsequently, by rejecting and replacing it with the masculine; second, by abstracting and technologizing reproduction as a prelude to its appropriation by the masculine. A reading of three of the most popular Vietnam representation narratives—Michael Cimino's *The Deer Hunter* (1978), Oliver Stone's *Platoon* (1986), and Francis Ford Coppola's *Gardens of Stone* (1987)—will illuminate the operations of presentations of the exclusion and appropriation of reproduction, showing the three phases of gendered representations of warfare in recent years: First, the exclusion of women from warfare in favor of the masculine bond; second, the appropriation by the masculine of the feminine role in reproduction, enabling the self-sufficient (re)production of masculinity and the reinstallation of the paternal family; and, third, the promotion of a revitalized patriarchal voice that can act as a stabilizing center for the reformation of U.S. society.

THE REPRESSION OF REPRODUCTION IN *THE DEER HUNTER*

Framed by the imagery of masculinity and structured by its bonds, the narrative of *The Deer Hunter* tells the story not of the war in Vietnam, but of gender. The feminine scenes of the wedding are explored in such detail in order to have them rejected so thoroughly by the scenes of masculine bonding that dominate the later sequences in Vietnam. Connections to and between women are, by the close of the film, all negated as sources of significant social and domestic relations: Stevie and Angela's marriage is tenuous, at best; Linda's proposed marriage to Nick is never discussed; no firm relationship between Linda and Michael is established; and the women who were found primarily in groups during the wedding are, at the close of the film, separated, frightened, and alone.

The first half of *The Deer Hunter* revolves around the promise of reproduction—the child that Angela is carrying and whose identity is so crucial to the narrative's progress. The second half revolves around that which denies reproduction, the promise of the masculine bond. As I have argued elsewhere (Jeffords, 1989), it is my contention that Nick is in fact the father of this child. This is the secret that Stash whispers to Michael and that prompts Michael to run off into the night, stripping himself of the wedding clothes that are now tainted by the birth the wedding was designed to hide. With subsequent scenes moving quickly to the remote mountains and then to Vietnam and the Russian roulette game, it is as if Michael runs from the wedding—scenes of a feminine community—to scenes that are ever more refined arenas for the expression of masculine bonding. He runs from the recognition of reproduction, a violation of Stevie's wedding vows, to a world where vows are not broken and reproduction is absent—the world of masculine-defined warfare.

The structure of the film rotates around the one figure, Nick, who links the two experiences of reproduction and warfare, of feminine and masculine bonding. Nick's graphically violent death is an indication of the stance *The Deer Hunter* takes toward men who attempt to balance these two worlds. Nick embodies the suppressed and yet insistent reminder of sexual difference that underlies Vietnam narratives. His is the point at which gender is made manifest, because he is a part of both the masculine and the feminine promise, having made a pact with Michael to "not leave me over there," as well as a proposal of marriage to Linda. His own sexuality mimics the ambivalence of his position. He is, on the one hand, fulfilling the demands of masculinity by going to fight in a war, and yet, on the other, linking himself to the feminine through Angela and Linda. In addition, while heterosexually defined through his link to Linda, Nick is also the most "feminine" of the male friends. His dancing in the bar is a type of erotic display in male company in which he becomes the "feminine" object of Michael's stationary gaze, as Michael sits and watches from his barstool.

Nick's position in relation to the oppositional structure of the masculine and feminine in *The Deer Hunter* might seem at first to be a deconstruction of that polarity offered by the film. Resting in neither the masculine nor the feminine worlds, Nick's character and function in the narrative take on the quality of what might appear to be what Derrida (1982) calls the "sexual otherwise," the point at which gender distinctions no longer determine meaning (p. 76). But the overt presentation and punishment of Nick in the film suggest that such androgynous positions are not only destructive but must themselves be destroyed. Rather than deconstructing gender oppositions, Nick's ambivalence and death assure their continuation.

Nick's feminine position in relation to Michael is so pronounced that it prompted Robin Wood (1986) to propose a reading of *The Deer Hunter* in which the tension of the film is not that of reproduction, but of homosexuality. In his reading of the film, "Nick both is *and knows himself to be* in love with Mike and Mike reciprocates that love but can't admit it, even to himself" (p. 294). Nick's fixation on the Russian roulette game is, then, a displacement of the moment at which he and Mike were most closely bonded, "a monstrously perverted enactment of the union he has always desired" (p. 296). Wood closes his reading with a plea for a resolution of the tension between the masculine and feminine that takes on an almost transcendental tone: The "problem" of the repression of bisexuality and the oppression of women "can only be resolved when the boundaries of gender construction become so blurred that men can move with ease, and without inhibition, into identification with a female position" (p. 291). Wood's reading of the film accepts Nick's sexual description as a positive feature of the *The Deer Hunter*'s portrayal of gender, one in which homosexuality would function as a deconstructive move towards the sexual otherwise. But I would suggest that Nick's ambivalent relation to the promises of masculinity and femininity does not constitute a moving beyond the categories of gender, but merely a blurring of them, a maneuver to avoid—both filmically and critically—the threat of reproduction.

The problem with Wood's "solution" lies at the heart of his reading of *The Deer Hunter* and, more important, is the nexus for Vietnam narratives' response to reproduction. Most important both for Wood's reading of *The Deer Hunter* and for a study of Vietnam narratives is that Wood depicts this desired change in gender structures *from the point of view of the masculine*. It is men who should gain ease and lose inhibition, men who should be able to identify with women, and men whose interests should be the goal of any move to alter the construction and operation of gender. It is because he does not interrogate this point of view that Wood accepts unquestioningly the male–male relationship as the center of meaning in *The Deer Hunter*. He, like the films and narratives of Vietnam, represses the matrix of reproduction in favor of the masculine bond. Wood's desire to "blur" the lines of gender is the hidden secret of Vietnam narratives: to confuse the categories of gender by asserting the masculine colonization of the territory of reproduction.

FATHERS NOT MOTHERS—*PLATOON*

As a further step in the gendered argument of Vietnam narratives, *Platoon* takes up where *The Deer Hunter* left off, beginning with and assuming the establishment of the masculine bond. *Platoon* then posits out of

this bond the production of the masculine subject as "the child of two fathers," thereby bringing the narration of reproduction to the point

where women are not only repressed but *replaced* as parents. With women effectively eliminated from the arena of war, and the masculine bond confirmed as the new "family," reproduction can now be taken over by men as the province of the self-sufficient father. This is "Vietnam, the way it really was" (Corliss, 1987).

Like so many other Vietnam narratives, *Platoon* depends on the eradication of difference through the institution of the masculine bond during wartime, what Broyles (1984) calls "brotherly love," a "love" "that transcends race and personality and education" (p. 58). Chris Taylor (Charlie Sheen), the movie's 21-year-old hero, dances with blacks, torments a Vietnamese villager to the encouraging "Do him!" of a red-neck Southerner, cleans latrines with California surfers, and smokes dope with lower-class men from the Bronx.

But, while *Platoon* disrupts barriers between blacks and whites, lower and upper classes, Southerners, New Yorkers, and Californians, the film establishes other lines of difference, ones that do not depend on social structures from the "world," but on a new set of values belonging to the "Nam," values defined along the lines of gender difference. Taylor's introduction to the "underworld" of the bunker is crosscut with scenes of the "outerworld" populated by other soldiers. Those in the underworld smoke dope, laugh, dance together, and seem to share a common vision of the war and its significance. With no tensions about race, these men put their arms around each other and sing Smokey Robinson's "Tracks of My Tears."

Their closeness and shared activity make their bond not only indiscriminate but erotic, as well, with the men's bodies framed by the small bunker that surrounds them. The leader of this world is Sgt. Elias, whose approach to Taylor in the underworld is laden with erotic connotations. After Taylor takes his first toke, Elias appears out of the haze and asks, "First time?" He then holds a rifle up to Taylor, saying "Put your mouth on this," after which Elias blows smoke through the rifle barrel into Taylor's mouth. In spite of *Time* magazine's phrasing it a "fraternal toke" (Corliss, 1987, p. 59), this act signals Taylor's virgin initiation into an underworld defined by homoerotic masculine bonds.

In contrast to the underworld, race is a source only of tension in the outerworld, where Junior calls Bunny's music "honky shit" and wishes he could hear some Motown, though he would not enter the underworld to hear it, underscoring his separation from other blacks. The erotic is also handled differently. Bunny is biting pieces out of beer cans, while delivering comments on the relative desirability of women: "Ain't nothing like a piece of pussy, 'cept maybe the Indy 500." In this heterosexual eroticism, differences that separate men are emphasized rather than overcome. There is no body contact, no touching, no signs of intimacy; there is only rape (when asked to join a card game, Lt. Wolfe says, "Wouldn't want to get raped by you guys"). The voice of authority in this world is not the seductive Elias but the death-decreeing Barnes, the alternate figure in the battle for Taylor's soul.

Time magazine tries to analyze this battle in the frame of good and evil and comes up empty: Can "Chris or the audience take moral satisfaction in" Taylor's killing of Barnes? "Which 'father' has he followed? Has Chris become like Elias?"

> Or has he emulated the enemy? Has he become Barnes in order to kill him? . . . A good man, and a murderer? It is a tribute to *Platoon*'s cunning that it can sell this dilemma both ways, and a mark of Stone's complexity that he can argue either side and believe both. (Corliss, 1987, p. 59)

Stone and his film seem to maintain *both* good and evil in Taylor's character, making it unclear who really "wins" the battle for his soul. And surrounding this confusion over the central tension of the film is its overall meaning, whether it should be interpreted as pro- or antiwar, for or against violence, as justifying or supporting American involvement in Vietnam (Sklar, 1987).

Reading *Platoon* through a gendered perspective (Jeffords, 1988b) produces an interpretation of the film that cuts through these confusions to a more systematic and coherent thematic shared by this film and other Vietnam representations. If, as the film's early schemes of difference suggest, the battle between Elias and Barnes—between what is called good and evil in the film—is a confrontation of the feminine and the masculine, then Barnes' murder of Elias is a direct attempt to eliminate these feminine qualities from the arena of Vietnam. Taylor's subsequent murder of Barnes as vengeance for Elias' death would then seem to be a clear reinstatement of the feminine over and against the masculine, with Taylor assuming Elias' role in this struggle. But Taylor's final soliloquy denies such a simplistic reading: "Elias is in me and so is Barnes. . . . I felt like a child born of two fathers." By killing Barnes he ends the film not in the position of the masculine *or* the feminine, but in both.

In addition to Robin Wood's reading of *The Deer Hunter*, several other recent critical analyses of American literature focus on just this scenario—the male bond as a source for a challenge to traditional gender constructions of man/woman. Joseph A. Boone's (1986) reading of 19th-century American quest narratives examines texts by Melville, Twain, and London to conclude that they offer "visions of individuality and mutual relationship that attempt to break down conventional sexual categorization by breaking through the limiting forms of culture and the conventions of love-literature'' (p. 191). In particular, they perform this by presenting communities of men that allow for ''the psychological connection between self- sufficient male identity and an acknowledgement of the 'feminine' within man'' (p. 195). Boone explains that American ''bonds simultaneously partake of brotherly, paternal, filial, even maternal qualities, without being restricted to one definition alone'' (p. 193). He labels Ishmael's character ''androgynous'' (p. 198) and celebrates Huck for being able to ''cross boundaries of class, race, and sex with startling ease'' (p. 200), qualities they seem to share with *Platoon*'s young hero.

Both Boone and Wood highlight a movement in current U.S. criticism that celebrates these ''androgynous'' tendencies in male character, encouraging and valorizing their possession of both masculine and feminine qualities, and praising their facility to incorporate both into their character, moving across gender boundaries with ''startling ease.'' And, as Wood's argument makes clear, this is not a worship of men who can do what women do only ''better,'' but a promotion of men who can carry *both* men's and women's characteristics, who can incorporate the two simultaneously and ''with ease.''

With these readings in mind, *Platoon*'s murder scene becomes clearer. When Sgt. Barnes kills Elias, he *is* killing the feminine in this film, eliminating it from the film's interpretive structures as a single force. Yet, when Taylor in turn kills Barnes, he murders the solely masculine, as well, suggesting that its frame cannot survive alone either. What does survive is Taylor, the ''child born of these two fathers.'' Why, then, is this not a truly androgynous ''solution'' like that proposed by Wood, Boone, and many feminists (e.g., Heilbrun, 1973), one that takes equally of the masculine and the feminine, and produces a third, perhaps better gender formation?

The answer lies in the fact that, while Taylor incorporates Elias' femininity and attitude toward the war into his final character, he uses Barnes' methods to do so. Where Elias stood passively while Barnes held the rifle to kill him, Taylor acts as Barnes did to murder Barnes himself. He must become Barnes—the masculine—in order to successfully create a space in which he can be ''born'' as the masculine/feminine child. In Rhah's words, ''only Barnes can kill Barnes.'' But, more significant, Taylor's character is not androgynous because Stone presents in *Platoon* the same kind of structure offered by Wood, one that enables men to occupy ''with ease, and without inhibition,'' the position of the feminine. This movement is seen in *Platoon*, as in Wood and Boone, only from a masculine point of view, one that allows the masculine to incorporate the feminine into itself—not to become feminine, but to ingest it as a means of (re)producing its own character.

Taylor's confession that he ''felt like a child born of these two fathers'' stands metaphorically in *Platoon*'s dialogue, but its literal meaning is equally accurate and indicative of the gendered frame promoted in this and other Vietnam films. He has no mother in this film, but only two fathers; he is (re)produced by two men. He goes to war to be "like grandpa in World War I and dad in World War II." Films like *Platoon* work out representationally what Gena Corea (1985) identifies as technologies whereby "fathers can be, or appear to be, the sole parent" (pp. 292–293), scenarios in which men can be the "child of two fathers," and women and the feminine are entirely eliminated or absorbed into the masculine/father.

Because both Elias and Barnes are incorporated into Taylor's character through the masculine point of view, the good and evil they represent are finally not challenges to masculinity itself but are reaffirmations of its powers of appropriation. In such terms, the possibility of a "good" that is defined outside the frame of the masculine being presented in this film is very remote. At the same time, because of its expansive plot structure and its far-reaching themes, *Platoon* presents itself as addressing issues not only of war but of life itself. What this film suggests, then, is that these issues can finally be resolved only through a masculine frame, a resolution born, like Chris Taylor, "of two fathers."

The "misunderstanding" that Corliss (1987) sees as the interpretive product of *Platoon*, so that antithetical meanings seem to be simultaneously and appropriately produced, is not so much a misunderstanding as a misdirection in which blurred categories prevent us from recognizing the film's basis of meaning. Out of this sea of "misunderstanding," Stone sends forth the veterans of this war, who "have an obligation to teach others what we know." What a gendered reading of *Platoon* shows is that what Stone's veterans are teaching is not truth, not justice, not good, not even how to win a war, but that "meaning to this life," Taylor's final desire, is to be found only within the frame of men, inside the "platoon."

PATERNALISM IN *GARDENS OF STONE*

The final stage in this strategy of masculine (re)production is best seen in Francis Ford Coppola's *Gardens of Stone* (1987), a film that shows not the "birth" of the father in combat, but the "duty" of the father at home. Though set during the time of the Vietnam War, *Gardens of Stone* shows no combat, but takes place entirely within and around Washington, D.C., as decorated Vietnam veteran Clel Hazard (James Caan) uses his assignment to the Old Guard Regiment at Arlington National Cemetery to prepare young men for what they will see in the war. These preparations find them battling not the Viet Cong, but the bureaucracy and inefficiency of the military and political systems. Clearly, in the language of the film, the young men Clel Hazard oversees are being prepared not for the war, but for the battles that take place back in "the world."

Clel's position as father in this film is specified not in relation to his own daughter, who is grown and separated from him, as is his divorced wife, now in a mental institution, but in relation to his troops, particularly the young Jack Willow, a new recruit who is on his way to Vietnam. Friends with Willow's father, Hazard becomes Jack's sole parenting figure when Jack's father dies early in the film of a heart attack.[5] Emblematic of his fathering role with other young soldiers, Willow's growing idolization and emulation of Hazard marks this as the key relationship of the film.

In contrast, the significance of male–female relations in *Gardens of Stone* lies in their reference to reproduction. None of the women in the film has children: Clel's fiancee, Sam Davies, is sterile; and Willow's new bride, Rachel, widowed when Jack dies in war, will have no children by him. Even Betty Rae Williams, wife of Clel's closest friend, Sergeant Major Homer "Goody" Williams (James Earl Jones), is eliminated from reproductive possibility through a crude joke recited in the film's opening scenes. During an inspection of the barracks, Goody asks recruits sexually explicit questions designed to embarrass them. When Goody asks Willow, "How do worms copulate?" Willow replies, "Asexual reproduction." Goody continues, "Who first came up with that idea?" Willow replies, "Your wife, sir?"[6]

The film places women's relation to reproduction only in the realms of sterility and asexuality. Having women's reproductive capacities negated, the territory of reproduction is left at the close of this film entirely to men, who seem to have the only functional relations to (re)producing children. Though Clel's daughter is not seen, he writes to her; the mother is, presumably, unable to communicate with her daughter due to her mental imbalances (only a crazy woman would have left this man). And Willow, whose father dies during the film and is replaced

[5] This displacement of the father marks an important distinction between films of the post-Vietnam era and World War II combat films. As Jeanine Basinger (1986) said of *Sands of Iwo Jima,* where Sgt. Stryker (John Wayne) becomes a father figure to a young Private (John Agar), "Wayne then becomes the father that Agar needs to become a man. This does not constitute displacement of the real father, since Wayne himself was created by that same father in military terms [Agar's father was Stryker's commanding officer], if not biological ones" (p. 165).

[6] It is important to note here that this exchange, in the context of reproduction, *must* be read as a joke. The threat of a female power, especially black female power, of independent reproduction—asexual and therefore without males—would be too great to assert in any other context.

by Hazard, has no mother; she died much earlier. Only men in this film actually have relations to children; women have been shown unable to have them; and the clearly significant relations in the film—Will–Hazard, Hazard–Goody—are all between men.

What we have here and in all of these film narratives is an arena in which the family is composed either exclusively or significantly of fathers, not mothers, and relations between fathers and sons, not daughters.[7] Fathers are shown in each case to be not only the key parenting figures for the nuclear family, but also the primary examples of parenting for the social family. Their position is, like that of Clel Hazard, to "teach others what we know," to reshape a sterile and insane family that had been dominated by women into a firm and stable family guided by men.

THE PRODUCTION OF FATHERS

The appropriation of reproduction by the masculine, according to Gena Corea (1985), is generated by the life-death boundary tension foregrounded in war narrative: to conquer the barrier of death through the creation of immortality by continuous self-production. Epitomized in projects like cloning and artificial wombs is what Corea describes as "the patriarchal urge to give birth to oneself, to be one's own mother, and to live forever," so that "the desire to control birth through the reproductive technologies, then, is also a desire to control death" (pp. 162–163).

By inserting themselves into the birth process, Vietnam's narrators endeavor to gain control over the moment of reproduction through technology, and thereby to control death. In doing so, they must eliminate women from the birth process—from war—altogether. This battle with death is thus not cooperative but competitive, a battle that, as Robyn Rowland (1984) suggests, centers on power itself: "with the possibilities offered by technology [men] are storming the last bastion [of women's power] and taking control of conception, fetal development, and birth" (p. 363). In such terms, the insistent exclusion of women from war, coupled with the foregrounding of technology in Vietnam narration, marks

[7] The pattern of father–son relationships in film is somewhat different in television, where the predominant pattern depicted in family relations is of father–daughter, as in *Who's the Boss?*, *Full House*, and *My Two Dads*. The shift has much to do with the medium itself, as the televisual apparatus is more oriented toward the placement of domestic relations within the home and consequently of male–female relations. Film, predominantly oriented toward the placement of external social relations, is generally more concerned with the father–son paternal and patriarchal paradigm that characterizes the definition of social relations within capitalism.

the cultural force of these representations—to respond to the anxieties of the boundary between life and death by repressing and repossessing those who traditionally have been assigned the social, cultural, and biological power over that realm—women and the femininity that has come to be associated with them. In Vietnam narratives, the masculine gives birth to itself as a technologized body (it is said of Rambo, "He's a perfect killing machine") that not only defies death, but incorporates—*embodies*—the very means by which death itself is to be conquered.

Vietnam narration interposes itself at the point of (re)production, generating the birth of the masculine subject, apart from the mother, *self-delivered*. It is far more significant to the (re)production of the masculine that its character can be produced during war so that the arena of the masculine and the masculine character can be joined together and not separated, as they might be if that character were to continue to be associated only with "home" or "career" or "fraternity." The bonds of other masculinities are drawn together and redefined to encompass these diverse personalities. (This is one of the functions of the belief that combat experience breaks down barriers between men of diverse backgrounds and personalities.) In Vietnam representation, the masculine subject *as subject* is (re)produced.[8]

It is to this end that Vietnam representation narrates the appropriation of reproduction by the masculine character—not simply to negate a traditional role of social power for women, or to create a "feminized" male hero, but to establish a masculine character who can incorporate into a revitalized figure of masculine consciousness the capacities to (re)produce itself, a figure that has been salvaged from feminism by the socially isolated Vietnam veteran. Through this role, gender positions are being restructured and restabilized in such a way as to reassert the primacy of the masculine point of view in determining definitions of difference.

While space does not permit a full discussion of the consequences of such developments in cultural productions, I would like to suggest briefly a few ways in which I think these narratives are relevant to an understanding of some of the operations of contemporary U.S. culture. Films like *Lethal Weapon* (1987) and *Rambo III* (1988) display this new Vietnam veteran as stronger and more active than his old image (see

---

[8] This discussion seems to fall in line with arguments made by the French feminists, particularly Luce Irigaray, that it is the mother in every woman that every male child works to repress, not as Bataille and Freud say, the sexual woman in the mother. What Vietnam reproduction reveals is that these activities are one and the same, that the repressed is not the mother *or* the whore, but women from social reproduction. As Domna Stanton's (1986) critique of the French feminists suggests, and as Vietnam narration shows, their use of the maternal metaphor is less of a "revelation" than a "revalorization" (p. 171).

Chapters 5 & 6, this volume). It is no accident that the regeneration of the Vietnam veteran as father-figure (in *Rambo III* a young, orphaned Afghan boy clings to Rambo) coincides with a resurgence of violent action films in recent years, many with the Vietnam veteran at their center. A major sector of dominant cinema is currently presenting images of masculinity that are equated with the ability to act, and this most often violently (along with Stallone, Arnold Schwarzenegger is perhaps the most productive figure of this type). In most cases, such abilities are posed as counter to the narrative's institutional strength—often represented by women—as the ability to repress action or the inability to decide how or when to act. Such are the plots of *The Big Easy* (in which a cop must use violence to battle a corrupt police force that is failing to halt drug trafficking), *Lethal Weapon* (in which a cop who can't seem to go through a day without killing is shown as superior to a desk-officer in defending family and society), *Rambo III* (in which Rambo is able to help the Afghan "freedom fighters" that the American government, its hands tied by bureaucracy, cannot), *Robocop* (in which a mechanized police officer is able to battle all but the corporation that produced it), and numerous others.

Such narratives of action intertwine with narratives of fathers not only by reinforcing images of decisive and active father-figures who are able to protect and reunite a frayed domestic scenario, but also by infantilizing viewers so as to put us all in the position of regarding these strong and thriving men as our own ideal social fathers. Feeling unable to accomplish such "missions" ourselves, concerned about not protecting our own domestic arena, and sensing the alienation from consequential action that is a thesis of postmodern cultural production, viewers of these films are positioned to look up to these men as hopeful reconstructions of the failed fathers of our own domestic scenarios.

While feminist film theorists would counter that such positioning is, at best, ambivalent for female viewers who would have a different relation to such narrations (see De Lauretis, 1984, Chapter 5), I would argue that contemporary dominant cinema is constructing a new subject position that, through infantilization, may be more gender neutral[9] than, and would fix historically, the male gaze identified by Laura Mulvey (1975) in dominant cinema of the 1950s and 1960s. (By "gender neutral"

[9] I want to distinguish this argument clearly from that made by Ann Kaplan in *Rocking around the clock* (1987) in which she suggests that there are certain MTV videos that present what she calls a "maternal gaze," a gaze that is pre-Oedipal and therefore not gender-identified. While I find her argument intriguing for the televisual, it may require the intimacy and immediacy of video viewing, and may not be transferable to the large cinema screen (though this distinction is made problematic by home video viewing). The relation of such a thesis to the domestic scenario of most American television viewing is key.

I do not mean that the process of infantilization in fact operates identically upon male and female viewers. Instead, I want to suggest that the viewer is positioned as non-gendered—not "un-" or "degendered"—by the filmic narration.) The idolizing and idealizing gaze of the camera as it watches Rambo is quite distinct from the male gaze of the camera identified by Mulvey that objectifies women in classic filmic narrative.[10] Quite the contrary, this gaze does not fix Rambo by viewing him *from* a position of power and control—from a male viewpoint—but by gazing at him as if he *were* the source of power and control himself. Through infantilization, the viewer is made to feel the helplessness of the child in the face of the dominant father,[11] a paradigm essential to the reproduction of patriarchal social constructions.[12]

In a key scene of *Rambo III*, one that stands out because of its narrative dislocation, we view members of an Afghan rebel village as Rambo enters for the first time. Amidst full and medium shots of villagers engaged in various activities, we see, suddenly and briefly, a close-up of a young woman's eyes, the remainder of her face veiled; as Rambo's guide explains, "They're not used to seeing men like him." In relation to violent action narratives of contemporary dominant cinema, we are those eyes, unaccustomed to seeing "men like Rambo." The glance is so brief because the cultural desire it articulates is so strong. What is significant is that this desire is translated in the remainder of the narrative into the admiring gaze of the Afghan boy who follows Rambo. Unlike previous narratives in which female viewers would be the repositories of male idolization (as in many classic World War II films), the female look here is transferred to the child, accomplishing two things: first, immediately infantilizing and thereby negating any expression of female desire towards Rambo as a sexual object (necessary in a film that depends for so much of its "action" upon close-ups of Stallone's muscular physique); and, second, positioning the audience within a look that is more acceptable than that of the female, that is, in the child. Activated

[10] The idolizing gaze directed toward the male hero is not to be confused with the "male" gaze of the camera directed at such Vietnam figures as Nick in *The Deer Hunter*, where Nick's body is objectified in the bar scene as if he were female.

[11] As I hope the terms of this discussion make apparent, I am not ascribing this infantilization to a psychoanalytic relation between child and father-figure, but instead wish to emphasize the socially constructed relations between child and father in dominant American culture. While psychoanalytic relations would be relevant here, I do not want to ground these observations in a psychoanalytic position.

[12] It is important to point out that these discussions of fathers, reproduction, and dominant cultural representations of the domestic are appropriate only to a dominant white culture. Cultural interpretations of domestic relations are shaped in significant ways by issues of race, as well as gender, and would produce different analyses than those presented here (see Spillers, 1987).

through the safe (heterosexual, raced, and passive) position of the feminine look, but unable to be maintained at that level because of its disruptive potential, the look is transferred to the child we are asked to become as viewers of this narrative, the child we are asked to become as viewers of this masculinity, this violent and triumphant fatherhood.

In such terms the ending of *Lethal Weapon* becomes paradigmatic of this new phase of Vietnam films. After protecting the daughter and family of his partner from violent criminals, Riggs, formerly viewed in his isolated mobile home, is invited into his partner's home for a family dinner. The film closes upon a shot of Riggs and his partner walking up the sidewalk to the front door of a middle-class, split-level, suburban home. These narratives thus record that the Vietnam veteran has finally "come home," not as a soldier of a distant war, but as the savior of the American family he has "come home" to protect. And we, positioned as the children anxious for the return of his protection, are to invite him in.

REFERENCES

Basinger, J. (1986). *The World War II combat film: Anatomy of a genre*. New York: Columbia University Press.

Boone, J.A. (1986). Male independence and the American quest genre: Hidden sexual politics in the all-male worlds of Melville, Twain and London. In J. Spector (Ed.), *Gender studies: New developments in feminist criticism* (pp. 187–218). Bowling Green, OH: Bowling Green State University Popular Press.

Broyles, W., Jr. (1984, November). Why men love war. *Esquire*, pp. 55–56.

Corea, G. (1985). *The mother machine: Reproductive technologies from artificial insemination to artificial wombs*. New York: Harper & Row.

Corliss, R. (1987, January 26). *Platoon*: Vietnam, the way it really was, on film. *Time*, pp. 54–62.

De Lauretis, T. (1984). *Alice doesn't*. Bloomington: Indiana University Press.

Derrida, J. (1982). Choreographies. *Diacritics, 12*, 66–77.

Eastlake, W. (1969). *The bamboo bed*. New York: Avon.

Hartsock, N. (1983). *Money, sex, and power: Toward a feminist historical materialism*. Boston: Northeastern University Press.

Heilbrun, C. (1973). *Toward a recognition of androgyny*. New York: Harper & Row.

Jeffords, S. (1986). The new Vietnam films: Is the movie over? *Journal of Popular Film and Television, 13*, 185–195.

Jeffords, S. (1988a). De-briding Vietnam: The resurrection of the white American male. *Feminist Studies, 14*(3), 525–1545.

Jeffords, S. (1988b). Born of two fathers: Gender and misunderstanding in *Platoon*. In W.J. Searle (Ed.), *Search and clear: Critical responses to selected literature and films of the Vietnam War* (pp. 184–195). Bowling Green, OH: Popular Culture Press.

Jeffords, S. (1989). *The remasculinization of America: Gender and the Vietnam War.* Bloomington: Indiana University Press.

Kaplan, E.A. (1987). *Rocking around the clock.* New York: Methuen.

Kitzinger, S. (1974). *The experience of childbirth.* Harmondsworth, England: Penguin.

MacPherson, M. (1984). *Long time passing: Vietnam and the haunted generation.* New York: Signet.

Mathieu, N. (1984). Biological paternity, social maternity. *Feminist Issues, 4,* 63–72.

Mulvey, L. (1975). Visual pleasure and narrative cinema. *Screen, 16,* 6–18.

Rowland, R. (1984). Reproductive technologies: The final solution to the woman question? In R. Arditti, R. Klein, & S. Minden (Eds.), *Test-tube women: What future for motherhood?* (pp. 356–371). Boston: Pandora.

Sklar, R. (1987). *Platoon* on inspection: A critical symposium. *Cineaste, 15,* 4–9.

Spillers, H. (1987). Moma's baby, papa's maybe: An American grammar book. *Diacritics,* pp. 65–81.

Stanton, D. (1986). Difference on trial: A critique of the maternal metaphor in Cixous, Irigaray, and Kristeva. In N. Miller (Ed.), *The poetics of gender* (pp. 157–183). New York: Columbia University Press.

Stiehm, J.H. (1981). *Bring me men and women: Mandated change at the U.S. Air Force Academy.* Berkeley: University of California Press.

Wiegman, R. (1988). *Negotiating the masculine: Configurations of race and gender in American culture.* Unpublished dissertation. University of Washington, Spokane, WA.

Wheeler, J. (1984). *Touched with fire: The future of the Vietnam generation.* New York: Avon.

Wood, R. (1986). *Hollywood from Vietnam to Reagan.* New York: Columbia University Press.

Part III

Vietnam and the Shaping of American Cultures

8

Cultural Communication Among Vietnam Veterans: Ritual, Myth, and Social Drama

Charles A. Braithwaite
Dept. of Communication Studies, New Mexico State University

I've frequently heard the assertion that the Vietnam veteran "should put the war behind" him. I have also heard that the welcome home parades, which started after the dedication of the Vietnam Veterans Memorial in Washington, D.C., meant "the war was over" and that the very presence of the Vietnam Veterans Memorial means that the Vietnam veteran has now been "reintegrated" into American society after 20 years of being ostracized. Few Vietnam veterans would be so naive as to accept any of these declarations completely. The Vietnam War has left a mark on the men and women who shared that experience, and it is an indelible mark. The lasting effect of participation in the Vietnam War is nowhere more evident than in the speech of Vietnam veterans when they organize themselves into Vietnam veterans organizations. A unique and communal experience for Vietnam veterans occurs when they come together *as* Vietnam veterans. In the talk generated through that experience we can see how distinct the Vietnam veteran is from "mainstream" America.

This chapter describes and explains some aspects of the distinctive use of speech by a specific group of speakers: an organization of Vietnam veterans. The goal of the study is to present the forms, meanings, and functions of speech usage among members of this particular community and to argue that these ways of speaking constitute a significant dimension of their cultural identity (Braithwaite, 1989). This study thus seeks to present a culturally sensitive interpretation of the speech of some Vietnam veterans.

The research presented here is grounded in the perspective and method of ethnography of speaking. The goal of an ethnographer of speaking is to discover, describe, and interpret patterns of speaking in particular speech communities. As I will describe in more detail later, the ethnography of speaking descriptive/theoretic framework was developed by Dell Hymes (1962, 1972) to discover and describe the "operating principles, strategies, and values which guide the production and interpretation of speech, the community ground rules for speaking" (Bauman & Sherzer, 1974, p. 7). This framework is designed to serve as a theory of speaking as well as a guide for examining and describing speaking in particular communities; it delineates the necessary and sufficient features present in all communicative interaction and guides our inquiry of speaking in specific contexts.

I begin by describing the rationale for why a specific organization of Vietnam veterans can be referred to as a distinct "speech community." Then, I describe the context of the study as well as the subjects and their speech activities. After a further introduction to the methodology, I turn to three forms of cultural communication, which I argue demonstrate how the speech surrounding Vietnam veterans' experiences creates and maintains a coherent cultural identity for some Vietnam veterans.

SPEECH COMMUNITY

Identification of a speech community is partially a reflexive process in that one needs to assess the presence of dimensions of a speech community before one can posit the existence of a speech community. As defined for this study, the observer can identify a speech community by discovering and describing the degree to which (1) a group of speakers share aspects of linguistic variation (i.e., covariation is present between language and social context), (2) a group of speakers share communication *rules* for speaking (i.e., the use of speech judged as appropriate by native speakers), and (3) shared meaning is present among a group of speakers (i.e., members successfully render coherent and intelligible speech in the community). This approach to speech community asks the analyst to make a case for varying degrees of community, rather than simply positing its existence.

The organization of Vietnam veterans that is the focus of this study is composed of men who share little in the way of ethnic, social, or other demographic features. What they do share is a commonality based on *circumstance and shared experience.* It is the common experience of the *group,* rather than common characteristics of the individuals, that makes this a distinct speech community. This can be seen in several aspects of the covariation of linguistic features and social context. Language features that were so prominent in the life-world of the Vietnam soldier can still be heard in the speech of those men 10, 15, and 20 years after their original use.

One distinction consistently made concerns the article "the" and its use in connection with references to Vietnam. There is a regular use of the phrase "*the* 'Nam" when Vietnam veterans describe Vietnam to one another—for example, "That's the way it was in the 'Nam." The 'Nam had a hold on me." "Getting to the 'Nam was something else." "Did you get that [wound] in the 'Nam?" "The 'Nam was not the place to fuck around." "When I was in the 'Nam alls I thought of was getting back to the world." This article has a way of directing attention to the significance of the location by setting it apart as a distinct entity in the life-world of the veteran. Prefacing the abbreviation of Vietnam with the article is used to distinguish the context from others. Additionally, it sets up a contrast when used in conjunction with its opposite, "*the* world," which refers to the United States. In the life-world of the Vietnam soldier there existed only "the 'Nam" and everything else. One could also say that by creating this linguistic distinction, the soldier places himself in a separate place from the "real world" by making Vietnam something that is outside "reality." Whatever semantic dimension "the 'Nam" represents, it is still used frequently by Vietnam veterans today.

The linguistic marker is also used as a way to distinguish veterans from nonveterans. As one veteran said, "I hate it when some people think it is cool to call it 'Nam; you can tell they don't know shit; they just be trying to make you think they do." He went on to say that nonveterans usually do not pronounce Vietnam or 'Nam "correctly," given that they use a short "a" instead of a long "a," and that nonveterans sometimes refer to Vietnam veterans as "Vietnamese veterans." From the perspective of linguistic variation as a degree of shared speech community, this linguistic distinction made by veterans would appear to implicate the presence of a common evaluative system regarding language use.

In a related way, the large number of terms, acronyms, place names, and military nomenclature familiar to the veteran, and his ability to use them in conversation, sets their speech apart from others. Fifteen years after the incident, one Vietnam veteran related the following story:

> We was *didy-bopping* a couple of *klicks over the fence* when we *spied* this *ville*. We saw a few *baby-sans* so we didn't think nothin' and just *humped* right around. Then our point tripped a *bouncing-Betty* and then we all was in *a world of hurt*. Seven *dinks* opened up with *47s* and *RPGs* and all that good shit, but I didn't see nothing else until I was *dusted;* I took an *AK* round in the hip and got *titi* in the legs so I couldn't move. And that, Bro, was the *million-dollar wound*.

The underlined words indicate a variety of indigenous terms from the speech of some Vietnam veterans (e.g., "over the fence"—in Cambodia; "bouncing-Betty"—a small antipersonnel mine that explodes approximately two feet off the ground; "million-dollar wound"—a wound that is not serious enough to leave the victim permanently disabled, yet serious enough to get the person shipped back to the United States; "AK" and "47s"—the AK-47 Russian assault rifle carried by many of the enemy forces; "dusted"—medical evacuation by helicopter).

These specialized terms, most of them unique to the Vietnam experience, are not commonly used by veterans speaking to nonveterans. For example, the word *dink* was used primarily as a descriptive term by soldiers, but nonveterans tend to see the word as a racial slur. Vietnam veterans speaking to other veterans in specified contexts can use the term as a way of describing rather than evaluating. And, unlike the argot of speech communities such as prostitutes or criminals, the terms are not used to exclude nonmembers of the community from understanding or participating in speech. Instead, in specified contexts, the terminology functions to allow the speaker to "enact" linguistic characteristics of being a Vietnam veteran. Just as the article *the* is used linguistically to separate and redefine the context of Vietnam, the specialized language of the war is used to mark the speech as that of a Vietnam veteran; it is speech that has distinctive terms, phrases, and structures shared by a specific population.

One of the limitations of the present study is that some of the powerful statistical tools that can be used to identify patterns of linguistic variation further in a social context were not employed (C. F. Sankoff, 1978). Although I repeatedly refer to the use of specified terms and linguistic markers, a more complete analysis of the linguistic features of Vietnam veterans is still needed. However, because of the reflexive nature of defining a speech community, it is my hope that the descriptions provided in this study will provide the necessary and sufficient detail for illustrating the perceived degree of speech community present among members of this organization of Vietnam veterans. Let me first describe the specific context, subjects, and speech situations of the speech community.

CONTEXT

Data were gathered in an organization of Vietnam veterans (i.e., those American men and women who fought and/or worked in or around the Southeast Asian nations of South and North Vietnam between 1963 and 1975, and who subsequently returned to life in America). For two and a half years, I participated in monthly meetings, informal "rap" sessions, political rallies, and other specific speech situations described below. As a participant-observer, I had complete access to all members of the organization and freely moved among various aspects of the organization. Additionally, as a participant-observer, I consider myself to be what Turner (1974) would call a "liminal man," living between two communicative worlds. My identity as a veteran allows me to participate in a community as "just another vet." However, my identity as an ethnographer of speaking allows me to make those experiences as a veteran understandable and meaningful to a community of scholars.

The organization will be referred to as VET (all the organizational names, locations, and members' names have been changed to protect the privacy of the natives), which was a nonprofit, autonomous group of Vietnam veterans. VET was not affiliated with the U.S. government, either on the local or on the national level, and was not affiliated with any other veterans' organizations (e.g., Vietnam Veterans of America, Veterans of Foreign Wars, etc.), although some veterans in the organization belong to other veteran groups. The term *organization* is used because the group was incorporated, had drawn up articles of incorporation, elected officers in accordance with the articles of incorporation, collected dues from members, and held regular monthly meetings.

VET began when two Vietnam veterans published an announcement in a local Veterans' Affairs office newsletter calling for other veterans to join them in an organization that would "try to make life better for the Vietnam veterans in our state." Twenty men showed up at the first meeting, a name for the group was selected, and the two "founders" volunteered to draw up the articles of incorporation. It was decided that VET would "not be political" but that, among other things, it would work to lobby all state legislators for the passage of bills that would aid Vietnam veterans and their dependents. The articles of incorporation state that VET would focus on "political action," "promoting a better life and image for veterans," and "giving support to fellow veterans and their families." Within a year VET had 50 dues-paying members and approximately 100 veterans on their mailing list. The "founders" left VET after a year, but the group continued to meet, elect new officers, and carry on the identified activities. Although there were over 50 official members, and three times organizational events drew groups of more than 100 veterans, the "core" of the organization never included more than 20 members, and, at times, only 10 members were actively participating in the meetings.

As indicated, the primary purpose of VET was to "help veterans," both politically and socially. The articles of incorporation for the organization make explicit that one of the central goals of the group was to "improve communication" and "unity" among veterans. A portion of the articles states VET's intentions: (a) to promote physical and cultural improvement, growth and development, self-respect, self-confidence, and usefulness of Vietnam veterans and others; and (b) to eliminate discrimination suffered by Vietnam veterans and to develop channels of communication, which will assist Vietnam veterans to maximize self-realization and enrichment of their lives and enhance life-fulfillment.

Although no VET member ever stated the purpose of the organization in terms such as those listed in the articles of incorporation, when asked, members stated that the group was designed to "help all of us" (Vietnam veterans), "make sure they [the government] gives what they should," "let them [the government and the people] know we are here," and "just make life a little easier for some of us." It should be noted that, except for initially working to help pass several bills in the state legislature and organizing two state and city "recognition" days for Vietnam veterans, VET had no explicitly stated long-term goals or projects. Most often, VET provided support by responding to events or issues of interest to veterans—for example, testifying at hearings, organizing trips to the dedication of the Vietnam Veterans Memorial in Washington, D.C., raising money to help some unemployed veterans, and writing letters to newspapers and magazines concerning the image of the Vietnam veteran. This is not to say VET had no purpose. Rather, the goals of VET's members were not always specifically articulated and, as a result, were not always clear in observation. However, clear differences did occur between behavior that was focused on directed action to "help vets" (e.g., political action, economic matters, etc.) and between behavior that I would call *social action* (i.e., behavior focused on interaction and "support" among veterans as an end in and of itself). This included meetings where members attempted to define what was needed in terms of "helping vets" and activities designed to let "vets just have a good time being with each other." At a superficial level one could distinguish among these differences as the official versus the informal focus of the organization.

Subjects

All members of VET were perceived as being Vietnam veterans (no person had to provide documents or testimony to prove they had served in Vietnam). Approximately 2.9 million Americans served in Vietnam; over 58,000 were killed, and over 300,000 were wounded. As early as 1970, organizations of Vietnam veterans were beginning to form (Vietnam Veterans Against the War, Inc., 1972), primarily for political reasons and because established veterans' organizations (e.g., American

Legion, Veterans of Foreign Wars, etc.) had not been receptive to the more politically active young veterans. Although many Vietnam veterans now belong to traditional veterans' organizations, others continue to form and join organizations geared directly toward the Vietnam veteran—the largest and most established of these is Vietnam Veterans of America (VVA). However, some veterans have felt that the large national organizations do not meet the specific needs of the veteran on the local level; some perceive that national organizations like the VVA are more concerned with national political issues than with those issues faced by Vietnam veterans on a day-to-day basis (i.e., unemployment, mental health problems, etc.). Therefore, local veterans' groups have formed around the nation (though no data are available on the number or membership of all Vietnam veteran organizations). The organization investigated in this study is one of the local organizations that began as an alternative to the larger national groups.

According to VET's documents, its members "come from all walks of life," including lawyers, carpenters, students, state legislators, unemployed veterans, and members of the business community, the media, the health sciences, and the construction trades. VET's members are all male, range in age from 29–46, and come from diverse socioeconomic backgrounds. What needs to be emphasized is that VET is very heterogeneous—its members share few common characteristics other than having served in Vietnam at one time or another. Some men served more than one tour voluntarily, others were drafted, some were discharged honorably, some received "bad papers" (less than honorable discharges), some were wounded or maimed, others had an uneventful tour of duty, and still others are dealing with the lingering effects of their service in Vietnam (e.g., mental disorders, illness traced to exposure to Agent Orange, etc.).

The following sample of VET's members (pseudonyms are used to protect members' identities) will help illustrate the diversity of the membership.

Able: 35-year-old Black male, presently employed as an alcohol abuse counselor for the Veterans Administration; served in Army infantry from 1966–1967.

Baker: 34-year-old Caucasian male, presently employed as a part-time copywriter for an advertising agency; served in Army Special Forces from 1969–1971 training counterinsurgency troops.

Charlie: 32-year-old Chicano male, presently attending a vocational school to become a welder; served as a helicopter door gunner from 1972–1973 and spent three months in a Cambodian prison camp.

Delta: 40-year-old Caucasian male, presently employed as a manager of a telephone company; served on river patrol boats for the Navy from 1967–1968.
Echo: 45-year-old Black male, presently employed in an insurance company; served as a radio teletype operator for an artillery division from 1968–1969.
Fox-trot: 32-year-old Chicano male, presently employed as a police officer; served in the military police from 1971–1972.
Golf: 33-year-old Caucasian male, presently working as a free-lance artist; served as a forward observer from 1968–1969.
Hotel: 33-year-old Caucasian male, presently working for the postal service; served with the air cavalry from 1968–1969.
India: 30-year-old Caucasian male, presently attending a vocational rehabilitation center; served in the military police in 1972, received a traumatic amputation of the leg.
Kilo: 42-year-old Caucasian male, presently working for an air cargo firm; served as a helicopter pilot from 1965–1966.

Within this eclectic group of men, the organization can be divided into different "types" of members based on their degree of participation in VET. (These are observer's terms, not native terms.)

Actives were those who served as officers in the organization, attended meetings regularly, and would always participate in discussions.
Regulars were those members who would attend most meetings, were willing to participate in activities organized by the group, but did not take an active role in VET and could not always be counted on to participate in discussion at organizational meetings.
Irregulars were those who would only occasionally show up to meetings, sometimes not coming for several months, would attend some VET activities, primarily the informal activities, and would not participate in discussion in the organizational meetings.
Inactives were those who would show up to activities, such as ceremonies and informal activities, but would not participate in the organization.
The last two types would always be encouraged to attend whatever aspect of the organizational activities they desired and were rarely criticized for not being more active in VET.

Speech Situations

Six specific contexts for interaction among organizational members were studied: official meetings, informal meetings, public activities, internal activities, official ceremonies, and informal ceremonies.

The official meetings of VET began in the homes of the founders. By the third meeting they had moved to a room provided by a local veterans affairs office. By the sixth meeting rooms were being reserved at a local community college. These were the meetings where "business" was conducted and decisions were discussed (e.g., officers were elected, assignments were drawn or volunteered, logistical information was handled, decisions were voted on). For the first year and a half, official meetings were assumed by members to be held at least once a month unless "officially" cancelled. After that, meetings were not held unless there was a call for a meeting in response to some perceived need. The official meetings were not limited to covering a specific agenda in a certain order. Often, one or more of VET's officers would have an item that was described as "something we *have* to cover tonight," but that was not used to restrict the interaction of the members. Just as agendas were not obligatory, there was no set format for interaction—for example, no chair called the meeting to order, members did not need to be recognized before speaking, there were no set prescriptions for running meetings.

These meetings emphasized maximum participation by all present and avoided inhibiting interaction. For example, while discussing how to raise money to help some unemployed veterans, one member who had recently been released from a detoxification center for alcohol abuse started to describe how they could raise money by salvaging pipe from condemned buildings. His monologue was lengthy, often rambling, hard to follow, and included several long pauses where he stared intently at a wall across the room. However, the member was not interrupted, nor was he asked to "stick to the point." Instead, the member was given the floor and allowed to talk apparently as long as was necessary for him to say what he needed to say. After this member stopped speaking and appeared to have completed his monologue, the discussion resumed with occasional references to the previous suggestion. What is significant is that all members were allowed the same freedom to speak and "have their say." This speech situation was characterized by participants sitting in a circle with VET officers raising issues for discussion (without imposing restrictions on the discussion or restricting topics discussed), by all participants being encouraged to speak (although not all would speak), and by speech focusing on the *public* aspects of VET and Vietnam veterans (i.e., what VET should "do" regarding issues affecting Vietnam veterans). The official meetings never lasted more then two hours, and were usually followed by 5 to 10 members going out for coffee afterwards.

What could be called *informal* meetings were held by VET officers either as a prelude to holding an official meeting or as a follow-up to an official meeting (e.g., to carry out and discuss decisions reached at the official meetings). These meetings were always held at someone's house or at a coffee shop (it should be noted that, because so many members have drinking problems, meetings were never held in a bar, and liquor was never provided). These meetings usually focused on trying to identify specific ways to accomplish the group's goals or to generate additional ideas for discussion. Unlike the official meetings, which were announced in the monthly newsletter and posted at locations where interested veterans would likely be present, the informal meetings were called by one or more members contacting other members, who would most likely be interested in participating either because of special interest or because they were thought to be potential assets to VET (i.e., because they might have necessary skills).

As with the official meetings, no specific guides were set down concerning interaction. However, because of the small number of participants, the meetings tended to stay "on track" more often. One representative meeting focused on how to implement a suggestion raised at an official meeting that a public event be held for Vietnam veterans where they could bring their families, spouses, and/or girlfriends. This issue was raised in response to the perception by families of veterans that previous events had been for veterans only, and family members/friends felt excluded from the activities. Therefore, this informal meeting was called to try to identify a way to "remedy" the situation. Going to baseball games, on camping trips, holding recognition banquets for families, and throwing "a party" were all discussed as possible events. And, as with the other informal meetings, much of the talk concerned "just what we are trying to do, anyway." That is, questions were raised as to the specific goal of such an event, regardless of exactly what was done.

As described earlier, talk centered on the social action dimension of VET: What was it, and where was it going? Decisions were accomplished in these meetings despite the fact that no consensus was ever reached as to exactly what was meant by the "social" function of the group. It should also be noted that these "unofficial" meetings, where organizational decisions were made and implemented, were never criticized by members who were not involved or did not attend. The fact that individuals at the informal meetings were not seen as trying to "take over" or bypass the official channels would indicate that the meetings were viewed as an adjunct to VET, not as a replacement or a means of control. This speech situation was characterized by fewer participants (4 to 10) than typically attended official meetings, by no set spatial ordering, and by initial focusing of discussion on specific topics with emphasis on the *internal* aspects of VET and Vietnam veterans (i.e., the "nature" of VET and its membership).

Public activities were those situations organized, sanctioned, and advertised as "official" acts of VET. This included receptions for specific individuals or organizations (e.g., to recognize a particular legislator, to acknowledge the contribution of another group), for fund raising, for public demonstrations, for testimony presented as representing VET, for meetings with government or private agencies regarding Vietnam veteran issues, for sponsoring speakers or informative events, and for arranging entertainment and banquets that were publicized as being for "all Vietnam veterans and their families and friends." These were all situations publicly acknowledged as being organized by the group and for the expressed purpose of "helping Vietnam veterans" economically, politically, or socially. These situations were characterized by announcing the purpose of the activity regarding Vietnam veterans prior to, during, and after the event, by involving selected participants, and by including speaking about Vietnam veterans and the Vietnam War as public issues (i.e., something that concerns all members of society).

Internal activities were those situations privately sponsored by members of the organizational contexts—that is, where they were not regarded as representing an organizational activity and were not announced or acknowledged as public events for veterans. These included parties given by VET members, attending sporting events, meals preceding and following public activities or VET meetings, and occasions where members met to assist another VET member (e.g., helping in moving, housepainting). These situations were characterized by informality, the presence of veterans and nonveterans, and a mixture of veteran and nonveteran and organizational topics in speaking.

In addition to official internal activities, VET instigated and attended *official ceremonies* designed to recognize, honor, and praise specified or all Vietnam veterans. VET was instrumental in having the local government declare a "Vietnam Veterans Recognition Day," which preceded the National Veterans Day. This event included: ceremonies for presenting awards to outstanding Vietnam veterans who served the community, or Vietnam veterans in particular; prayers and moments of silence to acknowledge the veterans who had died in Vietnam; music played by and for the Vietnam veterans; and statements made by veterans and their families thanking the city, or veterans praising each other, or veterans calling on the government or "the people" to aid veterans regarding employment, exposure to Agent Orange, or the image of the Vietnam veteran.

Other related official ceremonies included: participation in memorial parades, where Vietnam veterans from VET marched together wearing fatigues or civilian clothes and carried a banner displaying the organizational name and symbol; memorial services at local veterans' cemeteries;

keeping vigils outside a Veterans Administration office as a means of protesting cuts in the V.A.'s budget; and, during the week that the Vietnam Veterans Memorial in Washington, D.C. was dedicated, arranging for the names of all the veterans from the state who had died in Vietnam to be read publicly at a candlelight ceremony. These situations were characterized by a solemn atmosphere, specific references to the dead of the Vietnam War, public recognition and acknowledgment of having served in Vietnam, nonveterans calling attention to the service of the Vietnam veterans, and speeches by veterans that called for public concern by "the people," the government, and all Vietnam veterans for specific, more positive images of Vietnam veterans (see Chapters 5, 6, 7, & 8, this volume).

Out of the public context, members of VET attended *informal "ceremonies"* that may be characterized as events designed to recognize, praise, and honor other Vietnam veterans. These situations included privately sponsored events, such as "bachelor parties," private graveside services for recently deceased VET members, and "toasts" to friends who died in action or after having returned from Vietnam. These situations are central to this study because the issue of *being* a Vietnam veteran was central to some of the speech activity in the context. Additionally, in these and other ceremonial contexts, references to the dead of the Vietnam War precipitated speech reflecting the perceived "meaning" of the war and subsequent treatment of returning Vietnam veterans. This connection between ceremonial contexts and references to the Vietnam War was so strong that when one "bachelor party" for a VET member was proposed, he requested that we "all just have a good time; I don't want to spend the night before my wedding sitting around and rapping about the 'Nam." Nevertheless, these situations were characterized by references to the war, the "legacy" of Vietnam for veterans and the country, and concern over the identity of being a Vietnam veteran in contemporary America.

Method

Hymes (1972) begins his seminal essay on the ethnography of communication by stating that "diversity of speech has been singled out as the hallmark of sociolinguistics" (p. 39). He points to numerous instances across and within cultures where the speech repertoire and economy varies considerably from context to context, relationship to relationship, topic to topic, and so forth, so that "no normal person, and no normal community, is limited to a single way of speaking, to an unchanging monotony" (p. 38). Although we recognize that there is significant diversity in the speech of any culture, we also know that these diverse ways of speaking within a culture can be organized. Through the discovery and description of distinctive systems of symbolic forms, meanings, and functions, we can understand the relationship of seemingly unrelated patterns of speech usage. A variety of indigenous expressions can be heard as emerging from a unified cultural system that, when explicated, can render coherent and intelligible diverse ways of speaking.

The ethnography of speaking descriptive framework, as articulated by Hymes, was adopted to chart the communicative terrain and identify the patterns of speaking of this particular Vietnam veteran speech community. Use of this framework facilitates the discovery and description of specified sequences of communicative acts that have particularized meaning in the specific speech community under investigation (cf. Philipsen, 1972, 1975, 1976). Systematic observation of interaction using the ethnography of speaking framework was used to discover and describe the regularities in speech use among the group of speakers. By describing the relationship among the various components of the *etic* framework (a general system of categories that can be used to describe all specific, or emic, speech acts—cf. Pike, 1967), the researcher can explicate how speech is organized in a particular context. The etic framework provides the observer with meaningful categories by which to "translate" the emic data of the native's communicative life. Furthermore, the discovery of reoccurring patterns of communicative conduct among individuals was assumed to implicate a system of shared knowledge for the appropriate use and interpretation of speaking (i.e., a shared normative system pertaining to speech).

I began this chapter with a detailed description of the speech community, context, subjects, and speech activities of VET members because, according to Hymes, an adequate description of distinctive ways of speaking must clearly delineate the specific social world being analyzed. To begin to analyze specific acts of speech, those speech acts must first be located within a speech community. This must be a reflexive process because an important dimension of defining a speech community is the identification of a shared normative system. Therefore, the ethnographer must make an initial gross generalization as to the location of a speech community while, at the same time, recognize that this generalization will need to be modified as more data concerning the presence of the speech community are collected. The initial move usually is to identify a group of subjects who regularly interact in some specific ground or context. However, that aspect alone should not lead the ethnographer to label that group of speakers a speech community until a more explicit analysis has been completed concerning the degree of shared linguistic, normative, and cultural features.

After the initial identification of a speech community, the ethnographer must locate those contexts within the community that are considered primary situations for speaking (or the absence of speaking). Speech *situations* are those contexts in the speech community marked by the observer as places for speaking (e.g., parties, meetings, conferences, rallies, ceremonies, etc.). Equally important, one must also note those situations associated with the absence of speaking (i.e., those contexts where speech is usually proscribed or not preferred). However, in most contemporary American communities, the absence of speech is usually restricted to specific speech events or acts rather than being associated with entire genres or situations (cf. Philipsen, 1975, 1976).

Within most speech situations the ethnographer can identify specific activities of speaking that can be called *speech events*. This is the level at which particular "boundaries" on speaking are identified as a way of delineating the distinctive patterns of speech in the community. Speech events can include phenomena such as leave-takings, greetings, conversations, prayers, arguments, speeches, and so forth. As Hymes (1972) has stated, "the term *speech event* will be restricted to activities, or aspects of activities, that are directly governed by rules or norms for the use of speech" (p. 56).

The minimal unit of analysis in the descriptive framework is the *speech act*, which "represents a level distinct from the sentence, and not identifiable with any single portion of other levels of grammar, nor with segments of any particular size defined in terms of other levels of grammar" (Hymes, 1972, pp. 56–57). The speech event is usually made up of one or more specific speech acts that can be abstracted from the event (e.g., jokes in a conversation, complaints in a story, requests in a prayer, etc.). Identifying the variety of acts, and their forms and meanings, is an essential move in the understanding of speech in a community because "discourse may be viewed in terms of acts both syntagmatically and paradigmatically; i.e., both as a sequence of speech acts and in terms of classes of speech acts among which choice has been made at given points" (Hymes, 1972, p. 57). It is at the levels of speech events and speech acts that one uses the specific descriptive features of the ethnography of speaking framework to discover and describe how speech is used in the community.

As stated earlier, the components of the descriptive framework are posited as necessary and sufficient to describe the use and interpretation of all naturally occurring speech. In 1962, Hymes posited seven central components for analyzing speech events and acts: sender, receiver, message form, code, channel, topic, and setting. In 1972, these factors were elaborated to include 16 components, although they were grouped together into eight categories under the mnemonic SPEAKING: settings, participants, ends, act sequences, keys, instrumentalities, norms, and genres.

Although the descriptive/theoretic framework of the ethnography of speaking can be applied to any speech community, the particular manner in which it is employed will depend on the constraints of the specific context. That is, the degree of what can be observed, whom can be talked to, what explanations can be articulated by the native, and so forth will influence the way one "does" the ethnography of speaking. What follows is an analysis of three specific *speech forms* used by members of VET that were discovered using the ethnography of speaking descriptive framework. The use of the three forms of cultural communication demonstrate how the speech surrounding the Vietnam experience creates and maintains a coherent cultural identity for some Vietnam veterans.

RITUAL

According to Philipsen (1987), "the reality of a culture as experienced by those who live it moves along an axis with two poles at opposing extremes, one exerting a pull toward the communal, the other toward the individual, as the dominant themes and warrants of human thought, speech, and action" (p. 245). He further asserts that communication scholars interested in the cultural "forces" that pull people toward the communal end of the axis should study those processes among speakers that create, enact, and negotiate shared identity. Philipsen maintains that, "although the way the cultural function is performed differs from community to community, there are characteristic forms used to affirm and negotiate a sense of shared identity. Three of these which feature prominently in cultural communication are ritual, myth, and social drama" (p. 250). Philipsen also points out that these are universal forms in cultural communication that can be identified using the ethnography of speaking descriptive framework.

Ritual is a form used to affirm a sense of shared identity by providing a culturally prescribed ordering of behavior that members can follow. Building on the work of Goffman (1967), Philipsen (1987) defines *ritual* as "a communication form in which there is a structured sequence of symbolic acts, the correct performance of which constitutes homage to a sacred object" (p. 250). One can find in communication conduct a series of highly codified acts that, when properly played out, demonstrate the consensus of the players regarding their shared identity. An example of this communication form can be found in Katriel's (1985) " 'Griping' as a verbal ritual in Israeli discourse." She argues that "griping" (*kiturim*, or *kuterai* in colloquial Hebrew) "has evolved as a standardized communicative event and that as such it constitutes a readily available pattern for the structuring of plaintive talk for a considerable section of the community" (p. 22). Using the ethnography of speaking descriptive framework, Katriel identified the specific setting, participants, topics, act sequences, and purposes for the enactment of this ritual. This form of "griping" allows Israelis to complain about their community while, at the same time, to reaffirm ritually their commitment to the principles and ideal of their culture.

A communication pattern among Vietnam veterans can be identified that functions to "pay homage" to the relationship between the self and group identity. An important aspect of the communication of Vietnam veterans involves the *affirmation* of their identity as Vietnam veterans. Speakers establish their *legitimacy* as Vietnam veterans when engaged in talk with other Vietnam veterans. Legitimacy was discussed and responded to as a necessary element in veteran interaction. The belief was repeatedly stated that "only" a Vietnam veteran "really knows" what the war was like, and "only a vet" is competent and trustworthy enough to engage in talk about the war with other Vietnam veterans. Among Vietnam veterans, *who you are* and *what you were* become prominent features of spoken life. The central criterion for what counts as a credible speaker is the speaker's background as a soldier and veteran. In other words, is the person speaking actually a Vietnam veteran, and, if so, was that person a combat veteran with service "in country" (in Vietnam)?

The characteristics of the ritual, which establishes legitimacy for Vietnam veterans, can be outlined using the ethnography of speaking descriptive framework. The purpose is not to present a step-by-step reconstruction of veteran encounters, but to present the particular cultural pattern for the interpretation of what counts as affirmation of shared identity among some Vietnam veterans.

The scenes for the ritual of legitimacy include those *settings* where veterans are together because they are veterans—that is, where only Vietnam veterans are expected to be, and that being a Vietnam veteran is the necessary and sufficient condition for admittance. Of the six speech situations described earlier, the ritual was played out at the official meetings, the informal meetings, the internal activities, and the informal ceremonies. In these situations all those spoken to would be expected to be Vietnam veterans unless they demonstrated otherwise. In discussing why he came to some of the activities listed above, one veteran stated, "I feel like I don't have to censor myself, like I do around others [nonveterans]. These guys here understand, and I don't worry about scaring anybody if I talk about the war. I know I can talk here without getting a lot of shit." While the physical location is usually unimportant, the scene is defined by the members as one where "being a Vietnam veteran" is expected.

Just as the scene must be one where only a veteran is expected to be present, the *topic* of the ritual takes the form of discussions regarding areas of knowledge "only a Vietnam veteran would have." Topics that serve to initiate the legitimacy ritual are ones that require the "specialized" knowledge of the veteran. These are topics where the speaker's knowledge of the topic *is* the enactment of being a veteran. The clearest example of this emerged during discussion regarding the various modes, settings, implements, and specific units involved in combat in Vietnam. These areas are considered topics where only a "legitimate" Vietnam veteran would possess the knowledge necessary and sufficiently adequate to engage in conversation. It is assumed only a Vietnam veteran would know the proper acronyms, unit numbers, weapon nomenclature, and field tactics involved in Vietnam combat. The ability to discuss these specialized war-related topics is perceived as a clear "signal" that the participant is "one of us."

A related legitimizing topic concerns statements reflecting experience in dealing with the "V.A." (Veterans Administration). Members of VET repeatedly stated that it is "common knowledge" that the V.A. "always screws you over," especially if you are a " 'Nam vet." This concept that the V.A. is the "enemy" is clear when a participant attempts to define the actions of the V.A. among other Vietnam veterans. Any statement that began, "but the man at the V.A. said," typically provoked laughter, the shaking of heads, and a series of profanities. As with discussions of combat and being "in country," the sharing of one's frustrating experiences with the V.A., or almost any other federal agency that deals with Vietnam veterans, signals to those present that the speaker is a "real Vietnam veteran."

The *act sequence* of the ritual can vary, depending on the number of participants, but similar constraints apply to dyads as well as to larger groups. What follows is a sequence that occurred repeatedly in groups of four or more Vietnam veterans in scenes like the ones described above.

1. A topic can be generated by any participant of the group. The ritual is initiated if the topic falls under one of the categories of "vet" topics discussed above, or any other topic that "only a vet would know."
2. The topic is appropriate or initiating the ritual if it provokes a "collective" response from the other participants (e.g., exclamations of recognition, shaking of heads, derisive laughter, the pushing out of breath for signaling disgust or pleasure, etc.). This ackowledgment

provides the impetus for the speaker to continue speaking and is necessary for the ritual to continue.

3. The person who initiated the topic is allowed and encouraged to continue with his account, but is interrupted by comments for clarification, expressions of understanding, or expressions that their experiences differed to some degree (e.g., "we used willey-peter [white phosphorus] instead of cannister rounds"). Accuracy and completeness of description are essential at this phase in the sequence because the ability to give a "credible" account is the central criterion for legitimacy. If the participant is repeatedly called to account for inaccuracies or contradictions, the ritual is not completed.
4. If the initial speaker successfully completes his description, and therefore has enacted his legitimacy, the sequence is continued and completed by the remaining participants, each putting in "a word or two" about their experiences with the topic. Hence, turns at talk are taken so that each participant has the opportunity to demonstrate his legitimacy as a Vietnam veteran. Often this expectation for each member to contribute was explicitly stated, especially in groups consisting of veterans who served at different times of the war (e.g., a veteran who served in 1967 is asked to compare "notes" with a veteran who served in 1969). These do not appear to be instances of "one-upmanship," but seem to serve as instances that establish the equality and commonality of the speakers.

That this final phase of the ritual is expected was made noticeable by its occasional absence. In one such case a discussion centered on various forms of helicopter transportation used in Vietnam. Of the five speakers, four mentioned different uses or types of helicopters they encountered during their tour of duty "in country." The fifth participant remained silent after the others took their speaking turns; the four who had taken their speaking turns then remained silent, with two of the participants staring at the man who had not taken his speaking turn. The man, who had remained standing silently for almost one minute, then quickly explained that he had not actually been "in country," but had participated in the war through flight off of a navy ship. The discussion then continued on various other combat veteran topics, but the silent fifth member, although an "actual" Vietnam veteran, did not participate except by looking at whomever was speaking; he also looked away whenever it appeared to his speaking turn. The topic shifted several times, and then the silent member left the group without further interaction or comment. Although one might get the distinct impression that these veterans believed the man who could not participate in the ritual was not a "true vet," they did not call the man to account. Thus, there existed a strong norm to maintain as nonjudgmntal a climate as possible when it came to evaluating the actions of other VET members. At least at this point in time, members worked hard to prevent any breaches in the cultural fabric of the group.

All members present in the appropriate scenes are eligible for *participation* in the ritual, and, as discussed above, it was expected that each person participate in the ritual when called upon. No exclusion due to ethnicity, age, or physical condition was observed. However, it should be noted that those veterans with obvious physical disabilities were accorded more turns at talk and appeared to be the focus of attention if the group consisted primarily of nondisabled men. Because Vietnam veterans with combat experience were clearly considered to be the "most legitimate" among Vietnam veteran, and since a physical disability is usually an overt signal that the person did experience combat, disabled Vietnam veterans had the highest priority in participation.

If the sequence described above occurs in the specified scenes, with the specified participants, and on the specified topics, then the *purpose* or *function of the ritual is to affirm shared cultural identity.* Each veteran is given the opportunity to *proclaim* his identity as a Vietnam veteran. The combined performances of such proclamations serve to develop a unified sense of what it means to be a Vietnam veteran and, therefore, to develop communal identity. When examining the statements of veterans during and after these ritual exchanges, one can hear an increase in comments regarding the "uniqueness" of Vietnam veterans, as well as the value placed on being a Vietnam veteran. The uniqueness or difference of Vietnam veterans is expressed in statements that reflect an "us versus them" attitude. In commenting on the combat stories that were being told, one veteran said "it scares the shit out of people when we talk like this." There is recognition, then, that what Vietnam veterans say to each other would be inappropriate or misunderstood if shared with non-Vietnam veterans.

Additionally, VET members expressed feelings of value and pleasure that they can share these experiences with those who would not consider them "strange." As one veteran stated after a meeting, "it's nice to know I'm not the only one who felt that way," and another veteran then added, "yeah, we all know what it was like, brother." By revealing aspects of the self-regarding experiences in "being" a veteran, the ritual allows each participant to place themselves and others in the community and to form a community "bond." In a previous study of a staged, public meeting in which Vietnam veterans confessed to war crimes they witnessed or committed, I noted that the event was most effective in the "celebration" of group identity (Braithwaite, 1982). Spoken affirmation of group selfhood is accomplished through this ritual, which establishes the legitimacy of each speaker and, at the same time, forms a link that unites the participants by virtue of their shared experiences and talk.

MYTH

While ritual is used by speakers to enact and affirm shared identity, the communicative form of myth provides speakers with a way to apply and express significant aspects of their cultural identity creatively. According to Philipsen (1987), "myth is a great symbolic narrative which holds together the imagination of a people and provides bases of harmonious thought and action" (p. 251). Speech can be identified as mythic when individuals weave cultural themes and resources into their own stories and tales. Myths are not fairy tales or ancient stories of unknown origins; they are narratives told by members of a speech community in which distinctive aspects of the culture are embedded in the speech in order to "posit a supersensible world of meaning and value from which the least member of a tribe can borrow something to dignify and give coherence to his life" (p. 8). Members use the cultural resources of their community in their stories to affirm their place in the community and to apply creatively those valued aspects of the culture to their individual lives.

For example, Hannerz (1969) describes the mythic expression of Black males in some urban ghetto communities, where he found that, when the men gathered in the community, each told a tale of how he "beat the white man" through cunning and verbal wit. Each story becomes a myth in that the speaker places himself at the center of a tale where "the ghetto man" defeats superior forces of the white man's world. To label these stories myths is not to question their veracity, but to call attention to the particular function of this type of communicative form.

It is not difficult to see that the stories Vietnam veterans tell to one another also occur in this mythic form. As described above in the discussion of appropriate topics for the ritual of legitimacy, there are numerous cultural resources shared by Vietnam veterans that can be expressed in individual stories. Vietnam veterans can tell tales that reflect experiences with a variety of phenomena common to all veterans (e.g., "buddies," "dealing with the V.A.," "coming home," "being in the 'Nam," "talking about the war," "being a vet," etc.). But these stories are told as individual experiences. Like the stories told by the urban Black males, the stories told by Vietnam veterans regarding these common topics provide a ground for the speaker's beliefs in what moves them and their world. The stories allow the Vietnam veteran storyteller to articulate to himself and to his listeners the way he, *as* a Vietnam veteran, sees and experiences the world. The stories told about the problems encountered by one veteran, which are common to all veterans, help us to understand the forces transcending the fate of any particular man. Additionally, the stories give a certain coherence to life as a Vietnam veteran by allowing the storyteller to see his own acts as conforming to a pattern that is implicit in the patterned stories of other members of the community of veterans. The stories function to establish a sense of "place" for the speaker within a particular cultural milieu. As Philipsen (1987) notes, "Myth is the form wherein they creatively apply and discover the fit between past and present, community and individual" (p. 252).

SOCIAL DRAMA

Ritual and myth are, respectively, communication forms wherein the shared cultural resources or codes are used with a restricted sequence or are creatively applied. However, a third communicative form serves to challenge, test, and, most importantly, negotiate resources and codes. This form, the *social drama,* "consists of a dramatic sequence in which social actors manifest concern with, and negotiate the legitimacy and scope of the group's rules for living" (Philipsen, 1987, p. 252). Philipsen argues that we can use Victor Turner's (1974, 1980) concept of social drama to discover, describe, and explicate those instances in the social life of a group of speakers when the boundaries and identity of the culture are called into question. Turner (1974) states that, "When the interests and attitudes of groups and individuals stood in obvious opposition, social dramas did seem to me to constitute isolable and minutely describable units of social processes" (p. 33). Using social drama to explore the "aharmonic" or "agonistic" phases among a group of speakers thus focuses our attention on those communicative sequences that orient toward, examine, escalate, and attempt to resolve tensions or conflicts within a cultural group.

As I observed in discussing ritual and myth, there were communication forms among VET members that stressed and "celebrated" individual and group identity *as* Vietnam veterans. This affirmation and maintenance of communal identity were described by the veterans as necessary and sufficient for achieving both individual and group goals (i.e., the "helping of all vets"). There developed what I would call a *code of consensus* where "what is best for all vets," "backing each other up," and "sticking together" were used as some of the primary warrants for speech and action. This code of consensus functioned as a unifying force, particularly in public discourse among Vietnam veterans. However, the power of this code was severely tested when the Vietnam Veterans Memorial (VVM) was erected in Washington, D.C. From the time the VVM's design was announced and continuing up to and after the dedication ceremonies, both public and private discourse among Vietnam veterans revealed fundamental differences concerning the VVM.  Analysis of the talk among Vietnam veterans regarding attitudes toward the VVM using the four phases of the social dramatic concept allows one to hear the discourse not as a series of random arguments, but as a sequential progression that functions as negotiation of a significant aspect of veteran cultural identity.

In referring to response generated by some attempts at American urban renewal, Turner (1974) states that social enterprises that intended to integrate and be "harmonic processual units" are oftentimes perceived as *breaches* rather than progress; acts that have the stated intention of being "done *for*" a particular segment of society are sometimes perceived as being "done *to*" that social group. This describes some responses to the VVM. The stated goal of the VVM was to "honor those who gave their lives," "put Vietnam behind us," and act as a "national salute to Vietnam veterans." The chairman of the board of the Vietnam Veterans Memorial Fund was quoted as saying the VVM would be the "first step in the healing process" for Vietnam veterans. However, the VVM was not received as such by all parties involved (see Chapter 10, this volume). Rather than serving as a unifying symbol for all Vietnam veterans, the VVM became a focus for fundamental differences among veterans and functioned to divide the group.

We can describe this breach in the cultural fabric by identifying the divisive character of the veteran's discourse about the VVM. The polarized terms used to describe the nature and function of the VVM reveal clear division among veterans. Although there is insufficient space here to describe fully all the various arguments for and against the VVM, we can see that each cluster of polarized terms characterized in many of the arguments leaves little room for middle ground: *Impressive* versus *hidden, unique* versus *black scar; honor* versus *shame, homage* versus *defame; win* versus *lose, remember* versus *forget*.

As indicated, the breach over the VVM became a signal of "deeper" divisions among the veterans. The conflicting dialogues were not merely about the nature of the VVM, but about differences in the premises and assumptions surrounding the identity of being a Vietnam veteran. Specifically, the conflict over the VVM became a question of defining the Vietnam veteran as a "winner" or a "loser." A crisis can be said to have occurred in that the VVM was used by VET members as a symbol to represent opposing positions. Some stated that the VVM signaled "success" and an "accomplishment" for veterans, while others held that it signaled "failure" and was a "defeat" for veterans. It was not that the opposing position wanted "failure," but the the VVM symbolized failure to "America and all vets." Just as the conflict over the "Watergate" incident in American politics led to a collective questioning over what it meant to be a "President," the conflict over the VVM led to questioning the basic assumptions of what it meant to be a " 'Nam vet."

Turner (1980) states that an inevitable result of a group experiencing cultural crisis is "what one might call social or plural *reflexivity,* the ways in which a group tries to scrutinize, portray, understand, and then act on itself" (p. 156). This reflexivity can be identified in the methods used to limit the spread of a crisis and return the group to the "status quo." That is, the particular cultural resources brought to bear to "defuse" a divisive situation should reveal the manner in which a group assigns coherence to its own actions. In this case, those veterans who recognized the danger of continued dissension over the VVM made public and private appeals to repair or *redress* the damage wrought by the conflict over the VVM. Three types of appeals or redressive actions can be identified, each of which was an attempt to assign a particular meaning to the events surrounding the VVM.

One type of redressive action involves the use of a "scapegoat" to define the veteran's sense of responsibility for "losing" the war. By placing the "blame" on the "politicians," the "protestors," "Nixon," and even "Reagan," some attempted to unite Vietnam veterans by pointing to a common "enemy." This appeal stated that veterans should not view themselves as losers, or the VVM as a symbol of their loss, because the responsibility of the war belonged to someone else. A scapegoat is offered in symbolic sacrifice for any perceived "sins" by the members of the group. However, this redressive action could be accepted only if one also accepted the premise that the war was "lost," something many Vietnam veterans would not concede. This redressive action had little impact on most Vietnam veterans.

A second type of redressive action is an attempt to reaffirm the code of consensus. This was a call for veterans to "set aside" their differences and "stick together" and was based on the premise that the issue of whether or not the VVM symbolizes winning or losing was not "significant" enough to divide veterans, that the significance of "who lost" was not relevant to "being a vet." The common symbolic code of "we're all just vets" was invoked to reduce the tension among those veterans who disagreed about the nature of the war and the VVM. However, this redressive action could only be accepted if one also accepted the premise that whether the war was won or lost "really didn't matter," something with which many veterans refused to agree. Numerous statements revealed that simply "being a vet" was not enough for consensus over the VVM. This action thus had limited effectiveness because it relied on an attempt to reaffirm a code that was itself being challenged.

A third type of redressive action can be described as an attempt to *redefine* the symbolic nature of the VVM. Unlike other redressive actions, this attempt to manage the conflict called for Vietnam veterans to "remember why we are here" (i.e., at the VVM). The appeal suggests that, while the win/lose aspect was not meaningless or insignificant, other issues concerning the VVM should take precedence at the moment. Two symbolic concepts that emerged to redefine the meaning of the VVM were "we're home" and "our buddies." The first concept was evoked to highlight the views that the VVM stands for the "welcome home we never had," and that the VVM should stand as a reminder that what "counts now is that we've made it [home] and that many of our buddies did not" (see Chapter 4, this volume). Hence, veterans should view the VVM not as a reminder of the war itself, but as a symbol that soldiers who served in Vietnam, both living and dead, are now accepted "back home." A second and related concept asked veterans to think about the VVM and all of the related activities (e.g., reunions, parties, speeches, flowers, wreaths, etc.) as reminders that we care for "our buddies." One veteran organization leader stated that, "in the 'Nam, your buddies was all that was really important. It should still be like that here." Asking veterans to see the VVM as symbolic of the importance of "our buddies," both living and dead, works as a redressive action because the concept carried such moral weight when the men served together during the war. Remembering and standing by your "buddies" carries meaningful and unifying force when used by Vietnam veterans.

The use of these two codes appeared to have the most impact on reducing the dissenting forces. One reason for this is that the two codes do not demand that those with opposing positions on the VVM compromise their stance. To paraphrase one veteran who attempted to intervene between conflicting parties, "it's O.K. to feel whatever you want about the war, but remember what is *more* important than any of that." What was emphasized in these appeals was a *hierarchy of meaning* (cf., Cushman & Craig, 1976; Pearce & Conklin, 1979) regarding significant concepts and premises of Vietnam veterans. The redressive action can be said to have reintegrated the community because it used codes that transcended earlier meanings attached to the VVM. All positions can now be recognized as legitimate, but at least two aspects of Vietnam veteran identity, "we're home" and "our buddies," rank above all others.

CONCLUSION

What I have tried to do here is posit several ways to organize the content, form, and function of discourse among some Vietnam veterans. I have argued that a productive way to begin this task is provided by the ethnography of speaking descriptive/theoretic stance, which helps us to discover, describe, and explicate significant aspects of the spoken world of the Vietnam veteran. In doing so, I have tried to present what I believe is evidence that Vietnam veterans form a distinct cultural community in contemporary America. Using Philipsen's (1987) cultural communication theory, I have argued that there are communicative rituals present in the discourse of Vietnam veterans who came together *as* Vietnam veterans, and that these rituals function to affirm shared cultural identity. I also posit that the cultural resources used in these rituals and other aspects of veteran discourse occur in mythic form in that they allow individual veterans to "place" themselves in a specific cultural milieu. Finally, I argue that we can hear divisive discourse among Vietnam veterans, at least as it applies to their differing responses to the VVM, as additional evidence that many Vietnam veterans possess a considerable number of shared concepts and premises regarding the meaning and place of the Vietnam veteran in America today. Although the exact location of that place is difficult to determine, it clearly exists somewhere on the perimeter of "mainstream" contemporary society (see Chapters 1, 5, & 6, this volume). The experience of Vietnam, and the mark it has left on the men and women who served there, permanently separates Vietnam veterans, no matter how often reconciliation is attempted. As William Broyles, Jr. wrote in "Why Men Love War" (1984), an account of his understanding of the relationships among the warrior, the war, and the rest of the world, "I suffered, I was there. You were not. Only those facts matter" (p. 61).

REFERENCES

Bauman, R., & Sherzer, J. (Eds.). (1974). *Explorations in the ethnography of speaking*. Cambridge: Cambridge University Press.

Braithwaite, C. (1982, February) *Enactment as a form of protest: The winter soldier investigation.* Paper presented to the Language Behavior Interest Group Western Speech Communication Association, Denver, CO.

Braithwaite, C. (1989). *An ethnography of speaking among Vietnam Veterans.* Unpublished Doctoral Dissertation, University of Washington, Seattle, WA.

Broyles, W. (1984, November) Why men love war. *Esquire,* pp. 55–65.

Cushman, D., & Craig, R. (1976). Communication systems: Interpersonal implications. In G. Miller (Ed.), *Explorations in interpersonal communication* (pp. 37–58). Beverly Hills: Sage.

Goffman, E. (1967). *Interaction ritual.* Garden City, NJ: Anchor.

Hannerz, U. (1969). *Soulside: Inquiries into ghetto culture and community.* New York: Columbia University Press.

Hymes, D. (1962). The ethnography of speaking. In T. Gladwin & W. Sturtevant (Eds.), *Anthropology and human behavior* (pp. 13–53). Washington, DC: Anthropological Society of Washington.

Hymes, D. (1972). Models of the interaction of language and social life. In J. Gumperz & D. Hymes (Eds.), *Directions in sociolinguistics: The ethnography of communication* (pp. 35–71). New York: Holt, Rinehart, and Winston.

Hymes, D. (1974). Ways of speaking. In R. Bauman & J. Sherzer (Eds.), *Explorations in the ethnography of speaking* (pp. 433–451). Cambridge: Cambridge University Press.

Katriel, T. (1985). "Griping" as a verbal ritual in some Israeli discourse. In J. Jascal (Ed.), *Dialogue: An interdisciplinary approach.* Amsterdam: J. Benjamins.

Pearce, B., & Conklin, B. (1979). A model of hierarchical meaning in coherent conversation and a study of "indirect responses." *Communication Monographs, 46,* 75–87.

Philipsen, G. (1972). *Communication in Teamsterville: A sociolinguistic study of speech behavior in an urban neighborhood.* Unpublished doctoral dissertation. Northwestern University, Evanston, IL.

Philipsen, G. (1975). Speaking "like a man" in Teamsterville: Cultural patterns of role enactment in an urban neighborhood. *Quarterly Journal of Speech, 61,* 13–22.

Philipsen, G. (1976). Places for speaking in Teamsterville. *Quarterly Journal of Speech, 62,* 15–25.

Philipsen, G. (1987). The prospect for cultural communication. In L. Kincaid (Ed.), *Communication theory from Eastern and Western perspectives* (pp. 245–254). New York: Academic Press.

Pike, K.L. (1967). *Language in relation to a unified theory of the structure of human behavior.* The Hague: Mouton.

Sankoff, D. (Ed.). (1978). *Linguistic variation: Model and methods.* New York: Academic Press.

Turner, V. (1974). *Dramas, fields, and metaphors: Symbolic action in human society.* Ithaca: Cornell University Press.

Turner, V. (1980). Social dramas and stories about them. *Critical Inquiry, 7,* 141–168.

Vietnam Veterans Against the War, Inc. (1972). *The winter soldier investigation.* Boston: Globe Press.

9

Vietnam and the Second American Inner Revolution

Elizabeth Walker Mechling
Office of the President, California State University, Hayward

Jay Mechling
American Studies, University of California, Davis

America's involvement in Vietnam began and ended during an era of American culture that, extending a phrase invented by historian Thomas Cochran, we propose to call the "second inner revolution" (Cochran, 1964). Cochran saw that the collective effects of science, especially physics and psychology, at the end of the 19th century were to abolish certainty and absolutes, thereby demolishing the religious and other foundations of Americans' value structure. Rising out of "the rubble of once imposing structures of truth" was an American generation born after 1910, a generation characterized not by the inner-directed personality of the Protestant Reformation and the rise of capitalism, but by a personality type variously called "the marketer, the fixer, the organization man, and the other-directed man" (pp. 16–17). The experimental attitudes of science, argued Cochran, ratified the "inner revolution" by entering the realm of character formation: child-rearing, religious training, and schooling.

We believe we are not taking too many liberties with Cochran's thesis to say that there was in America a Second Inner Revolution that began to be felt after World War II. Whereas the first revolution set a trajectory for the American character, the second revolution has to do with the changing social structural context for that modern American personality. Put differently, there developed in mid-century America a sort of American individualism unlike earlier versions and one becoming increasingly problematic. The tendencies of American individualism born in the First Inner Revolution accelerated and became increasingly pathological with the simultaneous loss of strong communal contexts for that individualism. The full flowering of bureaucracy as a form of social organization in the 20th century, and the emergence of the powerful, centralized welfare state in the 1930s and 1940s, meant not that there was a "new personality type," but that the existing personality type developed its most unpleasant possibilities in the absence of social structures that would normally keep it in check. The Second Inner Revolution, therefore, is less exclusively about the American personality than about the changing relationship between American individualism and the social-structural context for that individualism in the last half of the 20th century.

The present chapter explores the collision between the Second Inner Revolution and America's involvement in Vietnam. We see in this meeting between American individualism and the war an unfair match. The Second Inner Revolution is such a powerful force in American culture that the Vietnam War was a mere blip, an historical hiccup, in its flow through American history. We shall argue that Americans understood Vietnam within the context of this revolution, not the other way around. Vietnam was a "text" to to be interpreted, but it was no mere text. Vietnam was a powerful text because the war forced to conscious consideration precisely those contradictions and ambivalences that lie in American individualism and community in the 1960s, 1970s, and 1980s. The enduring legacy of Vietnam is not that it changed anything in American culture, but that it provided a condensed version of our most troubling contradictions (see Chapter 10, this volume). Vietnam may be with us for as long as these contradictions play themselves out in our history.

We begin by examining briefly the role of character and culture in American thinking about foreign affairs in the years immediately following World War II. Against this background we bring together two recent bodies of writing about America—books about the fundamental transformation of American character and culture in the past four decades, and books offering a cultural explanation for, as one of the authors puts it in his subtitle, "how American culture led us into Vietnam and made us fight the way we did" (Baritz, 1985). Finally, we raise some doubts about our own generalizations by inquiring into the readiness of some American audiences to "read" Vietnam narratives as dramas of individualism.

I

The history of scholarly literature on the meanings of American civilization begins in the 1920s and 1930s, just when Americans were least concerned with global events and with the country's role in foreign affairs.

Postwar isolationism and prosperity in the 1920s set the stage for the reflexive commentary of Parrington, Lippmann, and others who saw in America a culture fundamentally different from the European cultures that had proven themselves decadent and untrustworthy by creating a world war (see Chapter 4, this volume). The Depression shattered American self-confidence and accelerated the desire of journalists, culture critics, and scholars to understand whether there was something wrong at the center of the civilization. Although the American Studies movement was born in the university during this period, much of the analysis was for a general audience. Karen Horney's *The Neurotic Personality of Our Time* (1937), Robert S. Lynd's *Knowledge for What?* (1939), and Margaret Mead's *And Keep Your Powder Dry* (1942), for example, all worked at developing notions of cultural patterning and national character in order to account for American values in the 20th century. The emerging consensus of these writers was that American culture and character featured certain cultural contradictions that explained our unique traits and beliefs.

The theme of cultural contradictions, signaled often by the key words "irony" and "paradox" in the American studies scholarship of the period, emerged naturally from the period's myth of the Puritan origins of American culture. Puritan theology stressed ironies and dualities, from the basic imponderable fact that God granted grace in the face of original sin, through the daily ironies of living a virtuous life. Most important, the Manichaeanism of Puritan thought established a pervasive and enduring pattern of dualistic thinking in American public rhetoric. The Persian sage, Mani, founded in the 3rd century a Gnostic religion that presented a strong challenge to early Christianity and that spread from the 4th through the 12th century. St. Augustine (345–430) himself was a Manichaean for nine years before converting to Christianity, and the strong strain of Augustinian thought in Puritan theology guaranteed a Manichaean cast to early American thinking. The Manichaeans viewed the world as a struggle between two kingdoms, a peaceful and good kingdom of light versus an evil kingdom of darkness; and they viewed history as a movement toward the time when the kingdoms would be separated. The Puritans held a very particular version of this struggle, reading all around them signs that God and Satan had chosen New England as the final battleground between good and evil. The Puritans quite consciously saw themselves as the new Israelites, God's chosen people, on "an errand in the wilderness," throwing themselves into this final battle and struggling to build, as John Winthrop announced, a redemptive "city upon a hill."

But an American did not need to be a Puritan to have a sense of the contradictions posed by life in the New World. Old/new, city/country, and more complex cultural "biformities," as historian Michael Kammen (1972) calls them, arose in American consciousness during the 18th century, and the coming of the industrial revolution in the 19th provided material for a whole new set of dualisms and contradictions, summarized neatly by Leo Marx's (1964) phrase, "the machine in the garden."

Given this intellectual history of Americans' strong sense of themselves as living in a civilization of dualities in tension, it was natural for scholars and culture critics in the 1930s to see America's predicament as the result of cultural contradictions. Psychoanalyst Karen Horney, for example, detected in American society at least four cultural contradictions that, in her view, contributed to neurotic symptoms appearing in large numbers of "normal" Americans. The first "is that between competition and success, on the one hand, and brotherly love and humility on the other" (1937, p. 288). Americans in the 20th century inherited a public culture and mythology wedding Protestant Christian values of brotherly love and obligation with commercial values of competition and success, and (as Horney says) the attempt to take seriously both sets of values can lead to some serious conflicts. The second contradiction Horney identifies "is that between the stimulation of our needs and our factual frustrations in satisfying them" (p. 288). The turn of the 20th century was roughly simultaneous with the great transformation of American capitalism from a production orientation to one of consumption, with the subsequent rise of advertising as capitalism's way of inducing consumer desire. It is the nature of the system to engineer social and psychological needs just beyond the ability of consumer goods to satisfy those needs. The consumer, especially the neurotic one, never has enough goods to allay the anxieties that stimulate the consumption of the goods. The third cultural contradiction Horney identifies "exists between the alleged freedom of the individual and all his factual limitations" (p. 289). Notions of individual freedom, of freedom of choice, and so on run up against real barriers of race, class, gender, and age. The high-achievement orientation of Americans presumes individual freedom and responsibility that may be largely a fiction, but in failure, the individual tends to blame himself or herself. Horney's argument, put most briefly, is that these cultural contradictions induce in most Americans neurotic conflicts that lead to neurotic symptoms (such as rationalization, denial, narcoticization, or avoidance) as strategies to allay the conflicts. As a psychoanalyst, Horney's primary interest is in the patterns of "character neuroses" she sees, and she keeps apologetically short her discussion of the cultural origins of the neuroses.

Robert Lynd, however, picks up the sociological argument in his *Knowledge for What?* (1939). Best known as the author (with Helen Merrell Lynd) of *Middletown* (1929) and *Middletown in Transition* (1937), Lynd offers a series of propositions he believes constitute the pattern of American civilization. Like Horney, Lynd (1939) tends to see the "assumptions in American life" in contradictory pairs (p. 60). Thus, American "individualism" and belief in "the survival of the fittest" stand alongside the notion that "people ought to be loyal and stand together and work for common purposes." The strong success ethic is contradicted by an equally strong sense that the "kind of person you are is more important than how successful you are." "Hard work and thrift" may be "signs of character and the way to get ahead," but "No shrewd person tries to get ahead nowadays by working hard. . . . It is important to know the right people" (p. 61), and so on, through now-familiar cultural biformities.

Margaret Mead's *And Keep Your Powder Dry* (1942) continues probing the cultural consequences of the American success ethic and the conflicts engendered by that ethic. Mead, the anthropologist, looks to socialization at home and on the playground as the source of characteristic American patterns of values and action. Like Horney, Mead sees a connection between the compulsive competitive individualism of Americans and their simultaneous neurotic need for affection. For Americans, the measure of achievement lies not in the self but in the judgments of others, an observation reinforced by David Riesman's notion of "other directedness" in *The Lonely Crowd* (Riesman, Glazer, & Denney, 1950). In her well-known phrase that "we are all third generation," Mead attributes Americans' attitude toward authority to the immigrant origins of most Americans, a condition that reduces American deference to tradition and produces strong conformist tendencies. The success ethic does lead to characteristic American optimism and faith in improvisation. Especially relevant to foreign policy questions, Mead notes under what conditions Americans will resort to violence. Americans resent bullying behavior, but also must be willing to stand up for themselves. Americans have, in Mead's (1942) view, a "chip on their shoulder," spoiling for a fight they'll not start but are willing to join and finish (p. 156). Thus, there is a certain unsureness in Americans' engaging in a fight.

Gabriel A. Almond (1950) used these analyses of American character and culture to build his argument in what still stands as a unique accomplishment, his book, *The American People and Foreign Policy*. Writing deep in the Cold War, Almond proposed to interpret American public opinion polls about foreign policy issues with the help of the cultural analysis by Mead, Horney, and others. Almond distilled from the accumulating scholarship certain general value orientations, such as Americans' stress on "private" values, on competitiveness and achievement, on material evidence of success, and on innovation and improvement (pp. 48–49). Picking up on Horney's analysis, Almond argues that Americans' "intense individualistic competitiveness . . . produces diffuse hostile tension and general apprehension and anxiety," and that these anxieties drive Americans, on the one hand, to "an extraordinary need for affection and reassurance, and on the other, an extraordinary tendency to resort to physiological and spiritual narcosis," including mass entertainments (pp. 49–50). Discovering these patterns in American character and culture helps Almond make sense of the mass of public opinion data he has at hand as evidence of American attitudes toward foreign policy. American "moods" form policy, and Almond characterizes six movements of mood he sees as significant in understanding American foreign policy: withdrawal-intervention, mood-simplification, optimism-pessimism, tolerance-intolerance, idealism-cynicism, and superiority-inferiority (pp. 54–65).

The analysis of American national character and culture extended well into the 1950s, as important interpretations such as Riesman's *The Lonely Crowd* (Riesman, Glazer, & Denney, 1950) and David Potter's *People of Plenty* (1954) both drew on the work of Horney, Lynd, Mead, and others and added new observations and new causal explanations. In all of the writing about American character and culture the same themes recur, often in the familiar form of contradictory tendencies. Americans believe in competitive individualism, but suffer acutely the need to be liked by others. Americans believe an achievement ethic and economic abundance guarantee equal opportunity, despite real patterns of inequality and real failures in the economy to meet everyone's consumer needs. Americans will not initiate aggression, but they believe in the virtues of redemptive violence. It seems clear, in retrospect, that these culture critics are writing about a generation of Americans born during the first "inner revolution," but the analysis also hints at new tendencies barely detectable in the 1930s and 1940s. Not until the culture criticism of the 1970s and 1980s, to which we now turn, do we see the effects of the Second Inner Revolution.

II

The new scholarship on broad, synthetic themes in American culture of the 1970s and 1980s no longer speaks of "national character," but the aim still is to understand the relationships between the experiences of the individual American and the more general patterns in the public culture shared by groups of people. Indeed, the authors to whom we now turn see the emergent relationship between the individual and the group as the fundamental theme emerging in American culture for the remainder of the century. These authors find both continuities and discontinuities between the current and past concern about American individualism.

The new, synthetic scholarship on America includes Christopher Lasch's *The Culture of Narcissism* (1979), Daniel Yankelovich's *New Rules* (1981), Robert Bellah's collaborative (with four colleagues) *Habits of the Heart* (Bellah, Madsen, Sullivan, Swidler, & Tipton, 1985), and Frances FitzGerald's *Cities on a Hill* (1986). Although we shall draw upon additional contemporary culture critics as they assist in our inquiry, these are the books that bring to our analysis what Horney, Lynd, Mead, and Kluckhohn brought to Almond's—that is, a sense of the ways in which some fundamental patterns in American character and culture provide the interpretive framework for Americans' understanding of foreign affairs.

Our goal is to bring these texts together with a largely independent set of more recent texts striving to interpret the meaning of the Vietnam War and of the discourse surrounding the war. The "Vietnam critics" offer texts such as Frances FitzGerald's *Fire in the Lake* (1972), Myra MacPherson's *Long Time Passing* (1984), Loren Baritz's *Backfire* (1985), and John Hellmann's *American Myth and the Legacy of Vietnam* (1986). The first set of texts mentions Vietnam sparingly, while the Vietnam books mention some of the themes explored by the culture critics but never fully develop an analysis of the war against the background of larger patterns in American culture. Even Frances FitzGerald, who contributes a book to each group, has not brought together the two analyses (for good reasons, we might add, as an extended discussion of Vietnam in the *Cities* books would have been a distracting detour from her main thesis). Bringing together these two sets of texts establishes a conversation between them that explains a good deal more than either alone.

For the culture critics, the crucial event of the 1960s and 1970s was the emergence of an American ethic that believed that the individual could make his or her own identity. This great transformation really began at the end of the last century. Forces, now pretty well chronicled by historians, combined to create a new ethos that gradually has become dominant in 20th-century American civilization. The shift from an economy based upon production to one based upon consumption is implicated as an important cause of this change, as is the "inner revolution" (Cochran, 1964) in which Darwinian biology, non-Euclidean mathematics, the new physics, and psychology abolished absolute realities and certain knowledge. Religion declined not so much as a source of values, but as having a monopoly over all interpretations of reality. A symptom of the revolution is the shift in political, social, and literary discourse from 19th-cenutry talk about a person's "character" to 20th-century talk about "personality" (Sussman, 1984). Moreover, as psychology gained its scientific credentials and allied with advertising (Marchand, 1985), Americans were ready to think of the self as something to be fashioned.

Now, in one sense, this notion of making the self was not new to Americans. The very circumstances of the settling of America by immigrants meant that most white Americans were beginning anew, reinventing themselves, along with their communities and institutions. Mass-mediated culture in the 19th and into the 20th century touted the "self-made man." But, as Robert Bellah and his collaborators (1985) remind us in *Habits of the Heart*, even Alexis de Tocqueville issued early warnings that American individualism "might eventually isolate Americans one from another and thereby undermine the conditions of freedom" (p. viii). And de Tocqueville could not have predicted from his 1830s perspective the two 20th-century developments that would create the conditions he feared—namely, the weakening of the voluntary associations that moderated individualism and the simultaneous psychologization of American life.

Bellah and his colleagues (1985) take as their central concern the growing destructiveness of American individualism. Based on fieldwork conducted from 1979 to 1984, including interviews with over 200 informants, the authors are able to paint rather detailed portraits of four case studies whose life stories represent all the themes and complexities of American individualism. The authors actually see four strains of individualism in American culture. *Biblical individualism* works within the context of a religious, ethical community that works collectively toward redemption. "Success" within this tradition has meaning only against the communal, spiritual goals. Similarly, the founding of this tradition on holy scripture means that human actions are judged against transcendent truths, so that individual "freedom" amounts to freedom to do the right thing. And, like freedom, "justice" is "a matter more of substance than of procedure" under biblical individualism (p. 29). *Republican individualism* appeared as a second strain of American individualism at the founding of the federal government, and, even though this tradition introduced a more secular political theory and language into American civic thought, central concepts like "freedom" and "justice" still rested on the existence of a transcendent reality and values. "Success" still amounted to the leading of the virtuous life, but even Jefferson came around to the view that a strong economic base, including manufacturing, was necessary in guaranteeing equality (pp. 30–31).

Utilitarian individualism, some would argue, always coexisted with the first two traditions, but certainly this strain was ascending during de Tocqueville's visit to the United States in the 1830s, and became the dominant tradition in American society through the 19th century. Many Americans came to understand success, freedom, and justice within the framework of a philosophy that held that, "in a society where each vigorously pursued his own interest, the social good would automatically emerge" (Bellah et al., 1985, p. 33). The expressive individualism that Bellah and his collaborators identify as beginning with Walt Whitman was in some respects a reaction to utilitarian individualism. The *expressive individualist* declines to equate "success" with material acquisition and defines freedom as "the freedom to express oneself." For Whitman, the authors wrote, "the ultimate use of the American's independence was to cultivate and express the self and explore its vast social and cosmic identities" (p. 35). The emergence of expressive individualism marks the beginning of a tradition that matures in the 1960s and lies at the center of what we are calling the Second Inner Revolution.

Bellah and his colleagues (1985) find living Americans who embody all four traditions of American individualism, and each tradition poses contradictions and problems. But central to the authors' thesis is the argument that the utilitarian and expressive traditions are both dominant and out of control. The industrialization of America and the organizational revolution, prompted in part by the Civil War, led to dramatically new forms of social organization at the end of the 19th century. With the triumph of bureaucratic organization, American society saw the 20th-century emergence of two new character types, the manager and the therapist. Unlike the entrepreneur, the professional manager's "role is to persuade, inspire, manipulate, cajole, and intimidate those he manages so that his organization measures up to criteria of effectiveness shaped ultimately by the market but specifically by the expectations of those in control of his organization—finally, its owners" (p. 45). Following the logic of the bureaucracy, the manager tends to split the public world from the private, home sphere, perhaps viewing utilitarian individualism as appropriate to the public world and expressive individualism to the private. And to take care of the home sphere we have the therapist, the other character who defines the "bureaucratic consumer capitalism" of 20th-century American civilization (pp. 46–47).

The central problem in American culture of the 1980s, argue Bellah and his collaborators (1985), is "the lack of a fit between the present organization of the self and the available organization of work, intimacy, and meaning" (p. 47). The alliance of the utilitarian and expressive traditions creates a "deeply ambiguous" culture and a modern individualism inadequate for "sustaining either a public or a private life" (p. 143). The new individualism defines "success" according to the manager's standards, that is, the technical, rational solution to problems, but leaves maddeningly ambiguous the meaning of success in the private sphere. "Freedom" to the modern individualist "turns out to mean being left alone by others, not having other people's values, ideas, or styles forced upon one, being free of arbitrary authority in work, family, and political life" (p. 23), but this "freedom from" leaves open the question of how the individual may create bonds of friendship, affiliation, and even dependence within a community of equals. There may be ways out of the dilemmas posed by modern individualism, and Bellah and his colleagues channel much of their effort into examining the new strategies of commitment some Americans are adopting as they strive to ground their definitions of the self within "communities of memory." Still, the portrait they paint of American individualism in the 1980s is of an individualism developing all its worst potentials for lack of the social organizations that would tend to mitigate the effects of its ambiguities.

Daniel Yankelovich (1981) is something of a latter-day Gabriel Almond in his attempt to discover in American public opinion data patterns that will reveal the cultural base of those opinions. The "search for 'self-fulfillment' and the predicaments it creates for the individual and for the nation" explain, for Yankelovich (p. xviii), some of the major shifts he discovered in Americans' views of their lives from 1970 to 1980. Americans are taking more risks, taking an experimental view of their lives as things to be shaped and planned, and an important dimension of these "life experiments" is the drive of Americans to redefine or renegotiate the "giving/getting compact" that governs their everyday lives. Increasing numbers, for example, are questioning the economic core of the compact. There has been a "sharp drop in the number of college students who believe that 'hard work always pays off' " (p. 38), not so much because the students doubt the connection between work and reward, but because as they doubt whether it's worth all the trouble. Far fewer Americans in 1980 than in 1970 measured their fulfillment by competitive success. Instead, Americans increasingly sense an abundance of choices (p. 57) and believe themselves capable of reinventing themselves in the service of "self-fulfillment." Yet, the "psychological attitude" hinders the real search, leading more often to loneliness and anxiety than to fulfillment.

Sociologist Ralph Turner (1976) offers a useful way for talking about the economic, cultural, and psychological transformations identified by Yankelovich and others. Turner envisions a scale on which people locate the "real self," with one pole representing a self grounded in an "institutional" focus and the other grounded in "impulse." "There are suggestive signs," writes Turner, "that recent decades have witnessed a shift in the locus of self away from the institutional pole and toward that of impulse" (p. 990). The institutionally grounded "real self" emerges "when an individual adheres to a high standard, especially in the face of serious temptation to fall away"; it is something to be attained or achieved rather than discovered, and is revealed "only when the individual is in full control of his faculties and behaviors" (pp. 992–993). In contrast, the impulsively grounded real self "is revealed when a person does something solely because he wants to," is something to be discovered, and emerges most fully when inhibitions are abandoned (pp. 992–993).

A few keywords—hypocrisy, altruism, and individualism—reveal still more about Turner's (1976) distinction between the institutional and impulsive grounding for the real self. "For institutionals, hypocrisy consists of failing to live up to one's standards," whereas for the impulsives "hypocrisy consists of asserting standards and adhering to them even if the behavior in question is not what the individual wants to do and enjoys doing" (pp. 993–994). "Altruism," writes Turner, "in the traditional sense of responding to duty and setting one's own interests aside, is a penultimate hypocrisy, compounded by the probability that it is a dissimulated self-seeking and manipulation. The institutional goal is correspondence between *prescription and behavior;* the goal of impulsives is correspondence between *impulse and behavior;* hypocrisy in either instance is a lack of appropriate correspondence" (p. 994; italics in original). Finally, if we take the "individualist" to be the person who resists social pressure in order to assert true identity, Turner still distinguishes between the "institutional individualist," who is "most attentive to pernicious pressures on the side of mediocrity and the abandonment of principle," and the "impulsive individualist," who "sees clearly the social pressures in league with a system of arbitrary rules and false goals" (p. 995).

Implicit psychological theories inform the sociological analyses of Bellah, Yankelovich, Turner, and others, of course, but Christopher Lasch picks up Karen Horney's project by adding to the sociological analysis a psychoanalytic perspective on the relation between society and the individual. Many readers resist psychoanalytic approaches to culture criticism, but we believe Lasch's analysis significantly broadens our understanding of the Second Inner Revolution and its relationship to Vietnam. Lasch (1979) sees in the revised psychoanalytic notion of narcissism the key to understanding the way in which "the economic man" has given way to "the psychological man" in modern American culture. Like Horney, Lasch assumes that mild pathologies in a culture are intensified versions of natural tendencies, and that we can understand American culture by tracing the forces that give rise to a pervasive neuroticism in the American citizenry. The economic transformation described earlier has led to new institutional structures, which require new personality types for their functioning.

The bureaucracy, for example, values social skills as much or more than competence. The same historical forces that changed the institutional structures of the economy from an entrepreneurial to a bureaucratic form and style also changed the structure and dynamics of the American family late in the 19th century. The erosion of patriarchal authority, argues Lasch, weakens the superego so that its harsh, aggressive, punitive, irrational dimensions dominate the personality. "Secondary narcissism" emerges, then, not as self-love (as popular usage has it), but as the individual's defense mechanism against the anxiety, guilt, rage, and aggressive impulses of the superego. The narcissist conforms with others not out of guilt or anxiety, but out of a deep fear of punishment by the harsh superego. Part of this defense may take the form of fantasies of an omnipotent, good parent with whom one can identify the "good" self. Lasch quotes Melanie Klein approvingly with the observation that the narcissist builds fantasies of wealth, beauty, and omnipotence and lacks the ability to distinguish between the fantasized images and the self (pp. 83–84). The endless pursuit of these fantasized images, notes Lasch, is what makes the narcissist the ideal consumer for late capitalism.

The narcissistic personality of our time bears a new social ethic—self-preservation. The "new ideal of success has no content" (Lasch, 1979, p. 96) in a world where the style of "ironic detachment" seems like the only workable defense. Accordingly, the narcissist can feel no loyalty toward the group. The culture of competitive individualism, which Horney (1939) identified four decades earlier as a source of American neuroticism, frightens the narcissist, who lacks the strong superego that makes competition bearable and within bounds. Competition amounts to unbounded aggression. As might be expected, the weak superego in the narcissistic personality makes authority problematic. Moreover, therapy comes to replace religion in the modern world, and the therapeutic approach discredits authority in the search for an authentic self.

The therapeutic self involves more than the individual; at issue as well is the nature of community, of the connections between the individual and the group. Lasch's (1979) narcissistic individual has a great deal of trouble establishing intimacy with others, so friendship becomes increasingly problematic for Americans, who crave the bond of close friendship but do not know how to negotiate it. Gender matters here, as social psychologists view the male developmental problem as one of mitigating agency with communion, while the fundamental female developmental problem is gaining some agency beyond community (Spence & Helmreich, 1978). But, certainly for both sexes, the competitive individualism of American life poses many dilemmas of friendship.

Loyalty to the group, for example, becomes problematic in the new ethos. Lasch (1979) notes that the "organization man" of the 1950s gives way to "the bureaucratic gamesman" of the 1970s (pp. 92–94), as described by Maccoby (1976). "The gamesman" feels no loyalty to the organization, uses the corporation for personal ends, refuses to become close to others in the organization, and relies on power over others as a measure of success. Kanter (1977) comments on this same pattern in the organizations she has studied. Individuals chart their own professional life plans totally apart from organizations, seeking only instrumental bonds with others, as those bonds further the individual's career. Lacking is any loyalty to an organization or to a close group of colleagues within an organization. Mobility is everything on the upward trajectory, and close friendships would impede mobility.

American mass media narratives have kept pace with the cultural drama developing at mid-century, and they address quite explicitly the loyalty question. The most successful American Western films from the 1930s through the late 1950s featured a single hero and built narrative tension around the relationship between the individual-as-outsider and the community built on traditional values (Wright, 1976). By the 1960s, however, several successful Western films began to feature "corporate" heroes, wherein a pair of individuals (e.g., 1970's *Butch Cassidy and the Sundance Kid*) or even a larger group (e.g., 1969's *The Wild Bunch*) replaces the individual hero. The loyalties of these "professionals," as one media critic (Wright, 1976, p. 170) calls them, are to each other and not to the traditional society, and the commitments of these professionals are to professional values, not to larger social values. The "professional plot" introduces ambiguity into the usual opposition of good and evil in Western films. The fighting group of professionals is an independent, egalitarian, elite society completely set apart from traditional society, argues Wright, who attributes this change to the needs of an American economy overly managed by an elite group of technocrats. One might add that American espionage films of the 1960s and 1970s paint similar portraits of "professionals" whose loyalties are to the CIA or KGB rather than to the societies they are supposed to be defending.

Drawing together the insights of Bellah and his colleagues, Yankelovich, Turner, Lasch, and others, especially as they build on the earlier work of Horney, Lynd, and Mead, we are ready to say again what are the dimensions of the Second Inner Revolution that took form just as Americans had to confront the Vietnam War and all its implications and consequences. American individualism had been problematic for hundreds of years to the extent that it constantly embodies many cultural contradictions and ambivalences, but that individualism has always been balanced by social structures (such as de Tocqueville's voluntary organizations) and by public values that curbed its destructive potential. The First Inner Revolution, culminating in the generation coming of age just before World War I, destroyed faith in the eternal, transcendent truths and values that could contain the new individualism, and it initiated the process of infusing both private and public realms with a scientific, technical, and bureaucratic approach to organizing human affairs. The Second Inner Revolution, culminating in the generation coming of age after World War II, saw the ascendency of the impulsive self unfettered by social organizations and values larger than the individual. To some critics, the new self of the 1970s and 1980s shows neurotic, if not pathological, symptoms that threaten the foundations of private and public freedom.

We are concerned in this Chapter with the historical convergence between what we are calling the Second Inner Revolution and America's involvement in the Vietnam War. What happens, we want to ask, when the new American individualism collides with the war? We propose to sketch something of an answer organized around the themes or keywords used by Bellah and his colleagues and by Lasch, Yankelovich, Turner, and others. The keywords at issue are "success," "authority" (which permits talk about "freedom"), and "commitment" (which invites inquiry into "friendship," "altruism," and "community").

Success

The bureaucratic, managerial ethos of the Second Inner Revolution redefined "success" for the individual American. The "new ideal of success," writes Lasch (1979), "has no content" (p. 96). Rather, performance and process replace content. Baritz (1985) argues, for example, that despite the military's blaming the civilian government for the loss of Vietnam, it was the military's faith in technology and bureaucracy that doomed the effort. General Westmoreland rose to his position more for his understanding of the army bureaucracy than for his understanding of the Vietnamese people or of the war. The bureaucratic ethos and the sort of individualism it breeds led, in Baritz's view, to a range of problems—from interservice rivalries, to addiction, to advanced technology in weaponry, to the willingness to ignore or bury facts in order to report "progress." The mania for "body counts" stands as a grim artifact of the bureaucratic mentality in a war where progress could not be measured by ground taken. The wedding of technology's ethos with bureaucracy's ethos also tends to convert matters of quality into quantity. "The pattern of the way we fought the war is unmistakable," writes Baritz (1985). "When something failed to work, we did more of it. If a thousand troops failed, we used half a million; if grenades failed, we dropped 3,500,000 tons of bombs" (p. 233). Moreover, "careerism" within the military is indistinguishible from careerism in any bureau-

cratic corporation, though in the case of the military it has replaced an ancient code of honor. Baritz warns that the bureaucratic ethos is incompatible with "citizenship," a calling Americans must rebuild if they are to sustain democratic freedoms.

Bureaucratic individualism, in both its "normal" and its pathological, "narcissistic" versions, leads ultimately to the solipsism Baritz (1985) identifies as a core American trait revealed by the Vietnam War. "Our cultural perceptions failed," he writes, "when so many intelligent men in high positions simply assumed that our enemy's culture was sufficiently like ours that he would quit at a point where he believed he would quit" (p. 325). The bureaucratic individual so committed to rationality cannot fathom a cultural system built on other values. And, as FitzGerald (1972) and many other critics of the war make clear, Americans never understood Vietnamese culture.

Authority

Baritz (1985) opines that one of the legacies of the Vietnam era is a declining respect for authority, but Americans have a long history of skepticism toward certain sorts of authority (p. 339). A distinctly different sort of American "problem" with authority began in the generation before the war, in the Second Inner Revolution. As Americans moved from religious and civic individualism toward the utilitarian and expressive forms, from institutional sorts of individualism to impulsive ones, and as mid-range American institutions tempering those individualisms weakened, the meaning of "freedom" has shifted away from structured "freedom to" toward the contentless "freedom from," that is, freedom from the arbitrary dictates of others. Lasch's (1979) explanation for this trend, of course, rests on the notion that bureaucracy erodes patriarchal authority, thereby weakening the superego. The narcissist's subsequent "problem" with authority results from the fact that the weakened superego ends up projecting two fantasy versions of authority—one the harsh, punitive, aggressive version, and the other the idealized, omnipotent parent (p. 79). The first alternative, which leads to the rage and violence the narcissist must always work to repress, turns up in male fantasies of rape and violent destruction. The second alternative leads to surrender of one's freedom to the illusion of the protective "new paternalism" of the bureaucracy. Needless to say, neither "solution" to the problem of the weakened superego serves very well the avowed goals of a democratic society.

Several lines of inquiry suggest themselves once we recast the Vietnam War as an irritating event in Americans' increasing problem with authority in the 1960s. That the war, the draft, the resistance, and the student movement raised immediate questions about authority, we know already. What Lasch's (1979) analysis helps us understand is that Americans' "problem" with authority was not so simply a split between those who resisted the war and those who cooperated. Both sides worked from the same neurotic state of weakened superego, as becomes clear on rereading MacPherson's (1984) interviews from the perspective offered by Lasch's analysis. MacPherson talked to warriors and resistors, to deserters and commiters of atrocities. The reader is struck by the similarities among this cast of characters, as they alternately project harsh and idealized authority figures. The resistors freely admit their "hangups" with authority, and the veterans' stories of atrocities, of fragging officers, and of mutinies all make sense once we read them as symptoms of secondary narcissism.

In fact, the sexual content of much of the testimony by veterans supports Lasch's (1979) argument that the loss of the healthy superego drives men to exert their domination over women directly "in fantasies and occasionally in acts of raw violence" (p. 324). MacPherson (1984) so consistently came across two formula atrocity stories that she began to suspect their veracity. The first told of executions in which the victim's gonads were cut off and stuffed in his mouth, and the second told of counting a killed pregnant woman as "two" people for the daily body count (p. 569). The literal castration of the other in the first story and the violence directed against women (mothers) in the second provide apt symbolic content for the fantasies of an enraged self unable to build a healthy superego. The testimony of one of MacPherson's informants captures the fantasy of omnipotence, including sexual power, provided by the violence of battle: "I really believe there is no greater opportunity for tactile evidence of a sense of power than to get the M-16 working at full tilt. . . . There are two types of power. The power to create—and the power to destroy. We found that power to destroy in Vietnam. I know women don't understand it, but I don't think it's necessarily 'macho'—or male versus female. I couldn't understand it if I hadn't gone, hadn't seen it, experienced it" (pp. 207–208).

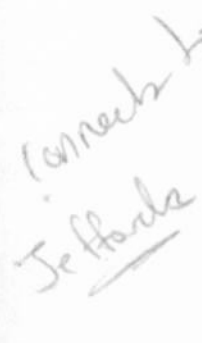

Oliver Stone's award-winning film, *Platoon* (1986), is an ideal Vietnam text for exploring some dimensions of the crisis caused by the Second Inner Revolution. Short of offering here a full critique of the film (see Chapters 5, 6, & 7, this volume), we can note a few of its elements relevant to our thesis. Chris Taylor (played by actor Charlie Sheen) feels a hovering meaninglessness in his life, so he drops out of college and volunteers for combat as part of a journey of self-fulfillment. In Vietnam he comes under the influence of two sergeants, one (Barnes, played by Tom Beringer) is the projection of a harsh and punitive father, the other

(Elias, played by Willem Defoe) is the equally unrealistic projection of a competent, kind, accepting father. Chris discovers his own rage and violence as he participates in an atrocity and eventually kills the evil father. Along the way, Stone's film touches on such issues as class and race differences among the fighting men, the absence of authority, and the attenuated, small community formed by Elias and held together precariously by the shared, ritual use of drugs.

Our point is that *Platoon* in no way raises or answers insightful questions about Vietnam. Rather, the film is about the plight of the hapless, modern American individual trying to find an identity and set of values in a world where individualism has lost its grounding in community and commitment. Vietnam just happens to provide a setting conducive to Stone's telling of this "mythic" narrative. In fact, there is no real difference between *Platoon* and Stone's next film, *Wall Street* (1987), which again features Charlie Sheen as a bureaucratic individualist (narcissist), who projects both a good father (played by his real-life father, Martin Sheen) and a bad father (played by Michael Douglas). The dramatic struggle is still about the central character's attempts to discover his "real self" and to fashion a system of values and standards of ethical conduct.

The Vietnam War, then, provided no special "legacy" regarding Americans' attitudes toward authority. Americans have a long tradition of distrusting certain kinds of authority, but the Second Inner Revolution destroyed the sort of legitimate, institutional authority (Lasch, 1979, p. 40, calls it patriarchal) necessary for a healthy superego. Without the strong superego, the impulsive side of the self runs unchecked, except by a harsh substitute for the superego. Vietnam did not create these conditions, but it did provide a stage for dramatic public narratives struggling with the tensions of this modern individualism.

Commitment

Vietnam also offers a challenging text about friendship, bonding, loyalty, and altruism. In many ways the Vietnam War and the public discourse about the war provided Americans the occasion to express their longing for community, for the intense bonding and friendship that the rise of the new individualism makes increasingly unavailable to Americans. The broad strokes of the longing are not new. Industrial capitalism was not even 100 years old in England and in the United States before antimodern movements began to fabricate an image of the world modern folks had lost (Lears, 1981). Even in the 19th century, these antimodern movements looked to medieval society, to oriental societies, and to

Native American societies as models of the close-knit community that modernity had destroyed. Yankelovich (1981), FitzGerald (1986), and the authors of *Habits of the Heart* (Bellah et al., 1985) all heard from their informants some nostalgia for lost community, and these authors devote considerable energy to identifying signs of new commitments to community.

"Alienation" is a common theme in analytical commentaries on the war. MacPherson (1984) repeatedly heard from her male informants variations of a common belief that fighting in the war would provide them with intense experiences of bonding and group loyalty they found missing in their everyday experiences with American institutions. Even some resistors romanticized the war and expressed regret that they missed the opportunity for such closeness under fire. Of course, the modern individualist rarely can find those bonds, unprepared as the narcissist is for intimacy. "It was a loner's war," writes MacPherson, "of isolated, private little battles, companies and squads, platoons and five man teams" (p. 64). And, as MacPherson (1984) and Baritz (1985) both note, the conscious military policy of keeping tours of duty short and fixed contributed to the lack of real bonding among the soldiers. Certainly, films about Vietnam portray only alienated individuals loosely connected as a group. During and immediately after the war, several of the the most successful television series portrayed the closely knit community that Americans longed for and that some thought they could find on the battlefields of Vietnam (see Chapter 6, this volume). *M*A*S*H* (1972–83) used the Korean War to comment in various ways upon Vietnam, but even series like *Barney Miller* (1975–82), while not explicitly about the war, presented an image of a group of male professionals sharing danger, humor, love, and loyalty (Schrag, Hudson, & Bernabo, 1981).

The belief that the war provided group bonding and loyalty that everyday American life did not provide relates to "altruism," one of the issues raised by Turner in his contrast between the institutional self and the impulsive self. Citizens are supposed to put the collective good above the self during wartime, both on the home front and the battle front. But the new ethic of self-preservation (Lasch, 1979) means that altruism represents the ultimate hypocrisy, the betrayal of the interests of the real self. President Johnson fought the war on credit, never asking the public to sacrifice for the war—perhaps he realized that Americans were no longer capable of such sacrifice after the Second Inner Revolution. And, from the impulsive's point of view, only fools took chances for others in battle; "short-timers" tended to avoid all risk. Again, suicide missions by the Vietcong puzzled Americans as much as it terrified them.

Our commentary on a few keywords linking recent culture criticism and texts of the Vietnam War by no means constitutes a full analysis of the meanings of Vietnam. Our goal has been to suggest what sorts of new insights we might gain by reexamining some leading scholarly and journalistic interpretations of the war in light of our thesis that a Second Inner Revolution over the past 50 years in America has resulted in a new sort of individualism unfettered by institutional controls. But we have written as if the cultural revolution in which Americans committed themselves to the pursuit of self-fulfillment affected equally all segments of American society. We need to examine now that assumption and modify our generalizations, for the fact is that the phenomena described by Lasch, Yankelovich, Bellah, FitzGerald, and others may be specific only to a particular social location in American society. If class, gender, race, region, and age matter as much as we suspect in the differential effects of the Second Inner Revolution, then scholars and journalists may need to revise many of their generalizations about the meanings of Vietnam for Americans.

III

One problem with much of the rhetorical criticism of the public discourse about Vietnam is that critics base their analyses exclusively upon the texts themselves without bothering to ask American audiences how they are understanding the discourse. We need a critical strategy that will do for Vietnam what Radway (1984) did when she combined fieldwork with textual analysis of the historical romances read by women. Distrusting the easy generalizations made by other feminist critics who judged the romance novels "bad" for women because of the roles and values portrayed in the novels, Radway interviewed readers individually and in groups and discovered that women "take" these novels in ways not easily predicted by the structural features of the texts alone. A complete analysis of the meanings of American public discourse about Vietnam must combine textual with contextual analysis, both informed by fieldwork among the audiences.

We cannot offer here a fieldwork-based analysis of the audiences for Vietnam texts, but we can offer some good reasons to question the assumption that there is one American audience for, say, Kubrick's *Full Metal Jacket* (1987). There are multiple audiences, and there are reasons to believe that many of these audiences know little and care little about the war, who agonize not one moment about the "meaning" of Vietnam, for whom the enduring "legacy" of Vietnam is a curious flood of discourse by others who apparently are agonizing over the war and its meanings (see Chapter 10, this volume).

The average consumer of Vietnam texts need not be a Marxist to understand that issues of *social class* pervade our public discourse about the meanings of the war. Baritz (1985) puts it simply: "The Vietnam War was fought by working-class teenagers" (p. 282). MacPherson (1984) provides more statistical and anecdotal detail about the social class locations of the warriors and the resistors, but the conclusion is the same. From the inequality of the draft to the class hatred directed at officers, the Vietnam War is a disturbing reminder of one of those cultural contradictions mentioned by culture critics from Horney through Baritz—a civilization based on equality presents to individuals real barriers of class and race.

But the Second Inner Revolution thesis recasts the social class issue for the 1960s, 1970s, and 1980s. FitzGerald (1986) picks up on the new sort of class conflict at work in the experimental approach to self and community she finds in the 1980s. While there have been utopian and perfectionist experiments in the American past, the four communities FitzGerald studied—the Castro district gays, Falwell's Liberty Baptist fundamentalists, Sun City's retirees, and the Rajneeshpuram commune in Oregon—suggest to her that there is something more here than a mere status revolution going on in the 1980s. "Looking back," she writes, "it's apparent that in the sixties and seventies, white, middle-class society changed more decisively than it had in many decades—perhaps even since the turn of the century," and what the four communities had in common was American faith that "individuals could start over again, and if necessary reinvent themselves." But what distinguishes the fundamentalists (and, to a lesser extent, the retirees) from the Rajneeshee and Castro Street gays is their "cultural politics" (pp. 16, 23). FitzGerald uses historian Richard Hofstadter's own revision of his "status revolution" thesis to see that the conflict between older and newer middle classes is not simply a struggle for status. Rather, as Hofstadter points out, in "our political life there have always been certain types of cultural issues, questions of faith and morals, tone and style, freedom and coercion, which become fighting issues" (FitzGerald, 1986, p. 385). Though FitzGerald does not use the language of Ralph Turner, we can see that Falwell's fundamentalists and the retirees belong near the "institutional" end of the continuum of the grounded self, whereas the Rajneeshee and gays belong nearer the "impulsive end."

FitzGerald is getting at a class conflict peculiar to Americans in the late 20th century. A "new middle class" was born early in the 19th century in the economic revolution and in the religious revolution of the Second Great Awakening, the cradle of the 19th-century nuclear family and the American cult of domesticity. This new middle class fell into conflict with the older middle class that had controlled American institutions since the 17th century. But a "New Class," as sociologists have come to call it, was born late in the 19th century and came into power, really, only with the 20th-century emergence of "late capitalism" and its consumer-oriented, information-based political economy. The technological and economic transformation of the American superstructure, argues sociologist Peter L. Berger (1987),

> frees up, indeed compels, the growth of an occupational sector that is geared to miscellaneous services. . . . Within this sector there is what has been called the "knowledge industry," and within *that* there has been a very peculiar activity, devoted to the production and distribution of what may be called symbolic knowledge. The "New Class" consists of the people who make their living from this activity. These are the educators (from preschool to the university), the "communicators" (in the media, in public relations, in a miscellany of propagandistic lobbies), the therapists of all descriptions (from child analysts to geriatric sex counselors), and, last not least, substantial elements of the bureaucracy (those elements concerned with what may be called "lifestyle engineering") and of the legal profession. (p. 9, italics in original)

Berger's point is that the New Class holds and acts on "class interests," that it currently is the rising class in power, and that it is meeting resistance from an unprecedented alliance between the older, business-based middle class and the dwindling working class. It is this class conflict, for example, that lies behind the antagonism between fundamentalist and liberal Protestant denominations, and it is this class conflict that FitzGerald sees in her communities.

The New Class uses its strategic location in the symbolic knowledge industries to market its own mythology. Writing in 1976, Berger argued that the politics of the 1960s had become thoroughly institutionalized in American public discourse by the 1970s, and that the overriding myth of the 1960s radical politics was a "socialist myth" that synthesized modernizing and countermodernizing themes (p. 7). The appeal of the socialist myth lies in its promise of all the "goodies" of modernity without the costs, and the myth taps the powerfully felt loss of community that is one of the costs of modernity. The myth picks up a theme of "renewed community," a redemptive community projected into the future (p. 9). Berger's point, however, is that the countermodern movement of the 1960s is especially attractive to the New Class that simultaneously suffers the alienation of modernity and has control of the information institutions that control the public, ideological discourse in the society.

What all this suggests is that the Vietnam War may be a preoccupation only of the New Class or, perhaps, of those most committed to the struggle between the New Class and the alliance between the more traditional middle class and working class. The American *mythologies* that culture critics discover in mass-media texts, including texts about Vietnam (Hellmann, 1986), are narratives mustered in this new class conflict. So, the Protestant myth of "a City upon a Hill" that Baritz (1985) finds at the heart of America's intervention in Vietnam, or the American "Monomyth" (Jewett & Lawrence, 1977) that animates *Rambo* (1985), to mention only two examples, serve class ideologies in the contest for public perceptions of the meanings of Vietnam. The goal of mythological analysis of Vietnam texts ought to be to decode the class ideologies that find the mythological narratives to their liking.

There are good reasons for suspecting that *gender* matters as greatly as class in generalizing about the pervasiveness of the "psychologized self" in the 1970s and 1980s. Yankelovich tends to treat the sexes alike in his analysis, finding as many women as men in search of self-fulfillment, but the more complex analyses by Turner (1976) and by Lasch (1979) suggest that the personality transformation may affect men far more than women. Turner's description of the "institutional self," for example, possibly never did apply very accurately to American women, who historically have had institutional connections very different from men's. At least, it is an empirical question whether Turner's generalizations apply to women. Similarly, Lasch's psychoanalytic approach necessarily acknowledges gender differences in many of the psychodynamic processes, such as the creation of the superego. To be fair, Lasch attends to gender issues throughout his books, but it is also worth noting that Lasch's (1979) description of secondary narcissism, with its rage against authority and its violent fantasies of omnipotence, sounds much more like a male than a female symptom.

If we are correct in asserting that gender makes a great difference in the impact of the social and psychological transformations of the last few decades, then we would need to look anew at the public discourse about Vietnam and ask to what extent (if any) the war poses a troubling "puzzle" to women in the same way it does to men. Feminist culture critics are beginning to reexamine Vietnam texts, primarily films (Modleski, 1988; Jeffords in this volume), and we suppose this is just the beginning of a feminist critique of the legacies of Vietnam. On the mass media side, the 1987–88 television season saw the debut of a two-hour pilot and several hour-long installments of a new series, *China Beach,* which attempts to portray both civilian and military women in the Vietnam War.

The reader must look carefully to find any mention of *race* or ethnicity in the discussions by Lasch and Turner, while Yankelovich (1981, p. 91) and the authors of *Habits of the Heart* (Bellah et al., 1985, p. xi) admit frankly that their generalizations are primarily about white Americans.

The Second Inner Revolution at mid-century may be a phenomenon affecting mainly middle-class white males, or class and gender may be the crucial variables, so that race and ethnicity matter less in determining how a middle-class male feels the tensions of the new individualism. The absence of attention to race in the big idea books about transformations in modern American culture is all the more bewildering in light of the overrepresentation of minority men fighting the war in Vietnam. MacPherson (1984) notes, for example, that in 1965, blacks accounted for 24% of the combat deaths in Vietnam (p. 30), and she devotes a chapter of her book to the black experience. Only one book about the war, Wallace Terry's *Bloods: An Oral History of the Vietnam War by Black Veterans* (1984), addresses in detail the black experience in Vietnam, but, even so, Terry's book is more a primary document than an interpretation of the experience. There is in these accounts some tantalizing information relevant to the inner revolution thesis. MacPherson (1984) repeats the finding by the massive "Legacies" study of Vietnam veterans that black veterans were more troubled than whites when they participated in atrocities, and this difference might suggest a stronger institutional than impulsive individualism among the black soldiers (pp. 227, 603). Clearly, we need detailed, thoughtful analyses of the effects (if any) of the Second Inner Revolution upon people of color in America. Our own impression is that the Vietnam War is not the compelling cultural "puzzle" for racial minority communities that it remains for white, middle-class males.

Perhaps unexpectedly, even *region* is a variable that might affect the ways in which Americans feel the pressures of the new individualism. We know that certain sorts of mid-range institutions, especially religious and social, thrive more in stable communities, and the health of communities shows some regional variations. Again, MacPherson (1984) cites the large "Legacies" study in their findings that there are regional variations in the personality trends of Vietnam veterans (pp. 335–336).

Finally, *age* is the human variable that undermines much current popular and scholarly wisdom about the legacies of Vietnam. It is odd that historians, those scholars most attuned to time, so often forget to take into account in their generalizations a simple truth: People in a society are at different ages at the same moment in historical time. This simple fact means that events and forces supposed to drive history may have varying effects on the members of the historical population. The notion of "birth cohort," a concept increasingly valuable in writing the histories of childhood and the family, combines with the equally useful concept of "life cycle" to warn historians that the impact and meanings of historical events may vary greatly, depending on where in the life cycle of an age cohort the event occurs. One historical sociologist, for example, discovered that one birth cohort, adolescents, was spared most of the much touted impact of the Great Depression on the American world view (Elder, 1974). So, historical wisdom about the Depression as a "watershed" event in American society must be tempered with the observation that, for large numbers of Americans, the Depression had little impact on their lives.

We have little doubt that the Vietnam War had great impact on the lives of a great many Americans from the beginning of the involvement of the United States through the dramatic evacuation from the roof of the embassy in Saigon in 1975. But age cohorts and life cycles determined a great many of the meanings of Vietnam even during the war. MacPherson (1984) makes much of age in her book, *Long Time Passing*. Wars and drafts are about age cohorts in that young people fight wars, but MacPherson has more subtle things to say than this cliché about the "generation gap" of the 1960s. American soldiers fighting in the Vietnam War were younger (average age 19) than those who fought in World War II (average age 25.8) or in the Korean War (p. 62). Moreover, notes MacPherson, a soldier's experiences in Vietnam and the individual veteran's legacy from the war depended greatly on his or her age during the experience. Younger veterans express greater guilt and shame about their war experiences than do older veterans. The youth of the Vietnam soldiers denied them a "normal" late adolescence, especially the period in which they would be expected to negotiate normal intimacy with women. MacPherson heard the "arrested adolescence" theme from many of her informants, including some protestors who look back on their social activism as having robbed them of a normal period in their coming-of-age.

Inquiring into the ages of the audiences for the primary discourse on Vietnam forces the critic to see that simple generalizations about the meanings of the discourse simply will not do. For the sake of simplicity, let us think of four large birth cohorts in that audience. Oldest are those who were in their 50s and 60s from say, 1965 to 1975. Born between 1895 and 1925, this generation barely may have remembered World War I. They experienced the Depression during an important stage in their life cycles, but (as we have seen) even this experience depended heavily on much smaller birth cohorts than we are picturing here. The men in this cohort may have fought in World War II, and the women had their own experiences of the war, only now being chronicled. In 1965, some of these Americans had sons eligible for the draft. How these parents felt about the draft, about the Vietnam War, and about the protests against the war had to be worked out in their minds against their life experiences of the Depression and World War II. That was the war they knew and, as MacPherson (1984) points out, it was an odd accident of time that it is this generation that parented the bulk of the 18-year-old sons for the draft. If the Vietnam conflict had begun a few years later,

she speculates, so that the draftees would have been the sons not of World War II veterans but of Korean War veterans, then both the draftees and their parents might have felt very differently about the war, the draft, and draft resistance. In any case, this audience is elderly for most of the primary discourse about the meaning of the war.

Imagine a second birth cohort in their 30s and 40s during the same period of American involvement in the War. Born between 1915 and 1940, this group has some World War II veterans, but it also includes those teenagers relatively unaffected by the Depression and those who remember World War II only vaguely as highlights in their memories of childhood. This group's experiences with war are as much products of Korea as of World War II. Some had draft-age sons during the Vietnam War, while others are themselves just past draft age and have young children. Perhaps most important, these Americans are hitting their adult-life strides. They are supposed to be at the stage in their lives when they have established their adult identities, and the Vietnam War may create for them the sort of instability that makes them extremely anxious about losing what they have acquired. As an audience in 1975–1988 for the primary discourse on Vietnam, these Americans are in their 40s and 50s.

The Sixties Generation would constitute a third birth cohort for historical comparison. Born in the demographic boom following World War II, they were the generation who fought, who protested, who escaped, and who resisted in 1965–1975. So much has been written about this generation that we need add little here, except to say that these Americans are in their late 30s and 40s when they consume the books, films, and television programs that purport to explain Vietnam. They are also the teachers of high school and college students in the 1980s; they are the ones who create the courses on Vietnam.

A fourth cohort was born after 1960 or so, including those born after 1975. For most of this generation, which includes college students in the 1980s, there is no unmediated experience of the Vietnam War. They know the war only through theatrical films, television documentaries, nonfiction and fiction books about the War, and even through the increasingly popular college courses about the 1960s and Vietnam. Some parents of these young people were warriors, some protestors; in our experience neither sort of parent speaks often of the war to these young people. So, in many ways for those born after 1965, the Vietnam War poses no salient puzzle to be solved, no difficult "text" to be decoded for what it tells us about our lives and institutions in America. These young people know that Vietnam is "important" to their parents and possibly to the nation's history, but they feel no driving need to understand the War. The war is for them more a curiosity than a trauma.

MacPherson (1984) no doubt speaks for many when she claims that the

"Vietnam Generation remains a divided generation; there are no imminent signs of reconciliation" (p. 33). We concur that there is a division in this generation of Americans, but we think MacPherson is wrong about the issue that separates them. The division is not between the warriors and the protestors and not between the revisionist hawks and the doves who put "No Vietnam in Central America" stickers on their car bumpers. The division is between those Americans still holding out for an institutionally grounded self and those advocating an impulsive individualism (see Chapter 10, this volume). The division cuts across class, gender, race, region, and age cohorts in ways we understand only imperfectly. Social, cultural, and historical forces beyond the control of either group created a Second Inner Revolution that has made both positions increasingly uncomfortable and untenable in American civilization. Vietnam remains a salient text for the struggles between these two groups because the Vietnam War condensed so dramatically the tensions and contradictions created by the emergence of the new individualism of the 1960s.

Culture criticism too often narrowly interprets its charge as the debunker of myths. We think it is significant that the culture critics we have consulted here have gone beyond this negative approach to culture criticism. Bellah and his collaborators (1985), Turner (1976), MacPherson (1984), FitzGerald (1986), Yankelovich (1981), Baritz (1985), and Hellmann (1986) all strike a surprising note of optimism in their prognostications about America's future. Bellah's crowd, Yankelovich, and FitzGerald, especially, see signs of new American experiments with commitment and community, signs of a return to public, collective action as a workable strategy for making a meaningful life. And even Lasch (1979), whose culture criticism is the most gloomy in its diagnosis, clearly writes out of a desire to have Americans see the pathologies of their civilization and to resist them. The word "citizenship," long ago abandoned by the New Class intelligentsia as a sign of right-wing politics, reappears in these books, and there is increasing attention to the role of intellectuals in what one distinguished historian calls "the care and repair of public myth" (McNeill, 1982). Vietnam is a significant text in this new public debate, to be sure, but it is an expendable text and should not distract the culture critic from the real drama unfolding as Americans attempt to cope with the consequences of the Second Inner Revolution.

REFERENCES

Almond, G.A. (1950). *The American people and foreign policy*. New York: Praeger.

Baritz, L. (1985). *Backfire: A history of how American culture led us into Vietnam and made us fight the way we did*. New York: Morrow & Co..

Bellah, R.N., Madsen, R., Sullivan, W.M., Swidler, A., & Tipton, S.M. (1985). *Habits of the heart: Individualism and commitment in American life*. Berkeley: University of California Press.

Berger, P.L. (1976). The socialist myth. *The Public Interest, 44*, 3–16.

Berger, P.L. (1987). Different gospels: The social sources of apostasy. *This World, 17*, 6–17.

Cochran, T.C. (1964). *The inner revolution: Essays on the social sciences in history*. New York: Harper & Row.

Elder, G., Jr. (1974). *Children of the great depression: Social change in life experience*. Chicago: University of Chicago Press.

FitzGerald, F. (1972). *Fire in the lake: The Vietnamese and the Americans in Vietnam*. New York: Vintage-Random House.

FitzGerald, F. (1986). *Cities on a hill: A journey through contemporary American cultures*. New York: Random House.

Hellmann, J. (1986). *American myth and the legacy of Vietnam*. New York: Columbia University Press.

Horney, K. (1937). *The neurotic personality of our time*. New York: Norton.

Jewett, R., & Lawrence, J.S. (1977). *The American monomyth*. Garden City, NY: Anchor-Doubleday.

Kammen, M. (1972). *People of paradox: An inquiry concerning the origins of American civilization*. New York: Random House.

Kanter, R.M. (1977). *Men and women of the corporation*. New York: Basic Books.

Lasch, C. (1979). *The culture of narcissism: American life in an age of diminishing expectations*. New York: Warner.

Lears, T.J.J. (1981). *No place of grace: Antimodernism and the transformation of American culture, 1880–1920*. New York: Pantheon.

Lynd, R.S. (1939). *Knowledge for what? The place of social science in American culture*. New York: Grove.

Lynd, R.S., & Lynd, H.M. (1929). *Middletown: A study of contemporary American culture*. New York: Harcourt, Brace.

Lynd, R.S., & Lynd, H.M. (1937). *Middletown in transition: A study in cultural conflicts*. New York: Harcourt, Brace.

Maccoby, M. (1976). *The gamesman*. New York: Simon & Schuster.

MacPherson, M. (1984). *Long time passing: Vietnam and the haunted generation*. New York: New American Library.

Marchand, R. (1985). *Advertising the American dream: Making way for modernity, 1920–1940*. Berkeley: University of California Press.

Marx, L. (1964). *The machine in the garden: Technology and the pastoral ideal in America*. London/New York: Oxford University Press.

McNeill, W.H. (1982). The care and repair of public myth. *Foreign Affairs, 61*, 1–13.

Mead, M. (1942). *And keep your powder dry: An anthropologist looks at America*. New York: Morrow.

Modleski, T. (1988). A father is being beaten: Male feminism and the war film. *Discourse, 10*, 62–77.

Potter, D. (1954). *People of Plenty: Economic abundance and the American character*. Chicago: University of Chicago Press.

Radway, J.A. (1984). *Reading the romance: Women, patriarchy, and popular literature*. Chapel Hill: University of North Carolina Press.

Riesman, D., with Glazer, N., & Denney, R. (1950). *The lonely crowd: A study of the changing American character*. New Haven, CT: Yale University Press.

Schrag, R.L., Hudson, R.A., & Bernabo, L.M. (1981). Television's new humane collectivity. *Western Journal of Speech Communication*, *45*, 1–12.

Spence, J.T., & Helmreich, R.L. (1978). *Masculinity and femininity: Their psychological dimensions, correlates, and antecedents*. Austin: University of Texas Press.

Sussman, W.I. (1984). *Culture as history: The transformation of American society in the twentieth century*. New York: Pantheon.

Terry, W. (1984). *Bloods: An oral history of the Vietnam War by black veterans*. New York: Ballantine.

Turner, R.H. (1976). The real self: From institution to impulse. *American Journal of Sociology*, *81*, 989–1016.

Wright, W. (1976). *Sixguns and society: A structural study of the Western*. Berkeley: University of California Press.

Yankelovich, D. (1981). *New rules: Searching for self-fulfillment in a world turned upside-down*. New York: Random House.

10

The Vietnam Veterans Memorial and the Myth of Superiority

Richard Morris
The Annenberg School of Communications, University of Pennsylvania

The main thesis of this chapter is that the Vietnam Veterans Memorial (VVM) in Washington, D.C. and the vitriolic debate that its design engendered are best understood and explained as having resulted from an historically embedded cultural conflict over the correct form and function of memorializing.[1] As a means of orienting subsequent discussion, I begin with a brief discussion of memorializing. Following that orientation, I turn to an analysis of rhetoric and memorials produced by those who witnessed the births of two American memorial traditions, focusing particularly on their conflicting views of what would be an appropriate memorial to George Washington. This analysis then serves as a basis for identifying and explaining the memorial traditions that came into conflict over the VVM's design. Finally, the conclusion argues that the VVM and the public debate that it fostered were, in a fundamental sense, not only cultural legacies of Vietnam, but also cultural legacies of the myth of superiority.

ON MEMORIALIZING

Memorializing is a process wherein memory is engaged. This much we might discern from the Latin term *memoria* (memory) and its root *memor* (mindful). But memorializing is never merely remembering. To be mindful of something (of anything) by way of memorializing is necessarily to engage in a creative, third-order, symbolic process that is simultaneously a concrete, abstract, functional, incomplete, and evaluative

[1] This chapter is dedicated to Professor Edwin Black, to whom I owe a great deal more than the dedication of a Chapter. I also wish to thank Professors Jay Mechling and Philip Wander for their helpful comments and insights.

effort to evoke or establish memory of the "memorable" (i.e., the object of memorialization) in some specific way. At the risk of belaboring what may seem obvious to some, consider the matter further.

Memorializing does not simply come to be, nor is it passively coaxed into being. Neither is it the memorable or even memory of the memorable; it is the result of a process that requires the creation of symbols in order to represent memory of the memorable. As a respresentation, memorializing is also necessarily concrete (albeit, not necessarily palpable) because it is something one can experience and to which one can refer, and because it frequently yields something we can call a memorial. A statue, a monument, a tombstone, a highway, a building, a bridge, a mourning ring, a locket, a lock of hair, a room kept as it was, a speech, even a silent prayer—all are concrete manifestations, memorials, brought about through a creative process of symbolization.

At the same time, because memorializing is a third-order process, both it and its manifestation(s) are necessarily abstractions: Both are drawn away from the memorable through memory. And, as symbolic, both are also necessarily incomplete. Through abstracting and symbolizing, one is left with a distillation of one's memory of the memorable. Since any such distillation cannot be identical to the memorable or to one's memory of the memorable, manifestation and process alike must be incomplete representations. From this it follows that both manifestation and process are necessarily evaluative. The process is necessarily evaluative because distilling or abstracting invariably involves identifying features of the memorable that deserve to be in memory, which concomitantly identifies by negation those features that do not (i.e., since it is not possible to bring the memorable forward through memory *in toto*, even symbolically, one necessarily partializes the memorable evaluatively). The manifestation is necessarily evaluative, first, because it derives from a necessarily evaluative process and, second, because any such symbolic formalization serves to evoke or establish features of the memorable that deserve to be in memory.

Of particular note here is the implication that function discloses itself specifically through the form in which the memorable is symbolically but partially represented in order to evoke or establish memory of the memorable. Put differently, *form* (manifestation) *derives from function* (process), *and function* (evoking or establishing memory of the memorable) *is in turn signified through form* (that which deserves to be in memory). In practice, of course, correspondence between form and function is often ambiguous or vague: Not all memorials fully disclose the significance of the memorable through form. A locket, for instance, may function as a memorial for some individual, yet fail to evoke or establish in others what it evokes or establishes in the memorializer. Discerning what a memorial memorializes, why and how it functions as a memorial, or what memory a memorial evokes or establishes may be possible in such instances only by consulting the memorializer. Yet, none of this matters. Personal memorials are not public; they are not meant to be shared, to evoke or establish memory of the memorable in others. However idiosyncratically they may signify, the apparent or actual disparity between form and function is consequently and literally insignificant. But when memorials are meant to be shared, when they serve as memorials in the public domain, disparity between form and function can be of considerable significance, as we shall see by examining the heated public debate that erupted over the VVM (see Chapter 8, this volume).

Here, it will be sufficient to note that the concrete, abstract, functional, incomplete, and evaluative character of memorializing directs us to attend carefully to what a given memorial says, to how and why it says what it says, to what it fails to say and why it fails to say it, and to what metric it evokes in order to arrive at its specific evaluation of the memorable. Further, acknowledging that memorializing is a creative, third-order, symbolic process directs us to attend carefully to the creative manner in which a given memorial seeks to represent the memorable, which in turn directs us to comprehend the memorial tradition through which the creativity and symbolicity of that memorial find their "voice."

Perhaps Heidegger (1962) is correct in saying that the negative side of tradition is that it "takes what has come down to us and delivers it over to self-evidence; it blocks our access to those primordial 'sources' from which the categories and concepts handed down to us have been in part quite genuinely drawn" (p. 42). Yet, it is by coming to understand the tradition to which something belongs that we can retrace and revitalize in the present those very same sources, that we can begin to understand how the past manifests itself in the present by circumscribing the grounds of self-evidence, and that we can begin to outline how tradition enables the past to speak through the present by encouraging and enabling those in the present to see themselves as part of a whole. Memorial traditions do not exist simply because scholars discover them. Nor is it necessary for individuals or collectivities to comprehend their membership in a specifiable memorial tradition. Both memorials and traditions arise and persist because they continue to answer needs—because they are emotionally, psychologically, culturally, and/or rhetorically satisfying to those for whom they are literally significant—even if in answering those needs they obscure their own "primordial 'sources.' "

Finally, acknowledging in this particular instance that the VVM is a public memorial directs us to comprehend the public character and status of the effort—that is, to observe, for example, that placing the VVM in a position that is parallel with some of the most readily identifiable memorials in America accords it the status of a cultural institution (an isssue to which we shall return later), and that a large part of the VVM's public character derives from its public status. Unlike many personal or private memorials, public memorials "speak" publicly by attempting to shape and possess the affective norms of the present and the future by first shaping and possessing the past. And, as Dilip Gaonkar (1988) has noted in another context,

> to possess the past is to possess the people. For those who possess the past command the sense of the community that enables them to authoritatively recognize the meaning of the present and the possibilities for the future. Thus, history as a systematic understanding of the past unavoidably becomes a site of ideological struggle to understand the past and to direct the future. (p. 1)

The ways in which individuals and collectivities respond to death reveal world views, cultural premises—manners of organizing, parsing, combining, interpreting, and responding to the world. May and Becker were both correct. The "sacral power of death" (May, 1969, 1973) is so enormous that we marshal all our energies to cope with the chaos. In marshaling those energies we bring to bear all the resources at our command (Becker, 1973)—our knowledge, our beliefs, our principles, and our attitudes: the culture that has nurtured and perplexed and shaped our lives. In other words, human confrontation with the death of an intimate—with someone or something who/that matters—bodies forth concentrations of the culture(s) we are. Literal constructions of social reality, memorials "speak" through cultural form, and their "speaking" is a signification of the culture(s) to which they belong.

TWO AMERICAN MEMORIAL TRADITIONS

The first American memorial tradition that concerns us here, which I have called the romanticist tradition (Morris, 1986, p. 34), began to emerge as a dominant force during the middle decades of the 19th century, largely in response to the deficiencies that American romanticists saw in an older American memorial tradition.[2] Regarding that older tradition as simply

[2] Three points bear mentioning here. First, these are not the only American memorial traditions; they are, however, the only two that are germaine to our understanding of how and why a conflict errupted over the VVM's design. Second, the romanticist memorial tradition actually began to emerge as a dominant force during the middle of the 18th century. Because this memorial tradition did not become fully established until the consecration of its first cemeterial environment (Mount Auburn Cemetery; September 24, 1831), and because the specific details of this tradition's emergence are irrelevant to the present discussion, it will suffice to say that the romanticist memorial tradition emerged during the middle decades of the 19th century. Third, this discussion is based on research conducted across six years that encompasses approximately 4 million American memorials.

and thoroughly unacceptable, for instance, Henry Ward Beecher (1859) summarized a number of romanticist sentiments when he declared that it was impossible not to "be pained at the desolation" of the older tradition's gravescape (i.e., cemeterial and iconographic environment). "The fences," where there were fences, "are dilapidated, the headstones broken, or swayed half over, the intervals choked up with briers, elders, and fat-weeds; and the whole place" bears "the impress of the most frigid indifference" (p. 123). In addition to their dissatisfaction with the older tradition's sense of aesthetics, Beecher insisted, romanticists believe that it is "a shame and a disgrace" that the places "where the bodies of our sweet children, where father and mother, brother and sister, husband and wife" are memorialized are the same places where "cows and horses are often allowed to pasture on the graves; thus saving the expense of mowing, beside a clear gain in grass" (p. 124).

Echoing related romanticist criticisms, William B.O. Peabody (1831) maintained that the older memorial tradition is an insult to human intelligence, the result of a recently developed superstition, and an affront to the emotions and rights of the living and the dead: "The cold ghastliness of the sculptured marble,—the grey stone sinking, as if weary of bearing unregarded legends of the ancient dead; the various inscriptions showing, sometimes, what the dead were, but still oftener what they ought to have been, subdue the heart to sadness, not to gloom" (p. 398). To subscribe to the dominant memorial tradition is to subscribe to "an invention of comparatively modern times" that seeks only to promote the dread of death, which "is not a natural feeling" (p. 403).

What Americans need and deserve, romanticists insisted, is a memorial tradition that evokes the most sublime emotions, that affects healing through emotional response, that promotes contemplation by joining the best of art and nature so that "a visit to one of these [memorial] spots has the united charm of nature and art,—the double wealth of rural and moral association," to awaken, "at the same moment, the feeling of human sympathy and the love of natural beauty, implanted in every heart" (Downing, 1854/1974, p. 155). Realizing that they could not adequately reform the older memorial tradition to suit their own sensibilities, romanticists thus sought to create a memorial tradition of their own. On September 24, 1831, at the consecration ceremonies of America's first thoroughly romanticist gravescape, those efforts came to fuition. And, in delivering the consecration address to those gathered at Mount Auburn Cemetery near Boston, Joseph Story provided a clear statement of what romanticists sought to accomplish with the establishment of their new memorial tradition.

Places of and memorials to the dead, Story (1831/1859) proclaimed, ought to be such that the living can derive pleasure, emotional satisfaction, and instruction on how to live their lives. They should be carefully created amid sylvan scenes, where we can contemplate and sit listening to our beloved deceased "to hear the tone of their affection, whispering in our ears," "in the depths of our souls," where we may "shed our tears"—not "the tears of burning agony," but the tears of relief that would allow us to "return to the world," where we can "feel ourselves purer, and better, and wiser, from this communion" (pp. 148–149). All great civilizations, Story continued, have understood the true lessons of memorializing. "The aboriginal Germans," who "buried their dead in groves consecrated by their priests"; the Egyptians, who "satisfied their pride and soothed their grief, by interring" their dead "in their Elysian fields"; the Hebrews, who buried their dead in "ornamented gardens and deep forests, and fertile valleys, and lofty mountains"; the "ancient Asiatics," who "lined the approaches to their cities with sculptured sarcophagi, and masoleums, and other ornaments, embowered in shrubbery"; the Greeks, who "exhausted the resources of their exquisite art in adorning the habitation of the dead," who "consigned their relics to shady groves, in the neighborhood of murmuring streams and mossy fountains, close by the favorite resorts of those who were engaged in the study of philosophy and nature"; the Romans, who "erected the monuments to the dead in suburbs of the eternal city, (as they proudly denominated it,) on the sides of their spacious roads, in the midst of trees and ornamental walks, and ever-varying flowers" —all of these ancient civilizations have provided ample evidence of the value of creating beautiful memorials surrounded by nature (pp. 149–151).

Why, then, Story asked, "should we deposit the remains of our friends in the loathsome vaults, or beneath the gloomy crypts and cells of our churches . . . ?" "Why should we measure out a narrow portion of earth for" our memorials "in the midst of our cities, and heap the dead upon each other with a cold calculating parsimony,"

> disturbing their ashes, and wounding the sensibilities of the living? Why should we expose our burying-grounds to the broad glare of day, to the unfeeling gaze of the idler, to the noisy press of business, to the discordant shouts of merriment, or the baleful visitations of the dissolute? . . . Why all this unnatural restraint upon our sympathies and sorrows, which confines the visit to the grave to the only time, in which it must be utterly useless—when the heart is bleeding with fresh anguish, and is too weak to feel, and too desolate to desire consolation? (Story, 1831/1859, pp. 154–155)

We need not answer such questions, Story suggested, for the consecration of Mount Auburn announces to the world the arrival of America's newly found recognition of the need for a purer, more beautiful relationship between the living and the dead.

Americans will now realize that, "rightly selected, and properly arranged," romanticist memorials "preach lessons, to which none may refuse to listen, and which all, that live, must hear," for in the midst of nature, with time to contemplate and feel, the living will understand beyond all doubt that the memorial "hath a voice of eloquence, nay of superhuman eloquence" (Story, 1831/1859, p. 156). At last, mourners and others will be able to "revisit these shades with a secret, though melancholy pleasure. The hand of friendship will delight to cherish the flowers, and the shrubs, that fringe the lowly grave, or the sculptured monument." At last, "Spring will invite thither the footsteps of the young by its opening foliage; the Autumn detain the contemplative by its latest bloom" (p. 165). At last, we can banish "the thought, that this is to be the abode of a gloom, which will haunt the imagination by its terrors, or chill the heart by its solitude." At last, we can "erect the memorials of our love, and our gratitude, and our glory," for here we may "let youth and beauty, blighted by premature decay, drip, like tender blossoms, into the virgin earth; and here let age retire, ripened for the harvest" (pp. 166–167).

Judging from the rapid emergence of romanticist memorials and gravescapes subsequent to the establishment of Mount Auburn, as well as from Mount Auburn's immediate popularity, America's new memorial tradition quickly proved to be everything Story and other romanticists hoped it would. As Andrew Jackson Downing, "America's most influential writer on gardening and rural architecture" (Tatum, 1974, p. v), pointed out in 1849, "no sooner was attention generally raised to the charms of" the romanticist memorial tradition "than the idea took the public mind by storm." Within a matter of months, travellers from near and far began to make "pilgrimages to the Athens of New England, solely to see the realization of their long cherished dream of a resting place for the dead, at once sacred from profanation, dear to the memory, and captivating to the imagination" (Downing, 1854/1974, p. 154). As Jacob Bigelow (1859), the father of Mount Auburn Cemetery, proudly proclaimed, the new tradition was so "rapidly imitated in all parts of the United States" that even romanticists were surprised (p. iv). And, by 1849, only 18 years after the consecration of Mount Auburn, Downing was able to observe with due pride that "there is scarcely a city of note in the whole country that has not its" romanticist gravescape (pp. 154–155).

Yet, in the midst of the romanticist memorial tradition's enormous popularity, another memorial tradition, which I have termed heroist (Morris, 1986, p. 34), began to emerge, largely in response to certain excesses that the romanticist tradition promoted, excesses that even romanticists were willing to acknowledge. At the same time that Downing (1854/1974) was heaping praise on the beautiful union of art and nature that romanticists had effected, for example, he also complained that that natural beauty was severely diminished "by the most violent bad taste; we mean the hideous *ironmongery*, which [romanticist gravescapes] all more or less display." "Fantastic conceit and gimeracks in iron might be pardonable as adornments of the balustrade of a circus or temple of Comus," Downing charged, "but how reasonable beings can tolerate them as inclosures to the quiet grave of a family, and in such scenes of sylvan beauty, is mountain high above our comprehension." Worse, "as if to show how far human infirmity can go," Downing continued, "we noticed lately several lots in one of these [gravescapes], not only inclosed with a most barbarous piece of *irony*, but the gate of which was positively ornamented with the coat of arms of the owner, accompanied by a brass door-plate, on which was engraved the owner's name, and city residence" (p. 156; italics in original).

Beyond the disruptive and aesthetically unappealing presence of "hideous *ironmongery*," Nehemiah Cleaveland (1850) insisted, Americans also object to the "deforming effect of those little terraces and angular disturbances of the surface, which result from leaving this work to the taste and caprice of individuals" (p. 250). Increasing pressure, especially from heroists, eventually led romanticists to make certain concessions—for example, to institute rules governing what visitors and even memorial owners were allowed to do (see Bigelow, 1859, pp. 221–254; and Cleaveland, 1850, pp. 255–271). In turn, instituting such rules shifted much of the decision-making power from lot owners, who, in many instances, were also part owners of the cemeteries, to a newly created professional position, the cemetery superintendent.

One of the most important consequences of the romanticist admission that the form of their gravescape could be improved by restricting individualism, for purposes of this discussion, is that it provided heroists with the impetus to separate their tradition from the romanticists' tradition. And in 1855, heroists took full advantage of that opportunity. Only 10 years after Spring Grove Cemetery in Cincinnati had been redesigned according to the dictates of the romanticist tradition, Adolph Strauch submitted and put into effect a plan to alter its form to suit heroists' tastes. Initially, the plan to redesign Spring Grove appears to have been directed primarily at removing the "hideous *ironmongery*" and "little terraces and angular disturbances" that romanticists admitted were excessive. But Strauch took the plan several steps further.

Having removed "the numerous and crowded enclosures," Strauch then eliminated burial mounds, hedges, stone fences, numerous trees, and "the innumerable tombs and gravestones," which "break up the surface of the ground, cut it into unsymmetrical sections, destroy the effect of slopes and levels, and chop up what should be the broad and noble feature of one great picture into a confused and crowded multitude of what seem like petty yards or pens" (Perkins, 1871, pp. 841–842). The owners of Spring Grove then instituted rules to prohibit lot owners from altering their lots. Lot owners could still purchase "a single monument" to be "erected in the centre of each lot," but, because the lots had been arranged symmetrically to make the best use of the land and to make maintenance more efficient, small markers "rising but a little above the ground" were encouraged. Spring Grove's owners also encouraged lot owners to plant "a tree," instead of erecting a memorial, and disallowed "small isolated flower-beds and the like, managed by individual proprietors, . . . as they patch and deform the scenery" (p. 843). For those who felt the need to erect an individual memorial, heroists had this advice: "Quiet and simple memorials sufficiently indicate the places of interment" (pp. 843–844).

This new gravescape—"the landscape lawn method" or lawn cemetery, as it was later called—did not take "the public mind by storm," as the romanticist memorial tradition had, but to heroists it possessed several distinct advantages. First, it provided visitors with an open vista, unobstructed by fences, memorials, and flora, where "the mind is not disturbed by the obtrusion of bounds and limits that seem to claim superiority and respect, or to assert rights of ownership and contrast of station, even among the dead" (Perkins, 1871, p. 843). Second, it allowed cemetery superintendents to make the most efficient use of the land, thereby affirming the heroist principle that a memorial tradition "must be conducted under one general plan *dictated* by *educated taste*. Individual rights must be subordinate to this general plan," for "civilization consists in subordinating the will of the individual to the comfort and well being of all" (M.P. Brazil, in Farrell, 1980, p. 118; italics in original). Third, prohibiting individualism and adornment in order to promote efficiency and control made this gravescape extremely affordable, especially when compared to the romanticist gravescape. Finally, by eliminating romanticist excesses—fences, flora, individualism, art, homeopathic emotions, and so forth—and by requiring memorials to be small enough to be level or nearly level with the ground, so "they do not appear in the landscape picture" (Weed, 1912, p. 94), heroists were able to eliminate features that might suggest romanticist ties, thereby asserting the independence of their emerging tradition. From this perspective, such "improvements" allowed heroists to eliminate, albeit gradually, "all things that suggest death, sorrow, or pain" (S.J. Hare, in Farrell, 1980, p. 120).

Though eliminating "all things that suggest death, sorrow, or pain" allowed heroists to establish the independence of their memorial tradition, it did not allow them to promote their tradition positively—to promote those nonindividualistic sentiments for which the heroist tradition is so notable. Initially, heroists sought to promote their tradition positively by erecting heroist memorials within the confines of the romanticist gravescape. But the introduction of heroist memorials in romanticist gravescapes could no more reform that tradition than the introduction of romanticist memorials in the older gravescape could reform the older tradition. More important, because of the heroist tendency to equate size with the deceased's merits and significance, because heroist memorials are conspicuously silent with regard to romanticist themes, because romanticists strenuously objected to such "barbarous" memorials, and because romanticists owned and/or controlled romanticist gravescapes, there were only infrequent opportunities for heroists to develop their emerging tradition in a traditional setting. Further, because erecting heroist memorials in a romanticist setting might too easily diminish their capacity to establish or evoke memory heroically, because heroists objected to fundamental features of the romanticist memorial tradition, and because heroist memorials would have been incongruous with the design of their own gravescape, heroists had to look elsewhere to promote their tradition positively.

To effect this positive dimension, heroists thus took their tradition outside the familiar cemeterial environment to the centers of towns and cities, where their memorials could instruct an even larger audience in the ways of heroism. Rather than focusing the viewer's attention on the terror of death, as the older tradition does, or on the homeopathic sentiments associated with death, as the romanticist tradition does, heroist memorials beyond the gravescape shift the viewers' attention away from death to heroism by allowing memorials, like heroic actions, to speak louder than words, to speak for themselves through heroic form. This is, in large part, why heroist memorials are typically larger than life, why they tend to equate a memorial's size with the merits and significance of the deceased, why they emphasize those sentiments that promote action rather than words or homeopathic emotions, why they typically have nothing to say about death but much to say about the life of a hero, and why they are so often idealizations of a particular individual or of an abstract individual who could be anyone.[3]

While romanticists were willing to tolerate the construction of some

[3] The obvious disparity between heroist memorials beyond and within the gravescape requires explanation that goes well beyond the limits of the present discussion. Suffice it to say for the present that the heroist gravescape is a manifestation of individual heroism and immortality, whereas heroist memorials in cities and towns are manifestations of collective heroism and immortality. The disparity in this particular American memorial tradition is thus parallel to the disparity that one typically finds in other hero cults, where local heroes, who are transformed into heroes for the collectivity, are stripped of their local characteristics so that they become generic or abstract heroes.

heroist memorials within the romanticist gravescape, and while they were also willing to tolerate and, to some extent, even to support the establishment of a gravescape stripped of its romanticist features, that toleration did not extend to the construction of heroist memorials outside the cemeterial environment. It is one thing for individuals to prefer one type of memorial or gravescape over another; matters of choice are entirely consistent with the kind of individualism that romanticism actively promotes. But to promote heroism actively by erecting heroist memorials in cities and towns is, from the romanticist perspective, to threaten the very foundations of romanticism. That romanticists understood the fundamental conflict here is amply illustrated by their response to heroists' efforts to construct the Washington Monument in Washington, D.C.

A typical early heroist memorial, the Washington Monument is an unadorned obelisk that was begun in 1848. Measuring more than 555 feet from the ground to its crown, this white marble shaft clearly does not invite viewers to contemplate nature, art, or one's "finer sentiments." Quite the contrary. One need not indulge in fanciful psychologizing about the phallic appearance of this memorial to recognize that it is an accomplishment of labor rather than of artistic skill, that it equates size with significance, that it occupies the center of space so that (like all heroes) its symbolic heroism can be witnessed and confirmed, that it asserts its dominance over its environment, over nature. Rather than being an expression of our need to live in harmony with nature, against which all things are measured within the romanticist perspective, a structure of such monumental proportions announces both the dominance of the species over nature and the consequences of heroic immortality.

Drawing attention to the date when this structure was begun points us both to the fact that this was one of the earliest heroist efforts outside the gravescape and to the difficulties that heroists faced in attempting to develop their tradition in this direction. Though the Civil War and the logistics of constructing a memorial of this size undoubtedly contributed to the time that it took to build this structure, an equally important and more immediate reason that the Monument was not completed until 1884 is that heroists could not acquire the necessary funding. And one clear reason for this is that romanticists opposed memorials that substituted size for elegance. More, romanticists were concurrently seeking to establish at least one other romanticist memorial to Washington.

Speaking on behalf of the Mount Vernon Association, for instance, Richard Owen (1859), a professor at the University of Nashville, told Tennessee legislators and readers of the *North American Review* that "size, as an expression of reverence, is barbarous; expense natural, but cockneyish. The moment ideas of size and expense take the lead in the conception of a reverential structure, the result assumes at once the dignity and satisfaction of a stone-cutter's bill" (pp. 55–56). Americans do not want a mere "pile," Owen insisted, for "if a true conception of greatness fill the soul, a huge tumulus is to us as a child's garden, over which we tread unconsciously in gazing at a great, glorious landscape, flooded with dazzling sunlight" (p. 56). Rather than "a huge tumulus" that would fail to capture people's hearts and imaginations, Owen continued, Americans would prefer that "one grand leading idea govern, as it should, every part of the design" of our memorials; this "leading idea" demands that "nature, simplicity, and a truly rural grace will prevail throughout" (p. 60). America's memorial to Washington "must, then,

> be something exquisite,—expressive rather of thought, feeling, and skill than of labor; more suggestive than ambitious; appealing not to criticism, but to love; belonging at once to past, present, and future; meeting universal tastes, whether uncultivated or refined; enduring in its nature, yet susceptible of continual growth in elegance as Time shall unfold new resources; associated so intimately with the idea on which it is founded. (p. 56)

In sum, Owen concluded, Americans would prefer to turn Washington's home, Mount Vernon, into "one grand monument,—majestic, living," where visitors might sit "in some spot made beautiful alike by sun and shade, by nature and art" (p. 61). This conclusion is made all the more obvious by the fact that, while heroists cannot raise the funds to erect their "piles," "money seems the least part of the affair, in this case; feeling carries all before it." For, at this very moment, "ladies sitting at home have many hundreds [of dollars] poured into their laps in a day. A school-boy, in his play hours, gathers, in less than three weeks, nearly a thousand dollars" (p. 53).[4]

The differences between these two American memorial traditions should be sufficiently clear at this point that we can begin to understand how and why the construction of a public memorial might result in derisive public conflict. Memorials are, in a fundamental sense, sacred symbols, and, as Clifford Geertz (1973) has pointed out, "sacred symbols

[4] I do not submit these two disparate memorial efforts as somehow comprehensively representative of the American memorial traditions that are under consideration. The array of memorials that romanticists and heroists have produced is so mammoth that any attempt to describe them by pointing to representative instances here would be futile. The aim of the present discussion, however, is not to provide a catalogue, but to outline primary sources that contributed to and, thus, will help us to understand the VVM's design and the positions of those who conflicted over it.

function to synthesize a people's ethos—the tone, character, and quality of their life, its moral and aesthetic style and mood—and their world view—the picture they have of the way things in their sheer actuality are, their most comprehensive ideas of order" (p. 89). When a private or personal memorial fails to synthesize the ethos and world view of its viewers, conflict may emerge but will have a limited circumference, as when such conflict envelops only the members of a particular family. When a memorial is public, however, when it functions didactically to instruct viewers to be mindful of the memorable in some specific way that is consistent with the ethos and the world view of one group, but is contrary or contradictory with the ethos and world view of another group, then public conflict is virtually assured.

In the present case, romanticists and heroists concurrently sought to create public memorials in the name of George Washington. Had these efforts been private or regional, had they signified vaguely or ambiguously, then perhaps public conflict could have been averted. Memorials need not be seen as being in competition with one another, and public memorials that are sufficiently vague or ambiguous can sometimes conceal their identity by permitting a wide range of contrary or even contradictory interpretations. However, because each of these efforts sought to possess the present and the future by possessing the past, because each is a sacred symbol that clearly and unambiguously seeks to perpetuate the ethos and world view of the tradition to which it belongs, because the ethos and world view of these two traditions are historically and practically at odds with one another, and because both memorial efforts are very public, derisive public conflict was perhaps inevitable.

As we shall see, an examination of the public conflict over the VVM leads us to strikingly similar conclusions.

REMEMBERING VIETNAM?

Constructing a memorial to honor Americans who had been killed during the Vietnam War was first conceived by Jan Scruggs, a "former rifleman with the U.S. Army 199th Light Infantry Brigade" (Scruggs & Swerdlow, 1985, p. 7). Long hours, numerous political maneuvers, and a series of frustrating starts and stops eventually led to a proposal, which the U.S. Senate (April 30, 1980) and the U.S. House of Representatives (May 21, 1980) approved, and which President Jimmy Carter later signed (July 21, 1980). Having acquired a two-acre site in Constitution Gardens in Washington, D.C. on which to construct the proposed memorial, Scruggs and the other members of the Vietnam Veterans Memorial Fund (VVMF), who had struggled to advance their proposal to this point, then turned their attention to the matter of selecting an appropriate design for the memorial.

Keeping with the reasoning that had led them to fund the project through individual donations, and recognizing the need to appease the Fine Arts Commission, the National Capital Planning Commission, and the Secretary of the Interior, James Watt—all of whom had been granted the right of approval—members of the VVMF determined to hold an open competition from which a jury would choose an appropriate design. Because "certain notions were fixed" (Scruggs & Swerdlow, 1985, p. 49)—because the winning design would have to display the names of all who had died or were still missing in action, would have to be horizontal "so that it would not awkwardly compete with the Lincoln Memorial and the Washington Monument," and would have to be constructed in " 'a spacious garden setting' "—members of the VVMF carefully screened, interviewed, and selected "jurors to make sure they demonstrated sufficient sensitivity to what service in Vietnam had meant" (Scruggs & Swerdlow, 1985, p. 51).

After sifting through 1,421 entries, jurors Pietro Bulluschi, Grady Clay, Garrett Eckbo, Richard H. Hunt, Constantino Nivola, James Rosati, Hideo Sasaki, and Harry M. Weese unanimously selected a design that had been submitted by Maya Ying Lin, an undergraduate student of architecture at Yale University. Lin's design called for a simple memorial: two trapezoidal, polished, black granite walls, each approximately 250 feet in length, joined at an obtuse angle to form a chevron. Approximately 10 feet high at the vertex where they join, each wall diminishes in height until, at the outermost point from the juncture, it is no more than several inches in height. Constructed in a declevity, moving along the walls from either direction leads viewers down toward the vertex. Containing seventy panels each, the walls chronologically display the names of all Americans who were killed or are still missing in action.

In announcing the winning design, the jurors remarked that, "of all the proposals submitted, this most clearly meets the spirit and formal requirements of the program. It is contemplative and reflective. It is superbly harmonious with its site and yet frees the visitors from the noise and traffic of the surrouding city" ("Student wins war memorial contest," 1981, p. 20). Even more telling, the jurors also noted that they had explicitly "rejected concepts that were heroic" (Ayres, 1981, p. 5). In perhaps the most obvious sense, the jurors rejected heroic concepts because they were seeking a nonheroic form to represent the memorable. Yet, the form they selected is not merely nonheroic; it is antiheroic, the anthithesis of heroism. It does not announce the triumph of the species over nature by piercing the sky or dominating its surroundings. It does not invite us to join the great atomized society, to be inspired by our membership in the the larger reality of the species. It does not promise immortality through one's inherited membership in the species. It does not celebrate life as the triumph over nature, over death. It does not tell us that only the strong survive, that the strong, the heroic, will press on into the future. It does not announce the possibility of the species' conquest of death. Nor does it insist on heroic silence in the face of death.

On the contrary, the VVM's form announces the harmonious relationship between art and nature. It invites us to contemplate, acknowledge, and express the individuality of the dead. It presses us neither into the past nor into the future, but encourages serenity and contemplation, which hold us in the present where we can experience our emotions homeopathically. It speaks to us of nature and of death and, thus, signifies a yielding to death as natural and painfully inevitable. The slight declevity leads viewers gradually into the earth, into nature, where they can be freed "from the noise and traffic of the surrounding city," from the species and the artificies of the species, to contemplate. But what are we to contemplate? The memorable is unequivocal: We are to contemplate death by confronting thousands of individual deaths. Each of the dead has a name and cannot be summarized by or compacted into an heroic symbol, an abstracted abstraction. Once inside, the conclusion is inescapable: We are among the dead, who are brought forward through memory into the present by means of a union of art and nature. Outside is the world of heroism, the competitive atmosphere that sustains heroic meritocracy, that requires youth, stamina, vitality, fortitude, courage. Inside one is left alone with art, nature, security, serenity, emotions, and time to contemplate. Combined with the thousands of names that will not remain silent, this contemplative dimension disrupts heroism.

" 'It's easy to love it.' 'Visitors can come here and pay homage.' 'Not a thing of joy, but a large space for hope.' 'Quiet, a place speaking of acceptance.' 'Reverential' " (Scruggs & Swerdlow, 1985, p. 63). " 'This memorial with its wall of names becomes a place of quiet reflection and a tribute to those who served their nation in difficult times. . . . All who come here can find it a place of healing. . . . The designer has created an eloquent place where the simple setting of earth, sky, and remembered names contains messages for all who will know this place' " (Grady Clay, in Scruggs & Swerdlow, 1985, p. 65). "It seems to say, Vietnam was not theirs alone, it is all of ours; if you wish peace, love them" (Smith, in Scruggs & Swerdlow, 1985, p. xv). It is "contemplative and reflective," "superbly harmonious" ("Student wins war memorial contest," 1981, p. 20); "sober and eternal," "a lasting and appropriate image of dignity and sadness" ("Remembering Vietnam," 1981, p. 18); "uniquely horizontal, entering the earth rather than piercing the sky" (Ayres, 1981, p. 5); "a subtle yet powerful statement honoring the memory of those who were lost" (Corbett, 1981, p. 30); "a dignified and eloquent tribute" (Jack W. Flynt, commander of the American Legion, in "Around the nation," 1982, p. 10). These words of praise might belong to Joseph Story or to some other 19th-century romanticist, but they do not. They are the words of some of the many who believe that the VVM "says" what it ought to say, that it appropriately evokes what a sacred symbol ought to evoke, that it recapitulates the romanticist ethos and world view.

Though members of the jury, most of the members of the VVMF, and a great many others were obviously pleased with the VVM's form and function (see Scruggs & Swerdlow, 1985, pp. 97–99; Chapter 8, this volume), others were just as obviously displeased. " 'Why is it black? . . . Why is it underground?' " (James Webb, in Scruggs & Swerdlow, 1985, p. 80). " 'The Memorial is below ground, denoting shame.' " " 'It's black, a color of shame.' " " 'It is a tombstone, honoring only those who died.' " " 'It is unheroic.' " "Build the Memorial rising and white . . . Make it inspiring" (Scruggs & Swerdlow, pp. 82–84). It is "a black gash of shame and sorrow," "black walls sunk into a trench," "anti-heroic" (Carhart, 1981, p. 23); "a political statement of shame and dishonor" (Henry Hyde et al., in "Watt raises obstacle," 1982, p. 12); "a black ditch" (Scruggs & Swerdlow, 1985, p. 102); "a 'tombstone' that failed to take into account the valor and patriotism of the dead" (in Weinraub, 1982, p. 1). These criticisms might have been directed toward a 19th-century memorial effort, but, of course, they were directed toward the design of the VVM by 20th-century American heroists who clearly understand what the VVM says, but who deny that it says what it ought to say, that it appropriately evokes what a sacred symbol ought to evoke, or that it recapitulates the heroist ethos and world view.

The political and economic influence that critics of the VVM's design were able to exert was sufficient to bring the entire project to a halt. After the winning design had been announced publicly, for example, Republican congressman Henry Hyde (Illinois) and 27 of his colleagues drafted and "signed a letter to all Republicans in the House asking that they write to President Reagan requesting that Interior Secretary Watt not grant construction approval for the Memorial" (Scruggs & Swerdlow, 1985, p. 87). Watt then "put the Memorial on hold until further notice" (p. 88). Up to this point, different people had disagreed with one another over a variety of issues. Now, however, Americans were witnessing the eruption of a divisive public debate. The VVM had clearly and univocally identified how the memorable ought to be remembered.

Confronted with the possibility that heroists would manage either to destroy or to modify significantly the VVM and, more important to romanticists, confronted with the distinct likelihood that a prolonged public conflict would diminish the VVM's capacity "to heal a nation" (see Scruggs & Swerdlow, 1985, especially pp. 97–102), romanticists were compelled to compromise with heroists by adding a flag and a heroic statue. Through yet another series of frustrations and political maneuvers, members of the VVMF eventually authorized Frederick Hart to " 'begin work on a fully refined bronze model of the sculpture approximately 16 inches high showing all details' " (Scruggs & Swerdlow, 1985, p. 115). The end product, which was adopted and later erected near the VVM, is, in effect, a second memorial (VVM2) designed to appease heroists. Thus, next to the original VVM we now find three life-sized, Vietnam era soldiers (a white, a black, and an Hispanic—all males, all infantrymen) wearily but spiritually and courageously bonded together in an historical moment. Representationally, they might be anyone; yet, they are no one we know. They are inspiring abstractions, reminders of the bravery of those who fought for the freedom of their country. And this is the evaluation: These soldiers were brave, heroic. There is nothing suggested here about specific identity or individuality, about nature, or about the emotions occasioned by the death of an intimate. Neither speaking of death nor even inviting us to contemplate death, this second memorial encourages only heroism and the silence of heroes. Weary though they may be, these heroes are alive. And that is how we are to remember them: alive and heroic.

Predictably, conflict over the design of this second memorial immediately erupted. But now the roles were reversed: Romanticists assumed the role of critics, and heroists assumed the role of supporters. As Scruggs and Swerdlow (1985) recall,

> Robert N. Lawrence, president of the American Institute of Archetects called the addition of Hart's statue "ill conceived," a "breach of faith," and a "dangerous precedent." Paul Spreiregen, who had organized the design competition, called Hart's statue an "outrageous desecration." Juror Harry Weese told reporters, "It's as if Michelangelo had the Secretary of the Interior climb onto the scaffold and muck around." . . . Watt, for example, called for "a heroic sculpture." (p. 121)

Maya Ying Lin called Hart's statue "trite. It's a generalization, a simplification. Hart gives you an image—he's illustrating a book." "*New York Times* critic Paul Goldberger wrote, 'To try to represent a period of anguish and complexity in our history with a simple statue of armed soldiers is to misunderstand all that has happened, and to suggest that no lessons have been learned' " (Scruggs & Swerdlow, 1985, p. 129). And Constitution Gardens designer, Henry F. Arnold, insisted that "the proposed undistinguished, made-to-order statue is a sentimental response to a difference of opinion. The result is more likely to serve as a memorial to pettiness and corruptive endeavor. . . . It might be prudent and appropriate for the Commission to delay their decision until each member . . . and the detractors have had the chance to visit the [original] Memorial, after it is completed, and experience the mysterious power of this unprecedented work of art" (p. 132).

On the other hand, like "General Michael Davison, who had first suggested the statue and flag as a compromise," heroists understood their implicit victory and insisted that "this statue is breathtaking, because Frederick Hart, out of his genius, has captured that unique bond that ties men together in the face of danger" (Scruggs & Swerdlow, 1985, p. 132). Such remarks were all that heroists and romanticists needed to realize that the compromise had resolved the conflict—even if not everyone was completely satisfied. Resolution was assured because each of these two memorials functions as a sacred symbol for one group and not for another, because each says to some what they feel it ought to say and fails to say to others what they feel it ought to say, because each evaluates the memorable in a way that is consistent with the sensibilities of one group and fails to evaluate the memorable in a way that is consistent with the sensibilities of another group, because each conforms to the expectations of those who embrace one memorial tradition and does not conform to the expectations of those who embrace another, and because each was constructed on "sacred soil that is right next to our dearest and greatest patriotic memorials," which "is about the highest honor that this country can bestow" (J. Carter Brown, in Scruggs & Swerdlow, p. 133).

It is in this sense that public position accords each of these two memorial efforts the status of cultural institution. That is, if we understand with Geertz (1973) that the term culture "denotes an historically transmitted pattern of meanings embodied in symbols, a system of inherited conceptions expressed in symbolic forms" whereby individuals "communicate, perpetuate, and develop their knowledge about and attitudes toward life" (p. 89), and if we understand that memorials, as sacred symbols, function to recapitulate a people's ethos and world view, then we can also grasp the sense in which the conflict, its resolution, and both memorials are fundamentally cultural. At stake in the establishment of a national memorial are the very values that members of a culture wish to "communicate, perpetuate, and develop." To be granted or denied an opportunity to sustain and advance such values, therefore, is to be granted or denied an opportunity to sustain and advance one's culture. Returning once again to Latin origins, we may also say that each of these two memorials is an institution (*institutio:* education, instruction; *instituo:* to instruct, educate, train) insofar as each seeks to shape and possess the present and the future by first shaping and possessing the past. From this perspective, then, the public conflict, its resolution, and both memorials embody a moral struggle between historically and practically divergent cultural traditions each seeking to lay claim to America's past, present, and future through the establishment of a cultural institution that would "preach lessons, to which none may refuse to listen, and which all, that live, must hear."

Only time will tell whether these two memorials will continue to function adequately as cultural institutions for those to whom such matters matter most. Yet, we can say at least this much. The VVM2 is dwarfed by the VVM and by the heroist memorials that populate Washington, D.C.; and its diminutive stature (compared to others in the area) may well suggest to some that the significance of the Vietnam War and of the efforts of Americans during that war were less than monumental, less than fully inspiring, less than completely heroic. But those who comprehend the nature and magnitude of the public conflict from which the VVM2 was born, who understand that the heroist victory in this conflict was not that of having silenced another cultural institution but of having gained an opportunity to encourage present and future generations to see themselves as part of an heroic whole, and who recognize that, beyond the immediacy of the Vietnam War, the VVM2 lends its voice to a host of heroic memorials that continue to speak heroically, the size of the VVM2 will be of little consequence.

On the other hand, some may well suggest that the VVM's capacity to evoke or establish romantic memory is diminished by the presence of the VVM2. Again, however, those who understand the character and intensity of the public conflict, who appreciate the tradition that the VVM represents, and who grasp the significance of the VVM's public character and status will also recognize that its form fuels romanticist passions enthymematically. Supplying initial "premises" through its form, the VVM relies on viewers to provide missing "premises." Thus, for Jack Wheeler, one of the organizers of the VVMF, for example, the names serve as initial premises to which he adds his own: "there is no more sacred part of a person than his or her name. We have to start remembering real, individual names" (in Scruggs & Swerdlow, 1985, p. 562). Moreover, it is because the VVM functions enthymematically, because it romantically initiates an intimate dialogue, a whispering between friends, lovers, and relatives, that individuals frequently respond with anger and/or frustration when others intrude on their dialogue with the VVM (Ehrenhaus, 1985, p. 12).

Considered alone, the presentation of so many thousands of names—names to which visitors may bear personal witness—draws attention to individual loss, individual grief, individual pain, individual suffering, individual sorrow. Veterans of the Vietnam War thus confront the possibility of remembering not only the reality that their friends and comrads are dead, but also a magnificient confusion of emotions—of bravery and bloodshed, of innocence and victimage, of joy and sorrow, of guilt and reprisal, of fear and courage, of boredom and excitement, of regret and anticipation, of loss and gain, of anger, of hate, of love. With a truncated array of memories, perhaps, family members, friends, and even strangers confront a similar confusion of emotions.

Of course, not all who visit the VVM will or should experience it thus (see Chapter 8, this volume). Those who were touched marginally or not at all by the Vietnam War have little to remember, passionately. For them to be asked by the VVM to be romantically mindful is not necessarily to be asked to remember anything specifically passionate. And, as time passes, as the names and the Vietnam War fade, as the reasons for caring passionately decay, so will the VVM's capacity to evoke or establish homeopathic sentiments. Some present generations and very likely a good many more future generations will look at the names as names, not as memories of friends or loved ones (see Chapter 9, this volume). Already, the Vietnam War is gradually becoming but another war, and the VVM is becoming but another memorial.

This is not to say that the VVM is somehow fundamentally flawed as a public memorial, a sacred symbol, or a cultural institution. True, the VVM does not provide viewers with eternally pathetic images, and there are no exacting romanticist words inscribed on its walls. But no memorial—however public, however comprehensive—can evoke or establish what viewers deny, ignore, or do not possess. Being mindful requires being willing and able to engage in meaningful dialogue, enthymematically or otherwise.

CONCLUSION

In part, what our subject tells us about cultural legacies of Vietnam is that any effort to possess that set of experiences we call Vietnam cannot and will not obtain, at least presently, for two distinct reasons. The first is that we—that is, all those for whom Vietnam-related experiences are individually and collectively defining (see Chapter 9, this volume)—are possessed by the very "thing" that we seek to possess. This is not a metaphysical statement. It is a statement concerned with the relationship that individuals and cultures have with their past, with how the obsessive desire to resurrect, reinterpret, reshape, and, therefore, possess that which cannot be possessed can lead all too readily to mummification. The point here is not, as some would have it, that we must cast off the past so that we may live authentically in the present. Memory disallows that possibility, and our need to learn from the past and to see ourselves, our beliefs, our principles, our attitudes, our emotions, and our traditions as connected through time and space to past and future generations makes that variety of authenticity extremely undesirable. Yet, mummification of the past is perhaps even more undesirable; for the effort to relive the past obscures and stultifies the actualities of the present and the possibilities of the future. We must be certain, therefore, that our inheritance comes from a past that is vibrant, unpossessed, and unpossessing, not from a past that is merely an embalmed corpse propped up by fervent desires and empty hopes.

A second reason that the set of experiences we call Vietnam cannot be possessed—and a sign that the past is not, at the moment, ready to be wrapped—is that those experiences are far too significant to the various disparate collectivities that constitute America for anyone to propose to speak for the whole. Whether one's point of departure is memorializing, cinema (see Chapters 5, 6, & 7, this volume), television (see Chapters 2, 3, & 6, this volume), speech communities (see Chapter 8, this volume), literature and poetry (see Chapter 4, this volume), the manner in which political deliberations and policies are shaped by and infused with the specter of Vietnam (see Chapters 1, 2, & 3, this volume), the variety of ways that Vietnam as an issue of potent concern reflects equally potent cultural trends and manifestations (see Chapter 9, this volume), or any other means whereby individuals "communicate, perpetuate, and develop their knowledge about and attitudes toward life," the presumption that the perspective of any one individual or group can somehow paint a complete or even adequate portrait of how all ought to remember Vietnam implicitly issues forth a declaration and a threat to all those whose cultural values, whose sacred symbols are denied, ignored, marginalized, or repressed. As long as disparate American cultures view their experiences of Vietnam as central to their identity (see Chapter 8, this volume)—past, present, and future—the cultural legacies of Vietnam cannot and will not be possessed singularly. Conflict over who will and will not possess an inheritance that belongs to the whole, therefore, may not be inevitable, but the probability remains extraordinarily high.

Equally important is what cultural legacies of Vietnam tell us about the human condition. It is tempting to believe that there is a correct way to memorialize or, at least, that some ways of memorializing are superior to others. But the temptation to put faith in this myth of superiority, as I call it, must be resisted. First, it must be resisted because the myth of superiority is invariably articulated from a position that is itself the articulation of the internal metric from which the claim of superiority derives. The subject of this chapter is illustrative. Using the criteria of heroism as their metric, heroists necessarily find flaws in all other memorial traditions that do not "measure up" to the internal metric of heroism. Nonheroic memorial efforts simply are not heroic enough to satisfy the dictates of heroism. To heroists, therefore, heroist memorials are superior. The same may be said of memorial traditions and of dealing with the dead and one's death-related emotions, generally.

Second, the temptation must be resisted because the myth of superiority ignores the significance of audience in the memorializing process. While a locket, for example, may not function as a memorial to anyone save the memorializer, the fact that it does function as a memorial for the audience to whom its memorializing function is literally most significant is what makes it a satisfactory memorial. The obverse is not true. Nor is it true that an effort that fails to function as a memorial for anyone is somehow abstractly a memorial. Memorializing must satisfy its function for someone. As long as there are differences between and among individuals, there will be differences in their memorial efforts; and, as long as those efforts satisfy the needs of those for whom memorializing is most significant, the imposition of an internal metric on that which is external must remain vacuous.

Finally, the temptation must be resisted because the myth of superiority implies the possibility that memorializing might somehow be generalized so that, when its standards are appealed to appropriately, a generalized memorial effort could transcend individual or cultural differences. No doubt, Ernest Becker (1973) was correct:

> Man's best efforts seem utterly fallible without appeal to something higher for justification, some conceptual support for the meaning of one's life from a transcendental dimension of some kind. As this belief has to absorb man's basic terror [i.e., death], it cannot be merely abstract but must be rooted in the emotions, in an inner feeling that one is secure in something stronger, larger, more important than one's own strength and life. (p. 120)

Universalized or generic memorials—like universalized or generic speeches, suits, and creamed corn—may transcend individual or cultural differences, but they do so only at the expense of failing to satisfy anyone. In memorializing, generally, and in our understanding of cultural legacies of Vietnam, particularly, it is not audience, values, or cultures, but our faith in the myth of superiority that must be transcended.

REFERENCES

Ayres, B. (1981, June 29). A Yale senior, A Vietnam memorial and a few ironies. *New York Times, II*, p. 5.

Around the nation. (1982, January 26). *New York Times*, p. A10.

Becker, E. (1973). *The denial of death*. New York: The Free Press.

Beecher, H.W. (1859). *Star papers; or, experiences of art and nature*. New York: Derby & Jackson.

Bigelow, J. (1859). *A history of the cemetery of Mount Auburn*. Boston: Munroe & Co.

Carhart, T. (1981, October 24). Insulting Vietnam vets. *New York Times*, p. A23.

Cleaveland, N. (1850). *Green-Wood: A handbook for visitors*. New York: Green-Wood.

Corbett, P. (1981, November 11). Letter to the editor. *New York Times*, p. 30.

Downing, A.J. (1974). Public cemeteries and public gardens. In G.W. Curtis (Ed.), *Rural essays by Andrew Jackson Downing* (pp. 154–159). New York: Da Capo. (Original work published 1854)

Ehrenhaus, P. (1985). *Names not inspiration: When a memorial speaks non-discursively*. Paper presented at the meeting of the Eastern Communication Association, Providence, RI.

Farrell, J. (1980). *Inventing the American way of death, 1830–1920*. Philadelphia: Temple University Press.

Gaonkar, D. (1988). *The quarrel between philosophy and rhetoric: A case study in the self-understanding of a discipline*. Paper presented at the meeting of the Eastern Communication Association, Baltimore, MD.

Geertz, C. (1973). *The interpretation of cultures*. New York: Basic Books.

Heidegger, M. (1962). *Being and time* (J. Macquarrie & E. Robinson, Trans.). New York: Harper & Row.

May, W.F. (1969). The sacral power of death in contemporary experience. In L.O. Mills (Ed.), *Perspectives on Death* (pp. 168–196). New York: Abingdon.

May, W.F. (1973). The sacral power of death in contemporary experience. In A. Mack (Ed.), *Death in American experience* (pp. 97–122). New York: Schocken.

Morris, R. (1986). *Memorializing among Americans: The case of Lincoln's assassination*. Unpublished doctoral dissertation, University of Wisconsin-Madison, Madison, WI.

Owen, R. (1859). Honor to the illustrious dead. A lecture in behalf of the Mount Vernon Association, delivered in the state capitol, Nashville, Wednesday, December 4, 1857. *North American Review, 88*, 52–61.

Peabody, W.B.O. (1831). Mount Auburn cemetery. *North American Review, 33*, 397–406.

Perkins, F.B. (1871). Sepulture, Its ideas and practices. *The galaxy, XI*, 836–846.
Remembering Vietnam [Editorial]. (1981, May 18). *New York Times*, p. 18.
Scruggs, J., & Swerdlow, J. (1985). *To heal a nation*. New York: Harper & Row.
Story, J. (1859). An address delivered on the dedication of the cemetery at Mount Auburn, September 24th, 1831. In J. Bigelow, *A history of the cemetery of Mount Auburn* (pp. 143–167). Boston: Munrow & Co. (Original work published 1831)
Student wins war memorial contest. (1981, May 7). *New York Times*, p. 20.
Tatum, G.B. (1974). New introduction. In G.W. Curtis (Ed.), *Rural essays by Andrew Jackson Downing* (pp. v–xxvi). New York: Da Capo.
Watt raises obstacle on Vietnam memorial. (1982, Jananuary 13). *New York Times*, p. A12.
Weed, H.E. (1912). *Modern park cemeteries*. Chicago: R.J. Haight.
Weinraub, B. (1982, March 27). Ground broken in Capital for memorial on Vietnam. *New York Times*, p. A1.

Epilogue
Forms of Remembering, Forms of Forgetting

Peter Ehrenhaus
Department of Speech Communication, Portland State University

Richard Morris
The Annenberg School of Communications, University of Pennsylvania

This collection of essays, as we mentioned at the outset, originated with a conference, which brought together scholars from the disciplines of anthropology, art history, communication, political science, and sociology—as well as individuals who had contributed significantly to the "reawakening" of America's Vietnam experiences. Members of the public, particularly Vietnam veterans and those associated with veterans' issues, were also invited to attend and participate in the sessions.

Three points, which have helped to shape this work and our closing statement here, were crystallized during those sessions. The first concerns the merits of using the term "legacy" as a label for encompassing a multitude of concerns and consequences that Americans have inherited from the Vietnam Era. The second concerns the manner and consequences of preserving the past through cultural memory. And the third directs our attention to the astonishing diversity of concerns, passions, and positions that have been generated and/or sustained by the cultural legacy of Vietnam.

The first point—that is, whether the term "legacy" is adequate to encompass such a great multitude of concerns and consequences—suggests to us that our key term was both misleading and apt. In one sense, it was misleading because it suggested, as sociologist Todd Gitlin pointed out,[1] that Vietnam is now safely in the past. Yet, among other

[1] Comments by Professors Edwin Black (Communication Arts; University of Wisconsin-Madison), Murray Edelman (Political Science, University of Wisconsin-Madison), William Gamson (Sociology, Boston College), and Todd Gitlin (Sociology, University of California, Berkeley) are taken from the audiotaped round-table session at the conference, "The Cultural Legacy of Vietnam: Uses of the Past in the Present," which was conducted on April 26, 1986, at Rutgers University in New Brunswick, New Jersey. All subsequent attributions are taken from this session.

things, the contributors to this volume have consistently demonstrated that the America of today and tomorrow is an extension of the Vietnam War by other means. The venue has changed, the tools have changed; but the conflict persists, evolves. That persisting, evolving conflict serves to remind us that America's Vietnam experience is still very much with us. Little has been resolved or reconciled, and, within this society's "system of organized irresponsibility," as Gitlin also pointed out, the silence and disinterest of the many empower the few to shape the meaning of the past for all.

In part, the meaning with which we are concerned—the meaning of Vietnam—is, as Murray Edelman observed, "meaning read backwards." Only from the vantage afforded by some arbitrary end point can we reflect on prior "events" and give to them coherence and moral force. Meaning arises through the conflicts of diverse interests over how the past should be labeled and understood. The chapters in this volume examine some of those controversies and, we sincerely hope, contribute to the perpetuation of controversy. But if "legacy" suggests to some a comprehensive study of America's Vietnam-related experiences, or a sense that those experiences have been concluded, or that closure has been achieved, or that the divisiveness of Vietnam has been resolved or reconciled, then the term is misleading.

Nothing could be further from our intent. Our objective has been to *explore* both the shaping of remembrance in American cultures and the implications of the processes that have encouraged and continue to encourage that shaping. We have not sought to offer a definitive examination of the cultural legacies of Vietnam, and we do not presume that we have exhaustively treated the use of Vietnam as a political metaphor, Vietnam and the shaping of popular imagination, or Vietnam and the shaping of American cultures. Nor would we, even if we were so inclined, even if it were possible. We have sought to initiate—not suspend or conclude—serious dialogue. New strands of influence have emerged since the authors who wrote these essays formulated their positions. New strands of influence will continue to emerge because the issues involved extend well beyond a momentary crisis in national conscience. This is, in large measure, precisely what makes cultural legacies of Vietnam so significant.

The other two crystallized points—that is, the manner and consequences of preserving the past through cultural memory, and the astonishing diversity of concerns, passions, and positions that have been generated and/or sustained by the cultural legacies of Vietnam—suggest to us forms of remembering and forms of forgetting. As a consequence, each chapter in this volume in some way examines how the past is organized and construed to give shape and meaning to the present and the future. Each speaks to consequences of how Vietnam is and is not remembered.

Each chapter also tells us that war does not end with the cessation of combat. Diverse forms of symbolic expression—speeches and argument, prose and poetry, films, television programs, memorials, and private conversations, among others—all strive to give shape and significance to the Vietnam War and its relevant communities. All strive to shape cultural memory of Vietnam as a means of understanding the present and for guiding us toward a future. Contemporary American experience is, in many ways, a continuation of the war, which continues to be waged, and its repercussions continue to be felt, through symbolic process that form collective memory.

To reiterate a position argued throughout this volume, the past becomes meaningful through the selection of those "things" that are deemed worthy of remembrance; significance emerges most clearly not from past events, but from the dominant constellation of consensual social meanings that allow the past to become integral to the legitimization of present values and future policies. Once selected, these "things" are given the form of "events," while others are left to wither. It is inescapable that in giving form to remembrance we also give form to forgetting. What we cannot forget, however, are the implications of the production of that past: Who seeks to appropriate the past? For what purposes? Whose interests are served by such remembrance? At whose expense? What and whom do these remembrances overlook and set aside to be forgotten?

Consider the recent past. As American involvement in the Vietnam War came to an end in 1975, American political institutions and the American public turned away from closure. To be labeled a Vietnam veteran was to be anathema. For some Americans, veterans of this war embodied the failure of American will; for others they personified the immorality of American imperialism; and some considered them reminders of a nagging, chronic unpleasantness on the periphery of their daily lives—just as well forgotten. With the collapse of South Vietnam, an emotionally spent American public gratefully accepted President Ford's efforts to shift the nation's attention from its adversarial role in leading the "noble cause" of containing communist aggression in Southeast Asia to a more nurturing role defined by mastering technology for the good of all, thereby assisting individuals in their quests for self-fulfillment. America's "Vietnam Era" was supplanted, in the words of author Tom Wolfe, by the "Me Decade."

With rare exception, not until the early 1980s did Americans collectively redirect their attention to Vietnam. Coincident with the dedication of the Vietnam Veterans Memorial in Washington, D.C., and perhaps partly owing to it, came an outpouring of emotions and a return to issues that had been suppressed since the end of the war. Parades were held for veterans. Remains were interred in the Tomb for the Unknown of the Vietnam War in Arlington National Cemetery. State and regional Vietnam memorials (a total of 145 as of this writing) were erected throughout the nation. At the same time we see the beginning of a profusion of Vietnam-oriented publications—fiction and nonfiction—as well as a growing acceptance by the television viewing public of entertainment programming, either set during the Vietnam War or using the "Vietnam experiences" of characters as dramatic context, subtext, pretext, or pretense. The film industry during this time touched an apparently primal nerve in the American public's need for catharsis through jingoistic "return to Vietnam" movies offering revisionism as a solution to a recalcitrant past, after which came ostensibly "realistic" portrayals of the "real" Vietnam. After a portentous silence, then, public symbolic processes revived the war. But now the war is located in the American public conscience.

Jan Scruggs, founder of the Vietnam Veterans Memorial Fund, reveals a key dynamic by which these public symbolic processes help to shape American cultural memory. As he has often explained, his objective in creating the Vietnam Veterans Memorial was to separate the warrior from the war in order to enable all Americans to remember and honor those who sacrificed, regardless of one's feelings about the war. This same "weaning away" of human action from its sociopolitical environment—through which moral meaning constructs and is itself constructed—occurs in film and television, in parades and memorials, and in much of the Vietnam literature. We know of no reason to question the nobility of these acts of remembrance or the intentions behind them. But in separating the warrior from the war we run the risk of remembering one at the expense of the other: Remembrance is distorted by contextual dislocation. As a consequence, questions about war and peace, about the responsibilities and obligations binding individuals to their collective community, about American foreign policy and the legitimacy of American involvement in Southeast Asia (or elsewhere), about the very assumptions upon which foreign policy debate rests, pale and are lost and forgotten—obscured through remembrance of other "things."

One might argue that such questions are inappropriate—in poor taste—because they intrude on celebration of sacrifice and the human spirit; they shift attention away from reconciliation and reunification toward divisiveness and division. The resurgence of Vietnam in the public conscience, some would say, is laudable because it contributes to healing in the wake of Vietnam. And recent developments have been applauded by some for having restored the nation to an optimistic self-confidence and for having created a resurgence of public morale—a "national reconciliation" that is healing the nation's psyche. Insofar as this praise pertains to the healing of individuals, to reconciling the death of a loved one or a comrade-in-arms, or to confronting the guilt of survival, we wholeheartedly concur (see, e.g., Egendorf, 1985; Hendin & Haas, 1984; Lifton, 1973; Lopes, 1988; MacPherson, 1984; Scruggs & Swerdlow, 1985; Veninga & Wilmer, 1985).

But when "healing" implies a genuine social, political, emotional, or cultural convergence—when it manifests itself through individuals who have become particularly masterful in opportunistically capitalizing on the American public's yearning for a return to the illusions of national moral innocence and consensus—we cannot help noticing the equivocation, the effort to force a desirable outcome into being through mere assertion: "We are healed." At what expense do we acquire the warm glow of reconciliation? Thus far, the contentiousness of the past has been dissipated by repression and distortion. But national reconciliation at the cost of lies and a paranoic interpretation of history, as Edwin Black observed, is far too high a cost.

This warm glow of reconciliation masks the undesirable—those "things" that are just as well forgotten, that existed "before" our maladies were cured by reconcilable differences. But the differences persist, and the past manifests itself in the present, sometimes through the very things that we find easiest to forget—for example, that Vietnam was a war that took an estimated 1.5 million Vietnamese lives. Nowhere are their memories or interests represented in this great "national reconciliation." The implication is that we need not remember—that we can comfortably forget—the ruptures created by American actions, so long as those ruptures occur beyond national boundaries: The "foreign other" is expendable.

Within national boundaries, ruptures are all too easily dismissed as having resulted from a momentary lapse; they need not be addressed, therefore, by those with competing and incompatible points of view. As sociologist William Gamson observes, however, the difficulty lies in the system of institutional relationships of American society; a few dominant voices expropriate the experience of Vietnam for dubious, often cynical economic and political purposes. Ruptures disappear by mandate. We can forget that the Vietnam War was pursued at a disproportionate cost to America's poor, its working class, its minorities (Caro, 1988). Our forgetting can shield us from the reality that Vietnam was a laboratory for chemical warfare. When national purpose and national interests are discussed in terms of geopolitics and the clash of ideologies, the potential inclusion of the full range of Vietnam's human realities in cultural memory poses a grave threat to alternative expressions of American national will.

The reverie of mythic America to the contrary, reconciliation is not upon us, and responding to long-repressed voices with sympathetic understanding that borders on the patronizing is not healing. Acknowledging the contentiousness of the past does not confront its sources. Before we can begin to anticipate the prospects of reconciliation, we must first begin to ask and seek to answer some of the enormous questions we have been bequeathed: What are the rights and limits on our institutions to destroy life? Insofar as our institutions ostensibly act on our behalf, what is their obligation to heed our voices? What are the obligations of human beings to each other *as* human beings? When do those human obligations supersede institutional obligations? What is it in the nature of our system, as Todd Gitlin asks, that muffles and distorts these very questions?

Vietnam is not found in the past; it is enmeshed, in Edelman's words, within "a seamless web of social problems" that attend on us today. Through a myriad of forms of symbolic expression, we spin that web, shaping the past in the present. Our memory of the past is what we make of it, or what we allow others to make of it for us. And if we acquiesce to a past produced by others, then perhaps we deserve the future it bears.

REFERENCES

Caro, M. (1988, October 17). A Chicano in Vietnam. *Newsweek*, p. 10.

Egendorf, A. (1985). *Healing from the war: Trauma and transformation after Vietnam*. Boston: Shaubhala.

Hendin, H., & Haas, A. (1984). *Wounds of war: The psychological aftermath of combat in Vietnam*. New York: Basic Books.

Lifton, R. (1973). *Home from the war: Vietnam veterans, neither victims nor executioners*. New York: Simon & Schuster.

Lopes, S. (1988). *The wall: Images and offerings from the Vietnam Veterans Memorial*. New York: Collins.

MacPherson, M. (1984). *Long time passing: Vietnam and the haunted generation*. Garden City, NY: Doubleday.

Scruggs, J., & Swerdlow, J. (1985). *To heal a nation*. New York: Harper & Row.

Veninga, J.F., & Wilmer, H.A. (Eds.). (1985). *Vietnam in remission*. College Station, TX: Texas A & M University Press.

Author Index

Subject Index

Ch. 1 — POW pp. 22, 24 on that problem

Ch 2. — PBS series / AIM counter doc — ? of interpretation (32)

Ch 3 — PBS / AIM shows — politics of history

Ch 4. — "moral credibility" — Am mythology .. God's nation — and Vietnam

↓

our sense of moral superiority ... save the world

discuss poetry — Critique cultural mythology

Ch 5 veteranan and film — three stages — sense of metaphor?

Ch. 6. more Vets — "ideological struggle to assign meaning"

Ch 7 gender issues .. "appropriation of reproduction" (127)

Ch. 8. Vet organization / ethnography

Ch. 9 cultural / psychological history (C. Lasch?)

A. key quote 177

Ch 10 memorial — key passage p. 200